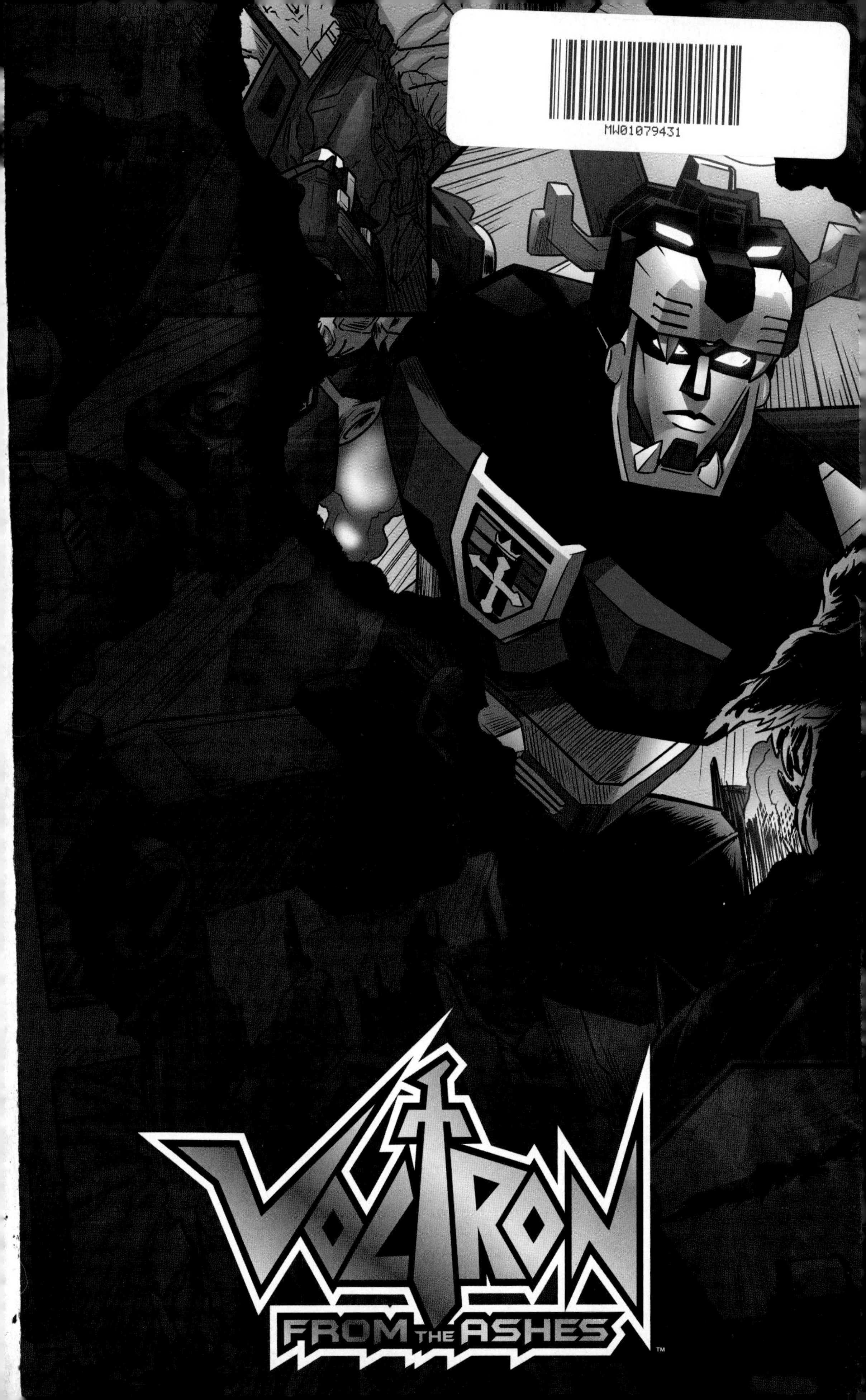
VOLTRON
FROM THE ASHES
™

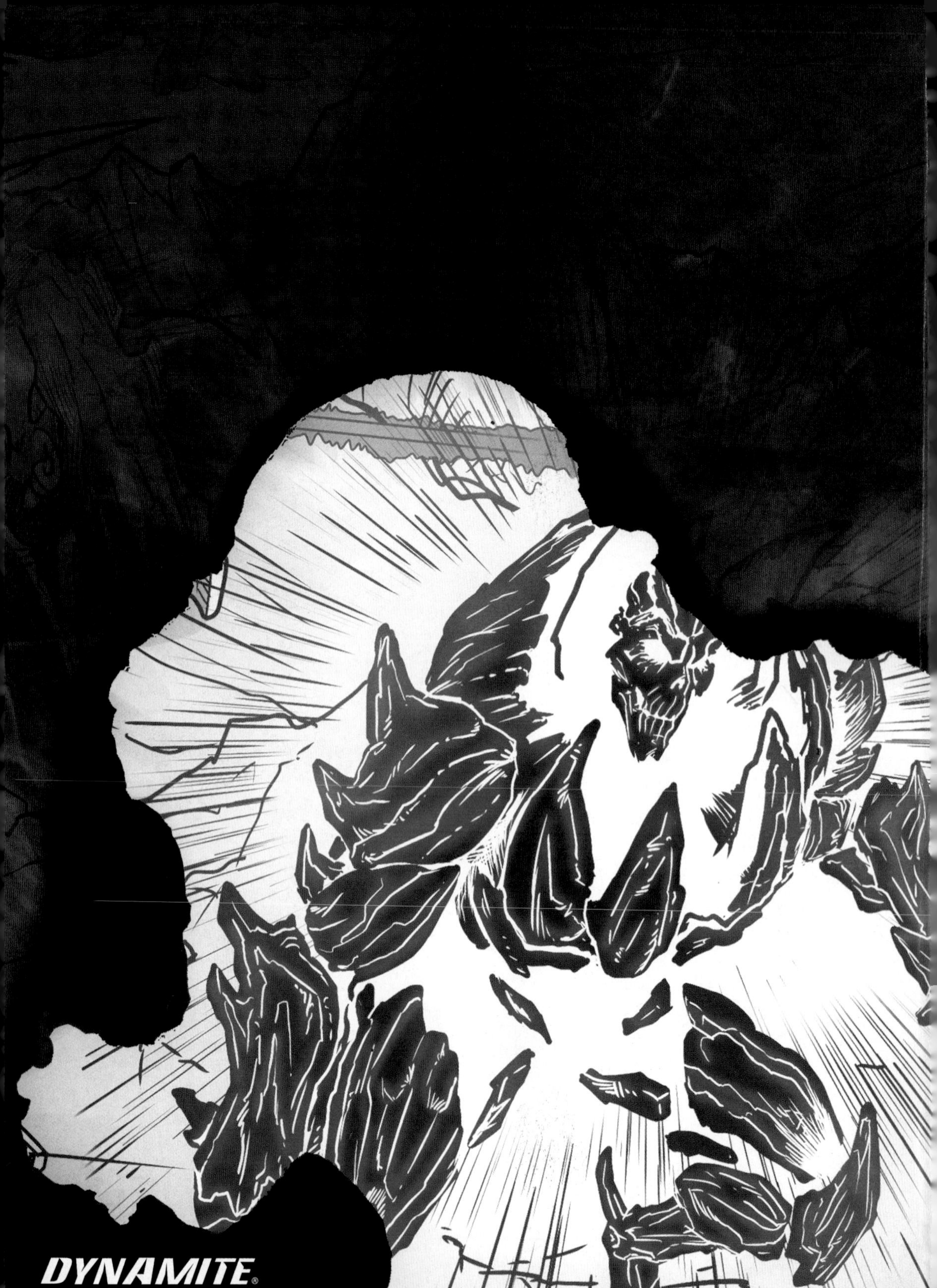

DYNAMITE®

**Nick Barrucci**, CEO / Publisher
**Juan Collado**, President / COO

**Joe Rybandt**, Senior Editor
**Rachel Pinnelas**, Associate Editor
**Kevin Ketner**, Editorial Assistant

**Jason Ullmeyer**, Art Director
**Geoff Harkins**, Graphic Designer
**Alexis Persson**, Production Artist

**Chris Caniano**, Digital Associate
**Rachel Kilbury**, Digital Assistant

**Brandon Dante Primavera**, Dir. of IT/Operations
**Rich Young**, Dir. of Business Development

**Keith Davidsen**, Marketing Manager
**Pat O'Connell**, Sales Manager

**Online** at www.DYNAMITE.com
**On Facebook** /Dynamitecomics
**Instagram** /Dynamitecomics
**On Tumblr** dynamitecomics.tumblr.com
**On Twitter** @Dynamitecomics
**On YouTube** /Dynamitecomics

# VOLTRON

## FROM THE ASHES

Written by: **CULLEN BUNN**

Illustrated by: **BLACKY SHEPHERD**

Colored by: **ADRIANO AUGUSTO**

Lettered by: **ROB STEEN**

Collection Cover by: **ALEX MILNE**

Collection Design by: **GEOFF HARKINS**

Special thanks to: SCOTT SHILLET, COLIN McLAUGHLIN, JEREMY CORRAY, DAMIEN TROMEL and BOB KOPLAR

First Printing
ISBN-10: 1-60690-857-X
ISBN-13: 978-1-60690-857-0
10 9 8 7 6 5 4 3 2 1

PEFC Certified
Printed on paper from sustainably managed forests and controlled sources
PEFC/01-31-106    www.pefc.org

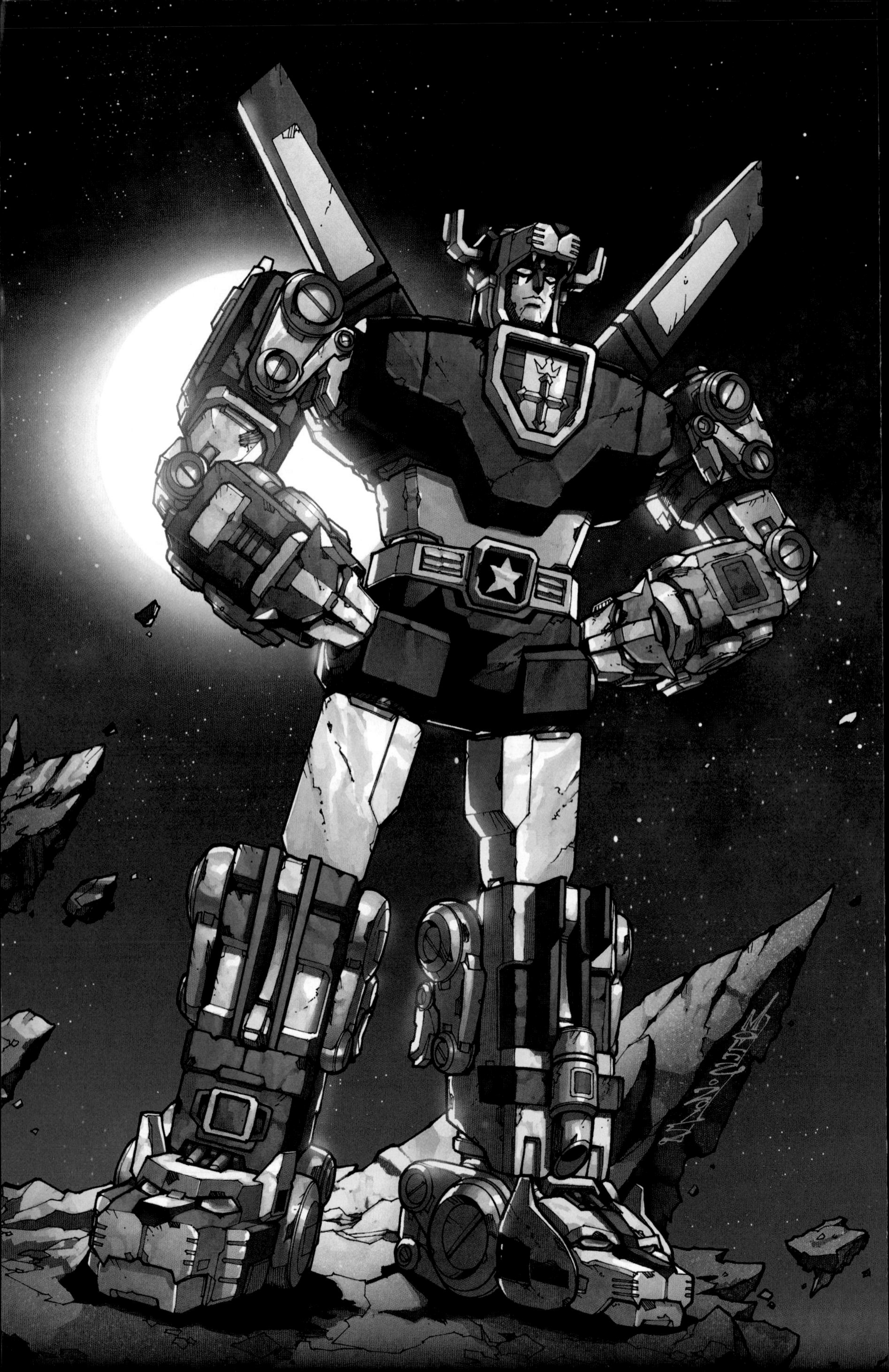

ISSUE 1 Cover by ALEX MILNE Colors by JOSH PEREZ

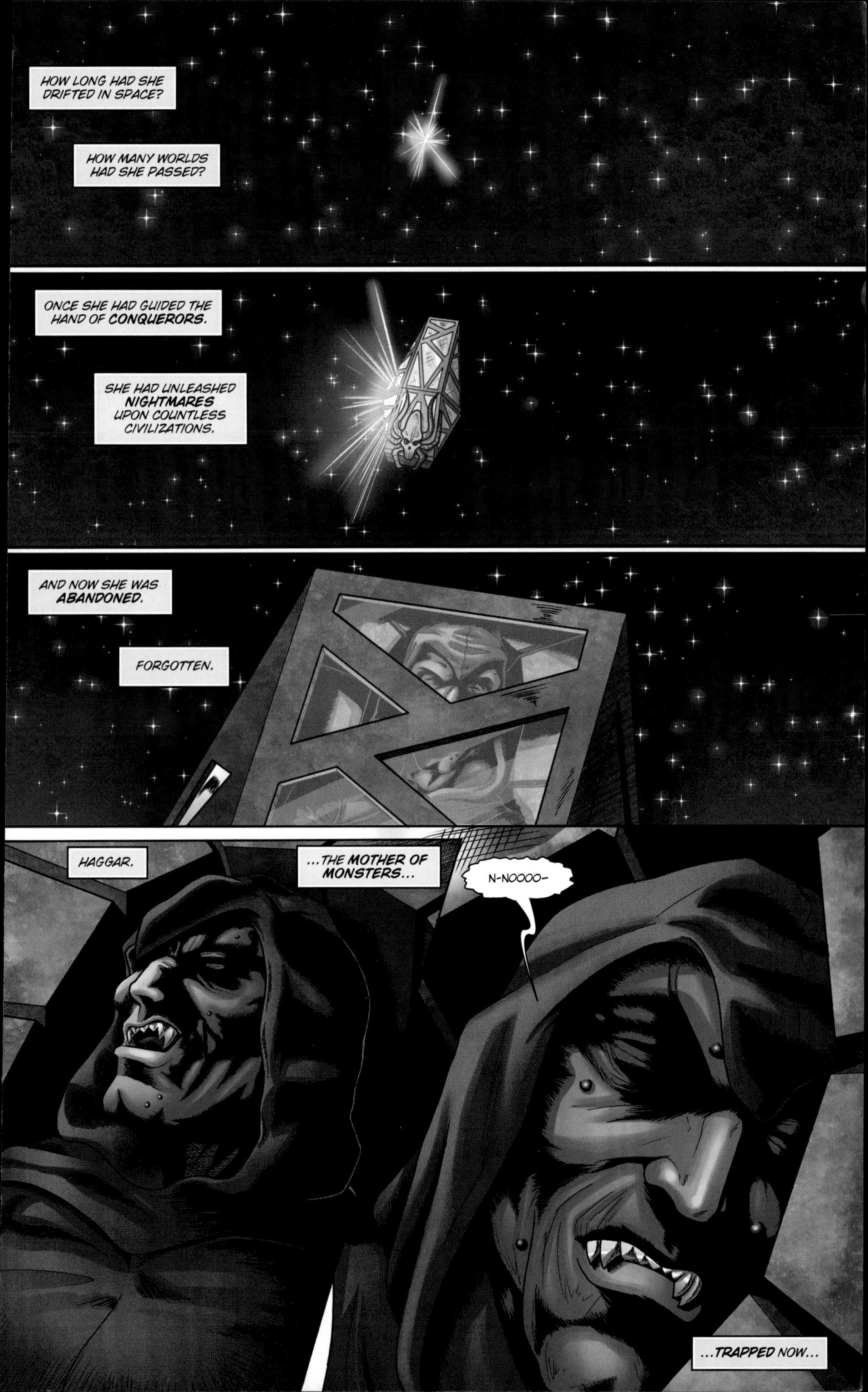
HOW LONG HAD SHE DRIFTED IN SPACE?
HOW MANY WORLDS HAD SHE PASSED?
ONCE SHE HAD GUIDED THE HAND OF CONQUERORS.
SHE HAD UNLEASHED NIGHTMARES UPON COUNTLESS CIVILIZATIONS.
AND NOW SHE WAS ABANDONED.
FORGOTTEN.
HAGGAR.
...THE MOTHER OF MONSTERS...
N-NOOOO-
...TRAPPED NOW...

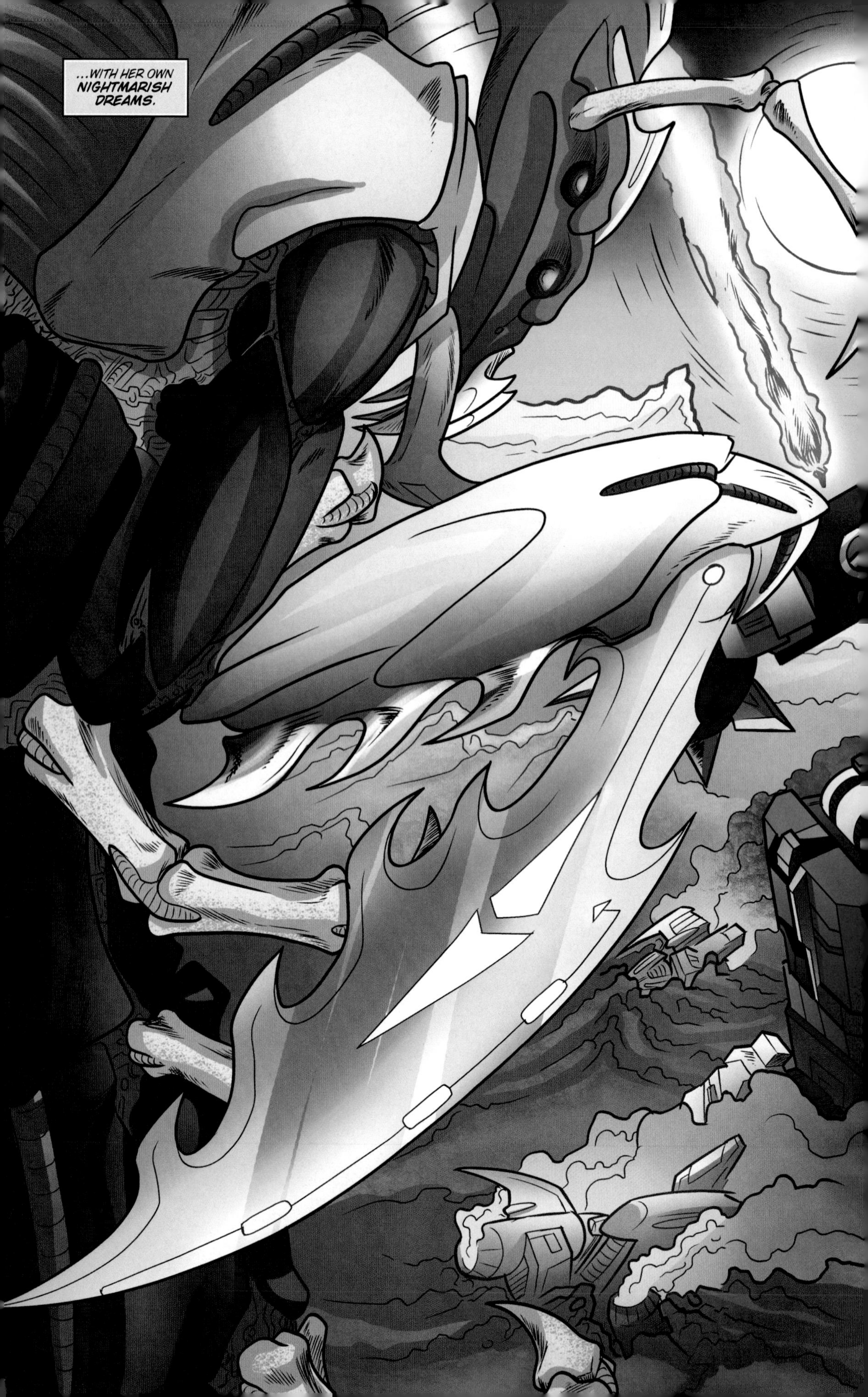
...WITH HER OWN NIGHTMARISH DREAMS.

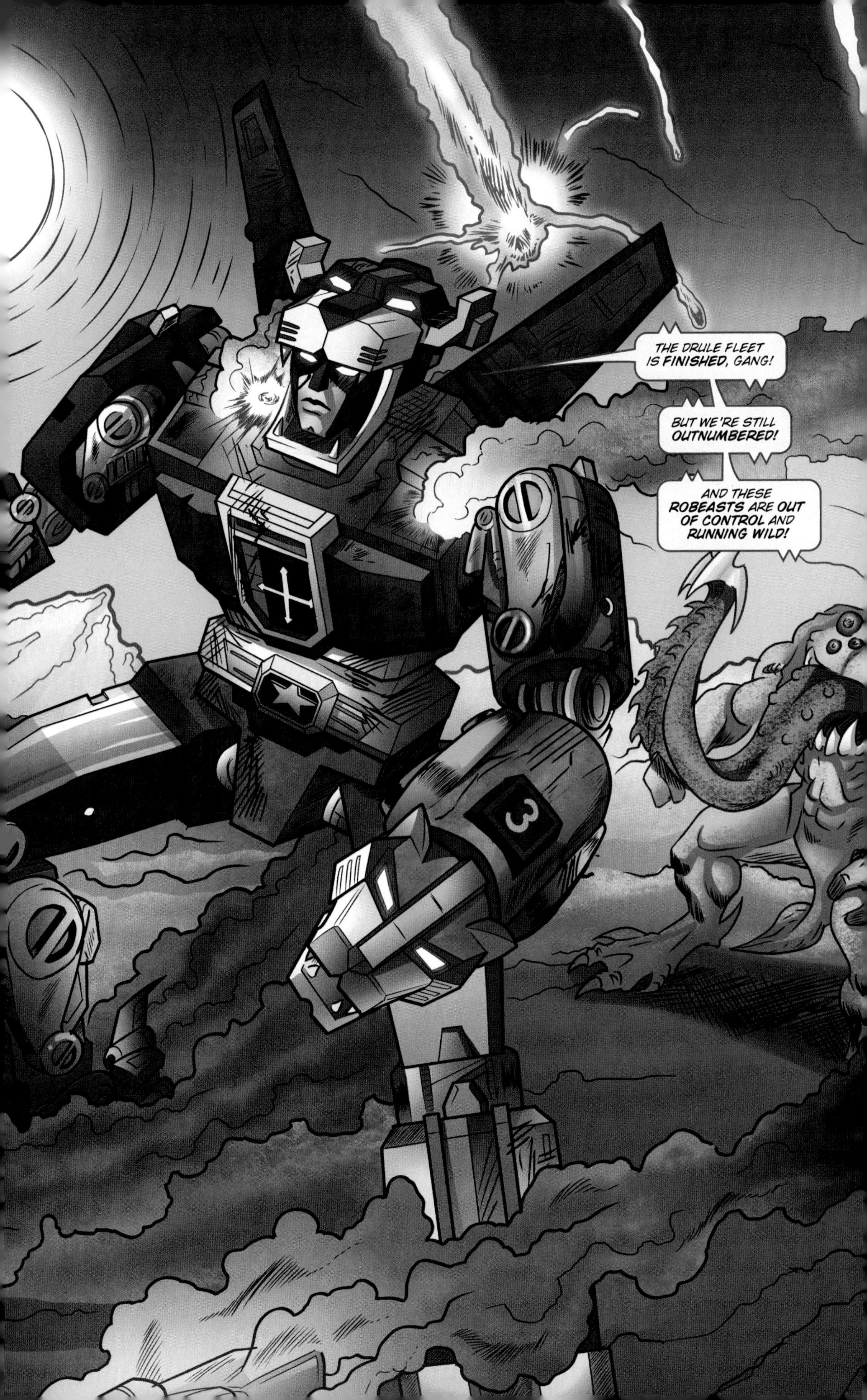
THE DRULE FLEET IS FINISHED, GANG!
BUT WE'RE STILL OUTNUMBERED!
AND THESE ROBEASTS ARE OUT OF CONTROL AND RUNNING WILD!

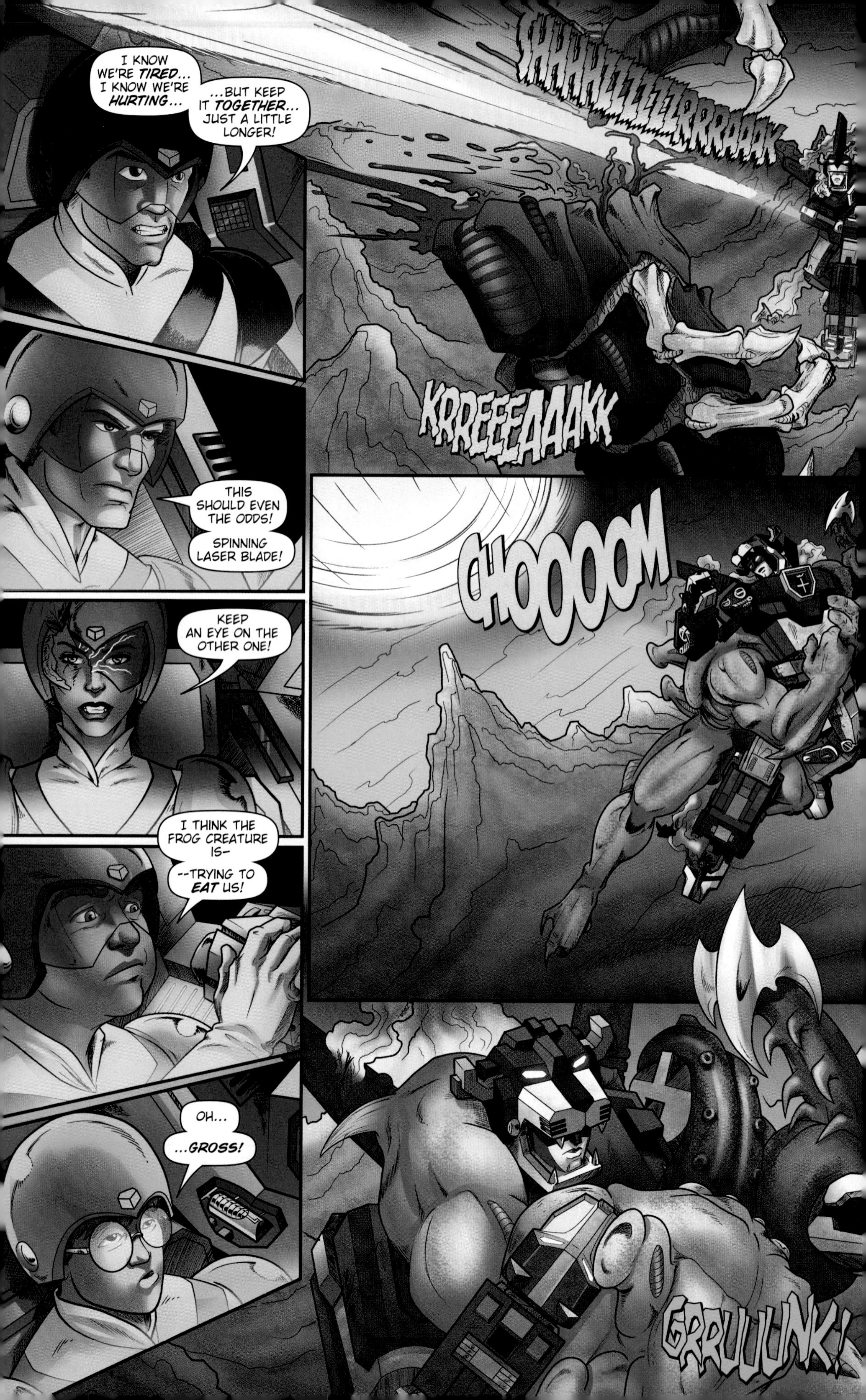
I KNOW WE'RE *TIRED*... I KNOW WE'RE *HURTING*...
...BUT KEEP IT *TOGETHER*... JUST A LITTLE LONGER!
SHHHHZZZZZRRRAAAK
KRREEEAAAKK
THIS SHOULD EVEN THE ODDS!
SPINNING LASER BLADE!
CHOOOOM
KEEP AN EYE ON THE OTHER ONE!
I THINK THE FROG CREATURE IS–
--TRYING TO *EAT* US!
OH...
...*GROSS!*
GRRUUUNK!

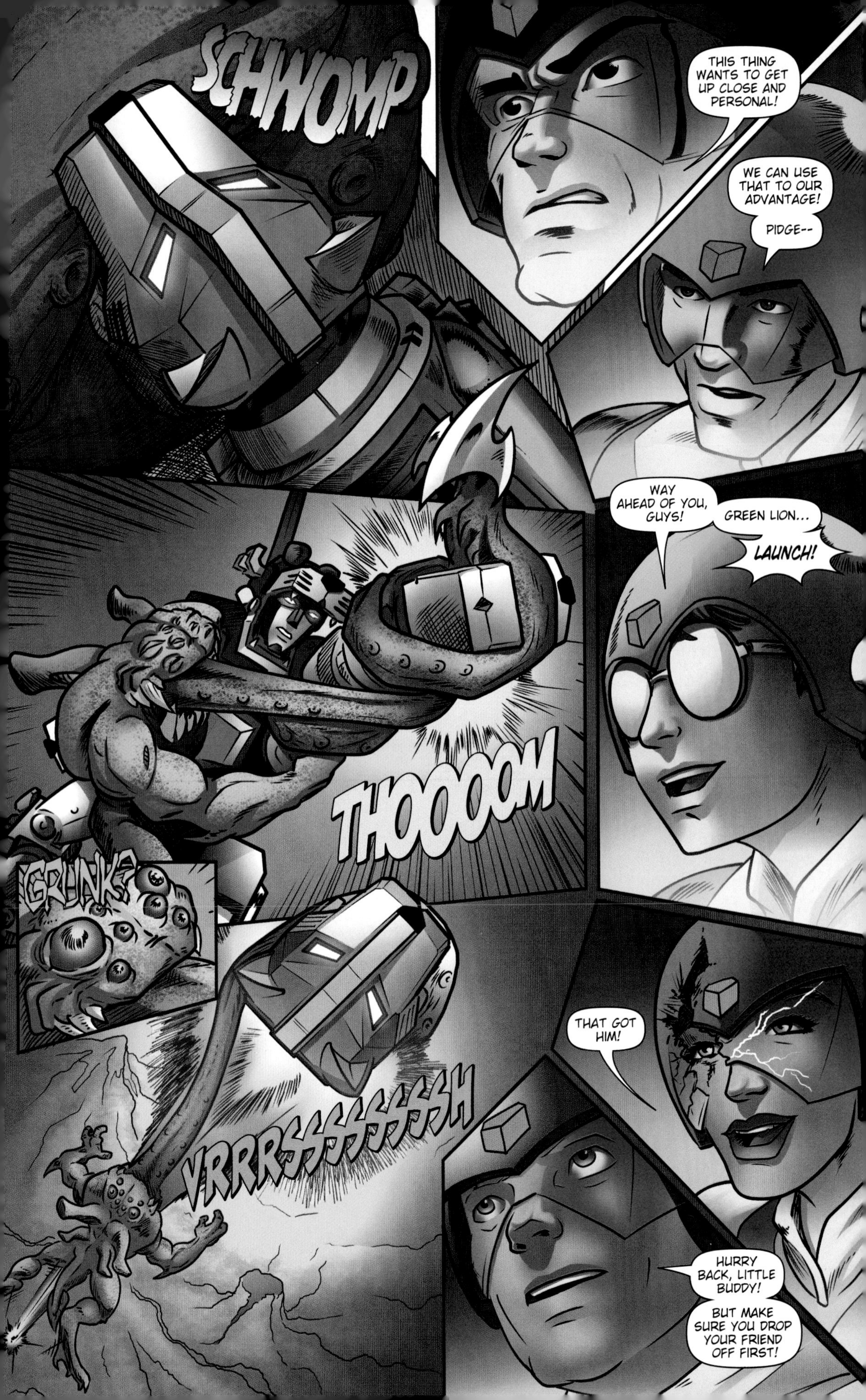
SCHWOMP
THIS THING WANTS TO GET UP CLOSE AND PERSONAL!
WE CAN USE THAT TO OUR ADVANTAGE!
PIDGE--
WAY AHEAD OF YOU, GUYS!
GREEN LION...
LAUNCH!
THOOOOM
GRUNK?
VRRRSSSSSSSSH
THAT GOT HIM!
HURRY BACK, LITTLE BUDDY!
BUT MAKE SURE YOU DROP YOUR FRIEND OFF FIRST!

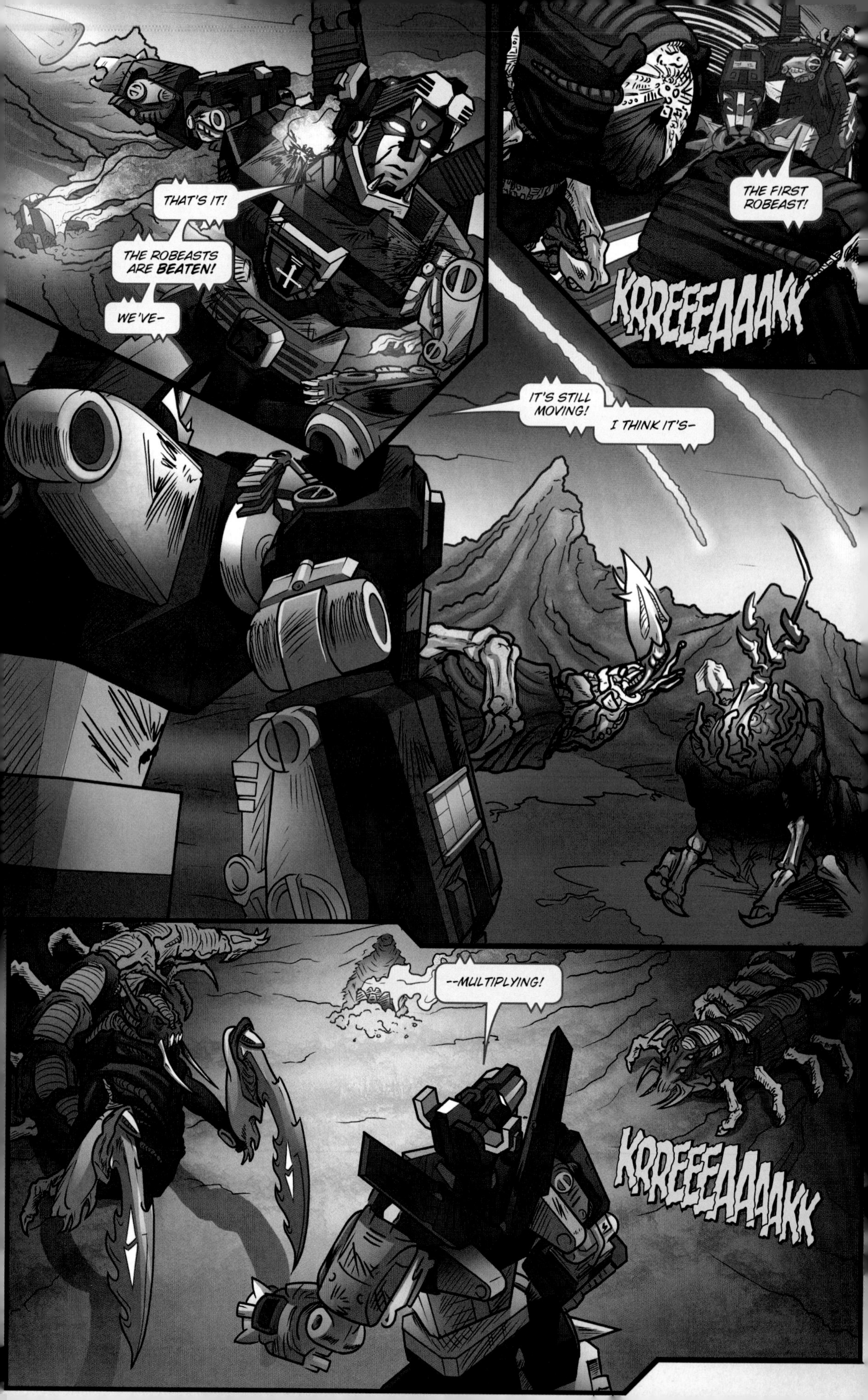
THAT'S IT!
THE ROBEASTS ARE BEATEN!
WE'VE-
THE FIRST ROBEAST!
KRREEEAAAKK
IT'S STILL MOVING!
I THINK IT'S-
--MULTIPLYING!
KRREEEAAAKK

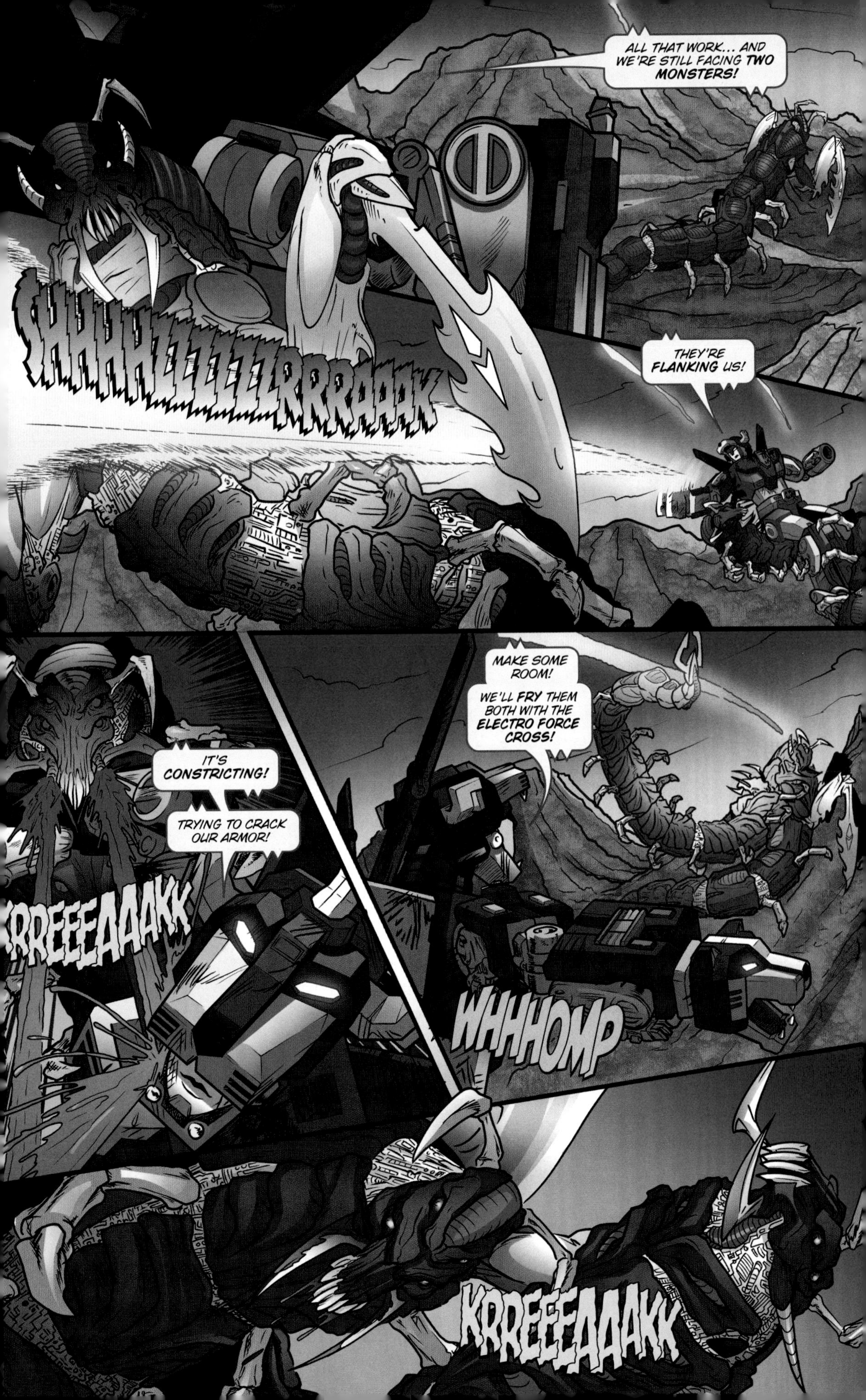
ALL THAT WORK... AND WE'RE STILL FACING TWO MONSTERS!
SHHHHZZZZZZRRRAAAK
THEY'RE FLANKING US!
IT'S CONSTRICTING!
TRYING TO CRACK OUR ARMOR!
KRREEEAAAKK
MAKE SOME ROOM!
WE'LL FRY THEM BOTH WITH THE ELECTRO FORCE CROSS!
WHHHOMP
KRREEEAAAKK

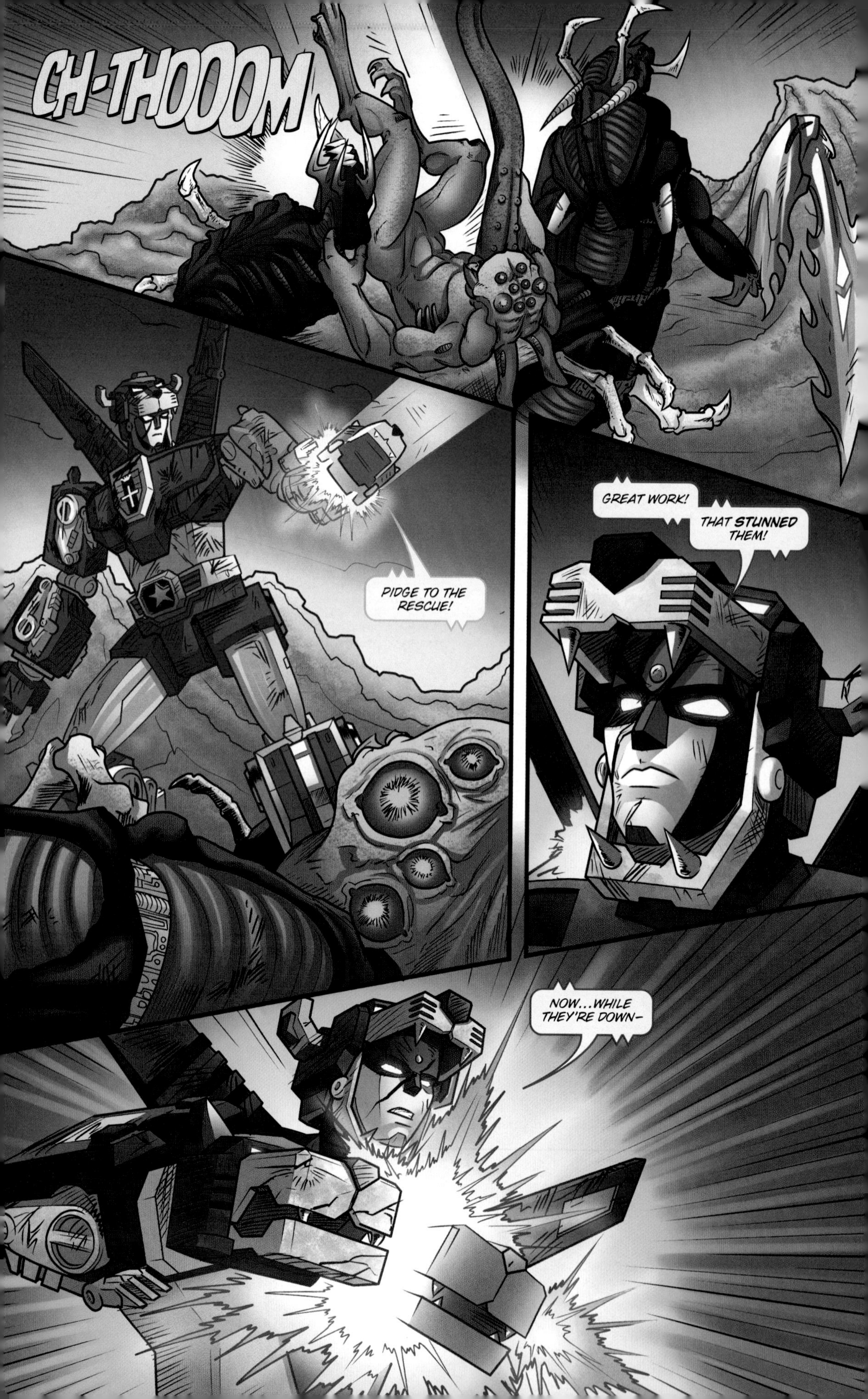
CH-THOOOM
PIDGE TO THE RESCUE!
GREAT WORK!
THAT STUNNED THEM!
NOW...WHILE THEY'RE DOWN-

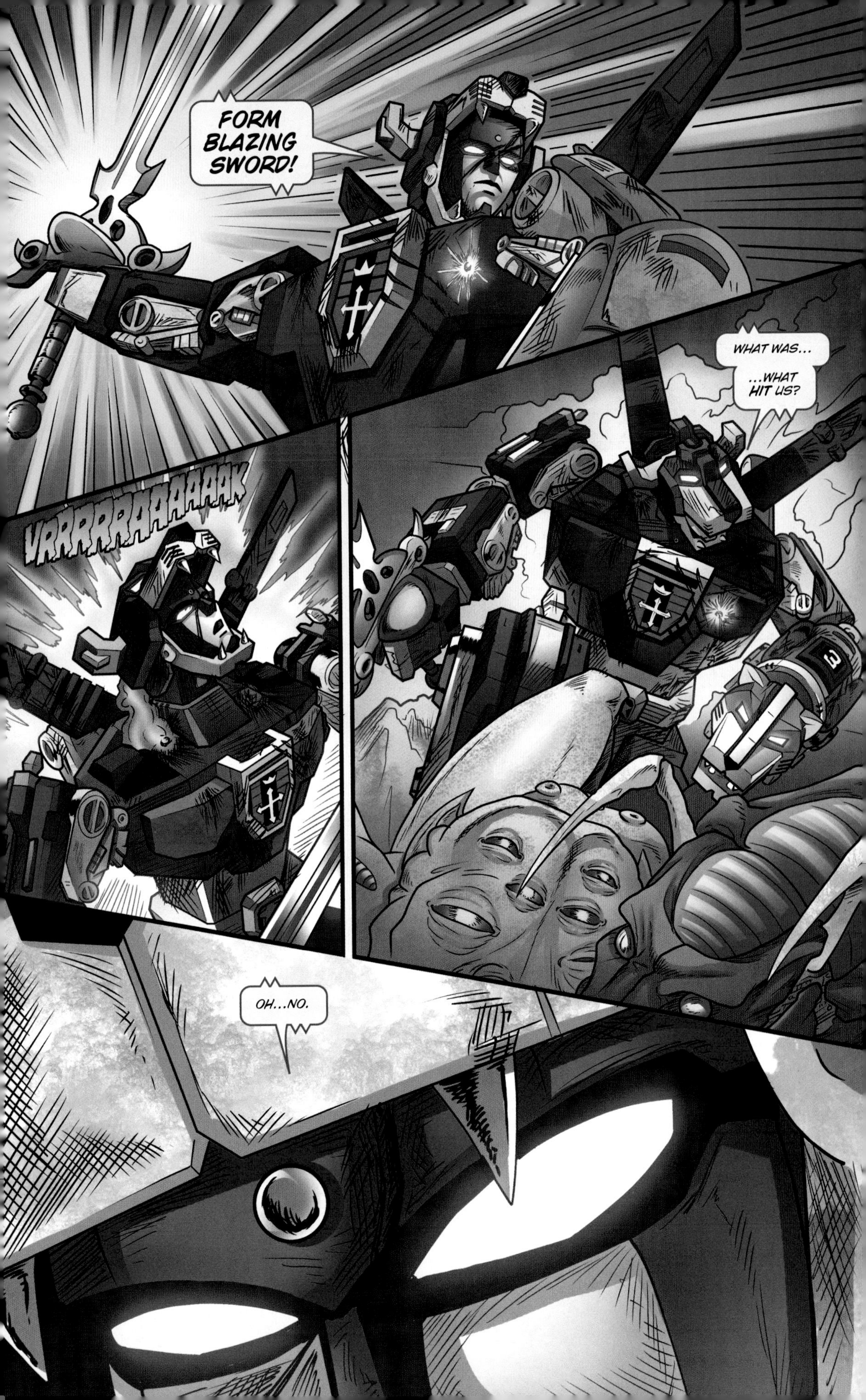
FORM BLAZING SWORD!
VRRRRRAAAAAAAK
WHAT WAS...
...WHAT HIT US?
OH...NO.

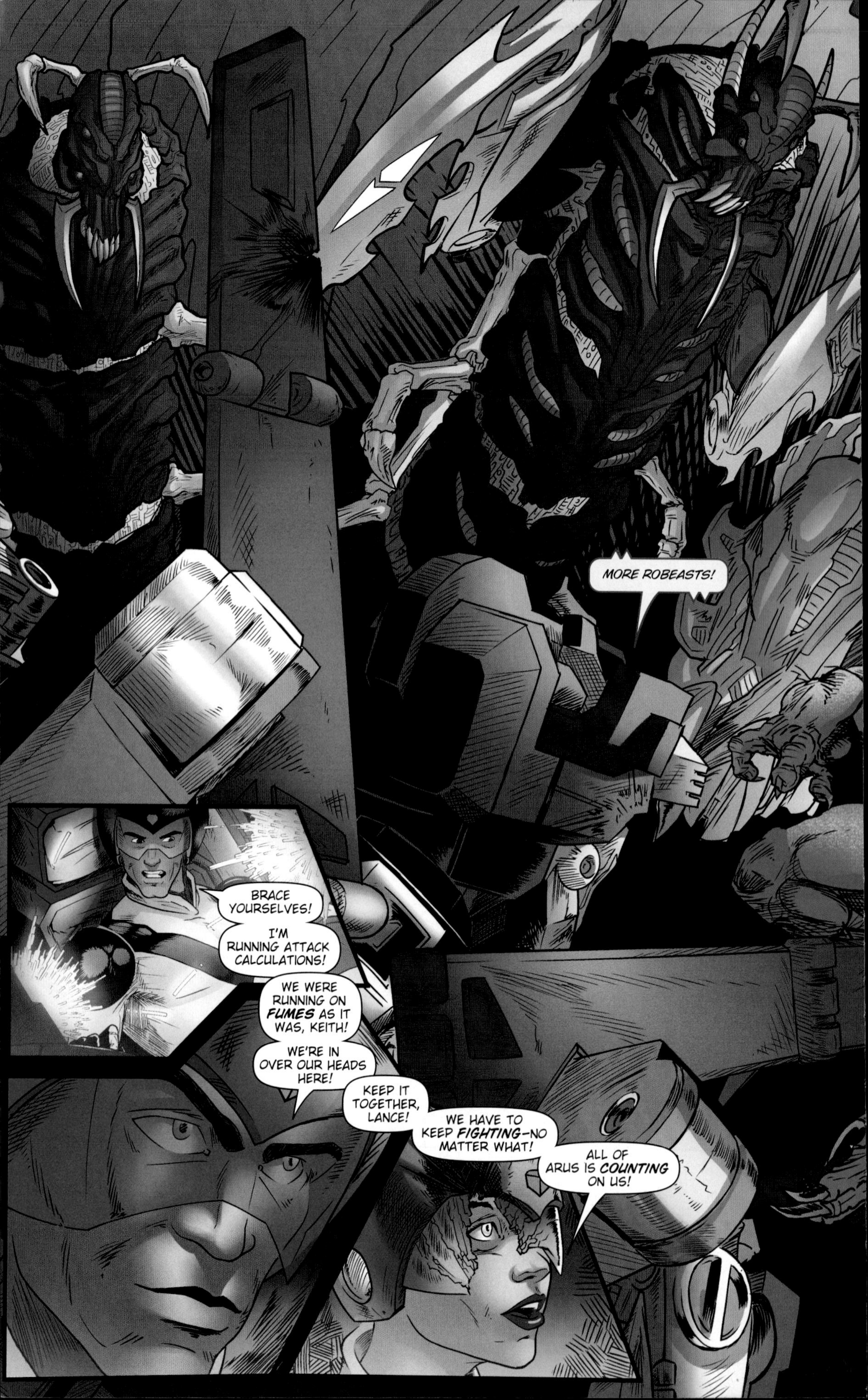
MORE ROBEASTS!
BRACE YOURSELVES!
I'M RUNNING ATTACK CALCULATIONS!
WE WERE RUNNING ON FUMES AS IT WAS, KEITH!
WE'RE IN OVER OUR HEADS HERE!
KEEP IT TOGETHER, LANCE!
WE HAVE TO KEEP FIGHTING—NO MATTER WHAT!
ALL OF ARUS IS COUNTING ON US!

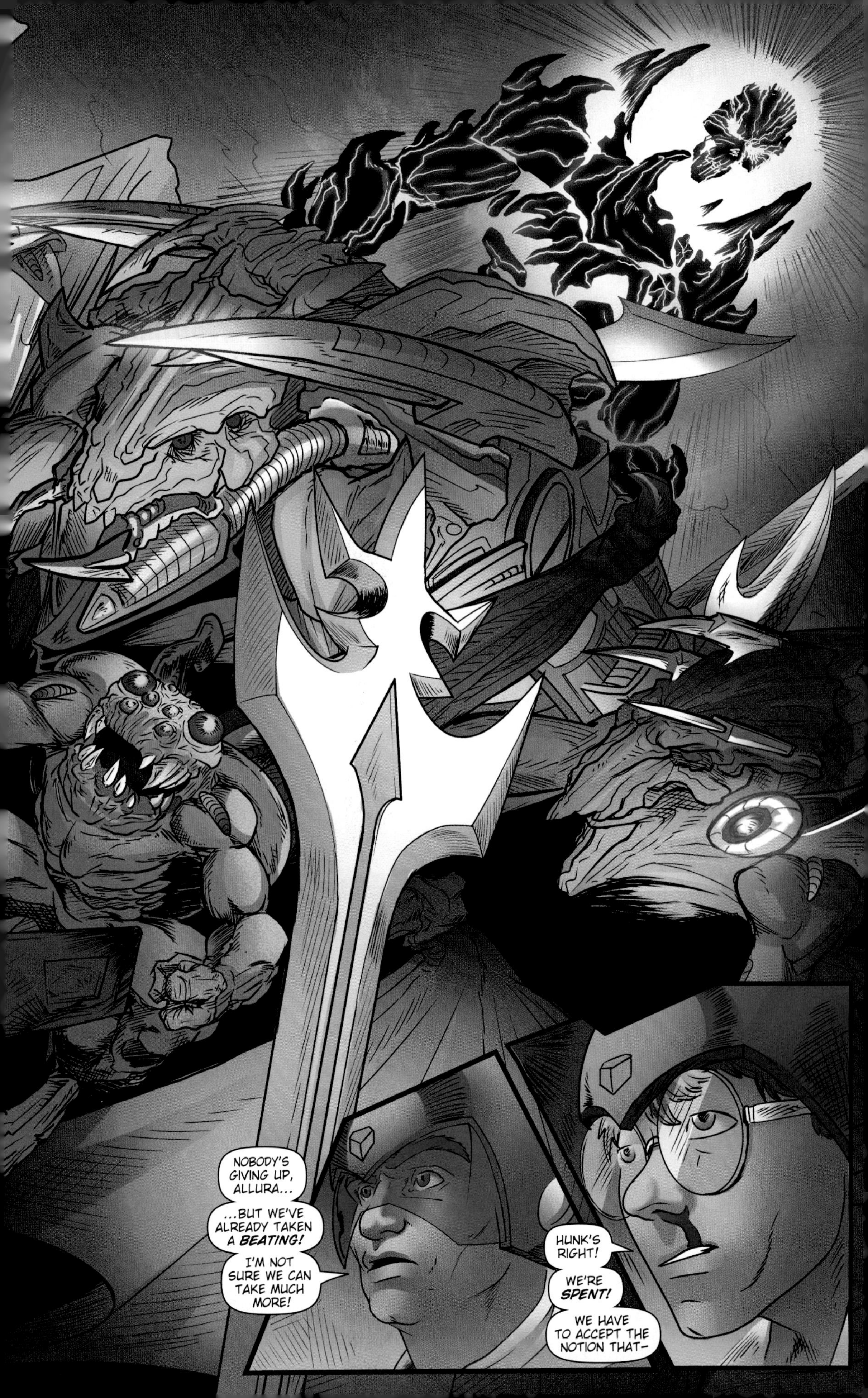
NOBODY'S GIVING UP, ALLURA...
...BUT WE'VE ALREADY TAKEN A ***BEATING!***
I'M NOT SURE WE CAN TAKE MUCH MORE!
HUNK'S RIGHT!
WE'RE ***SPENT!***
WE HAVE TO ACCEPT THE NOTION THAT–

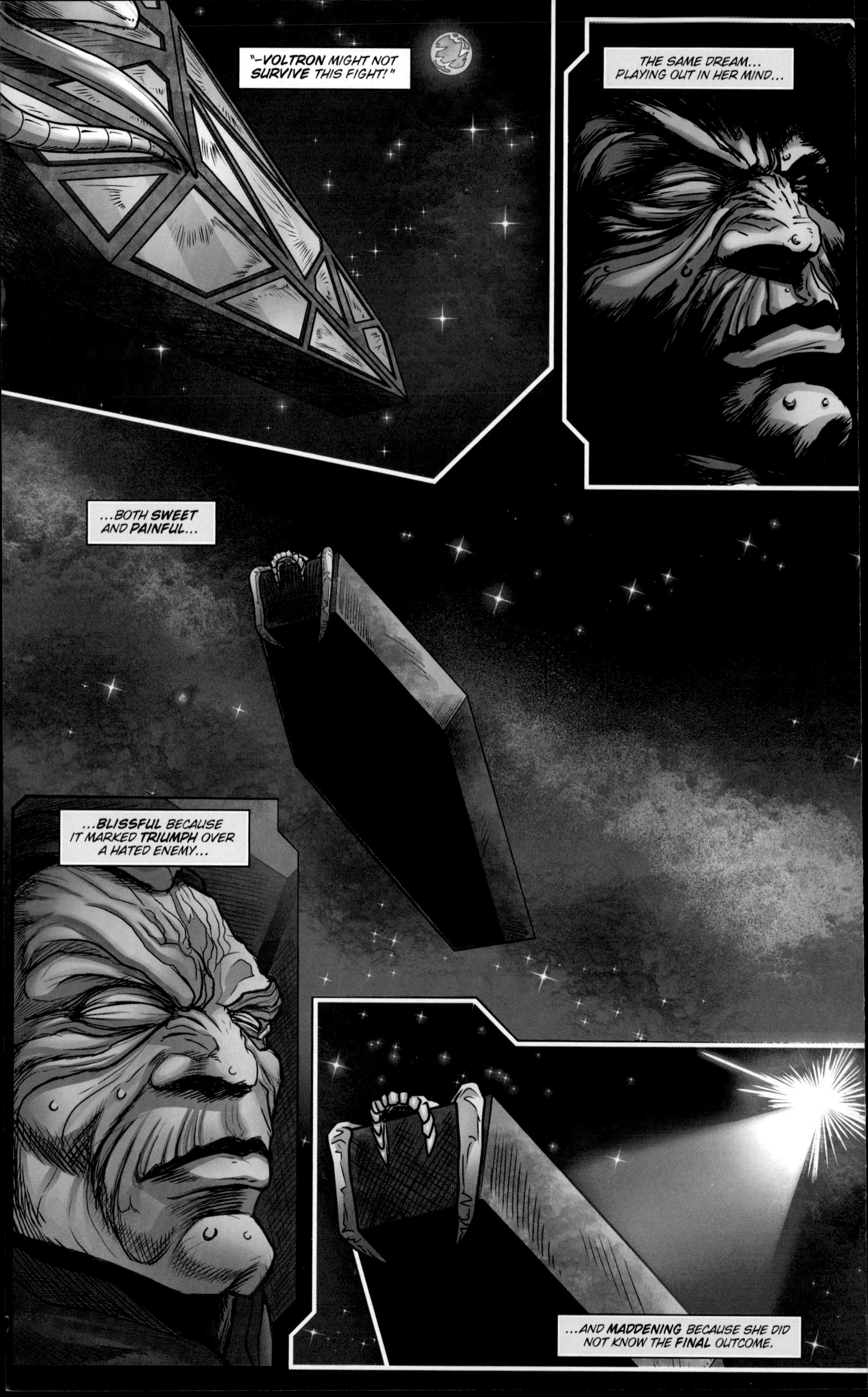
"–VOLTRON MIGHT NOT SURVIVE THIS FIGHT!"
THE SAME DREAM... PLAYING OUT IN HER MIND...
...BOTH SWEET AND PAINFUL...
...BLISSFUL BECAUSE IT MARKED TRIUMPH OVER A HATED ENEMY...
...AND MADDENING BECAUSE SHE DID NOT KNOW THE FINAL OUTCOME.

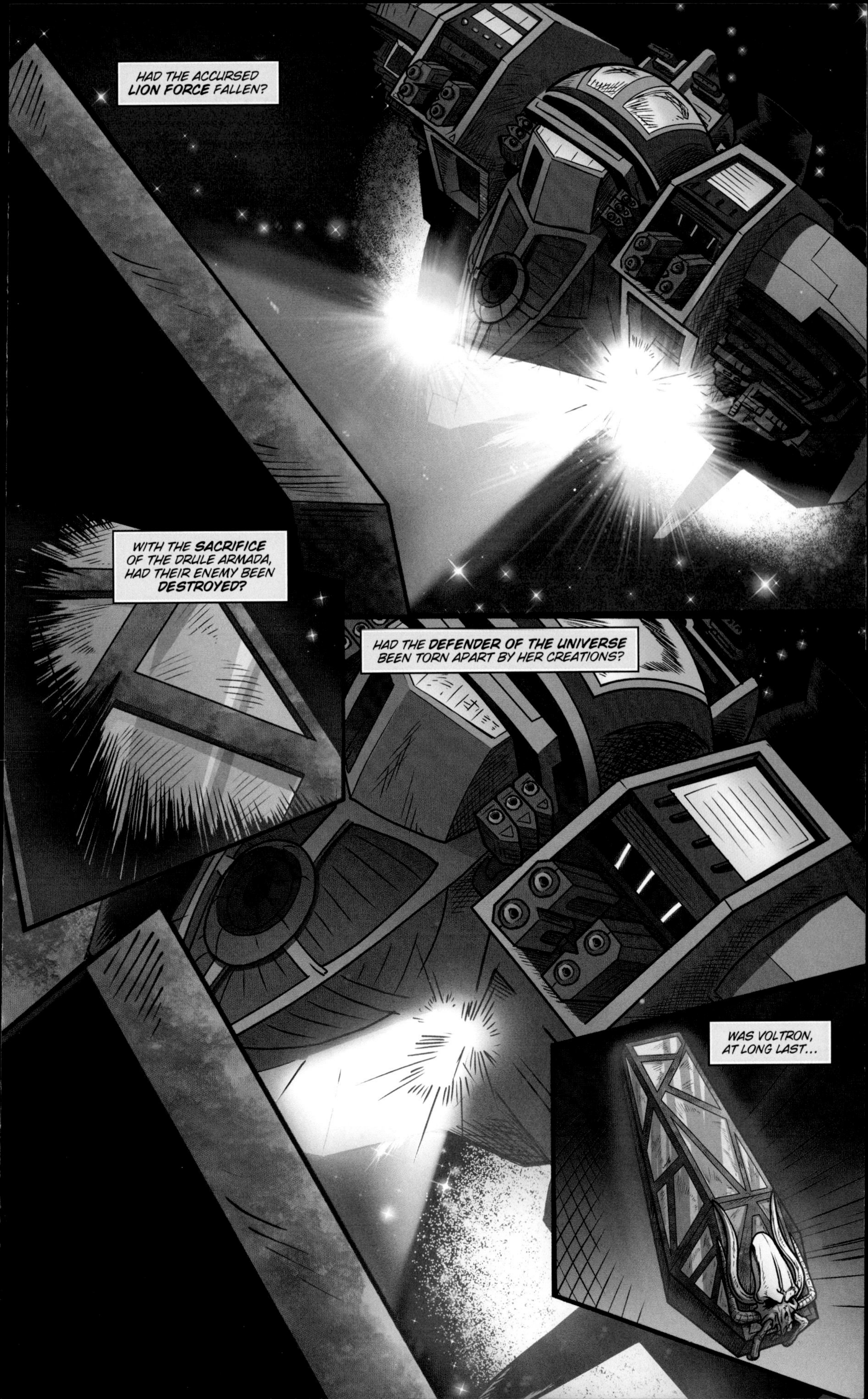
HAD THE ACCURSED LION FORCE FALLEN?
WITH THE SACRIFICE OF THE DRULE ARMADA, HAD THEIR ENEMY BEEN DESTROYED?
HAD THE DEFENDER OF THE UNIVERSE BEEN TORN APART BY HER CREATIONS?
WAS VOLTRON, AT LONG LAST...

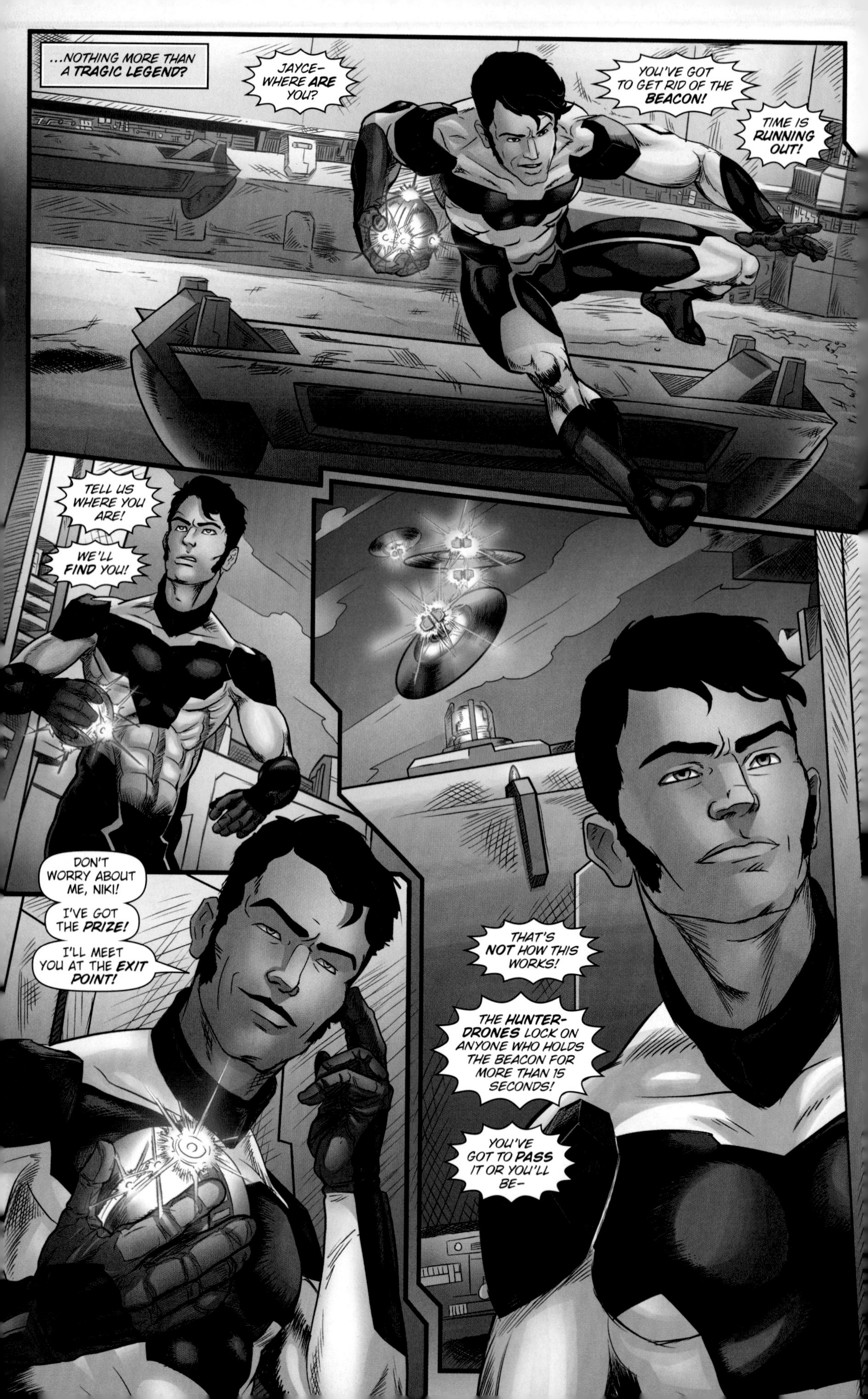
...NOTHING MORE THAN A TRAGIC LEGEND?
JAYCE-WHERE ARE YOU?
YOU'VE GOT TO GET RID OF THE BEACON!
TIME IS RUNNING OUT!
TELL US WHERE YOU ARE!
WE'LL FIND YOU!
DON'T WORRY ABOUT ME, NIKI!
I'VE GOT THE PRIZE!
I'LL MEET YOU AT THE EXIT POINT!
THAT'S NOT HOW THIS WORKS!
THE HUNTER-DRONES LOCK ON ANYONE WHO HOLDS THE BEACON FOR MORE THAN 15 SECONDS!
YOU'VE GOT TO PASS IT OR YOU'LL BE-

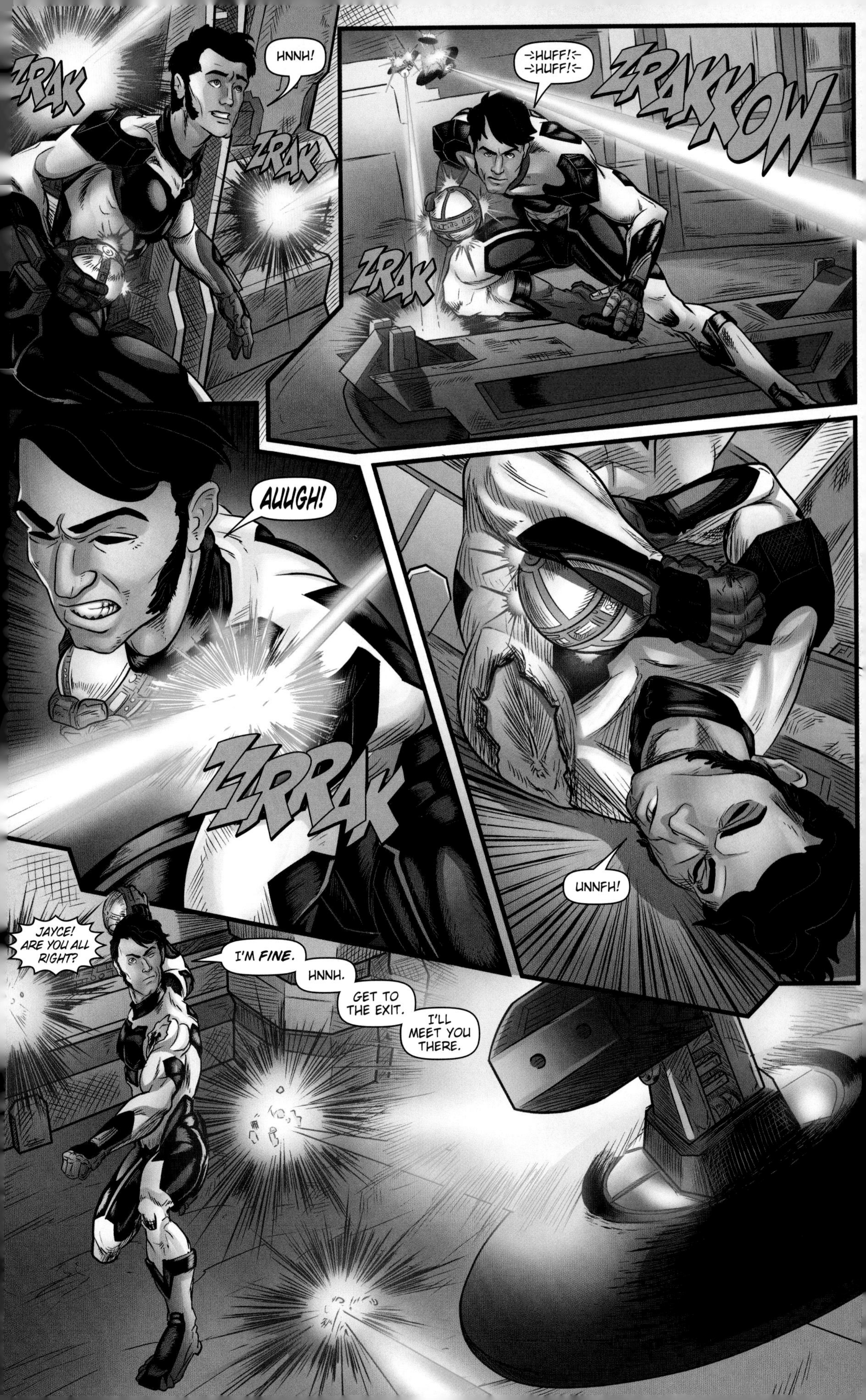
ZRAK
HNNH!
ZRAK
-HUFF!-
-HUFF!-
ZRAKKOW
ZRAK
AUUGH!
ZZRRAK
UNNFH!
JAYCE! ARE YOU ALL RIGHT?
I'M FINE.
HNNH.
GET TO THE EXIT.
I'LL MEET YOU THERE.

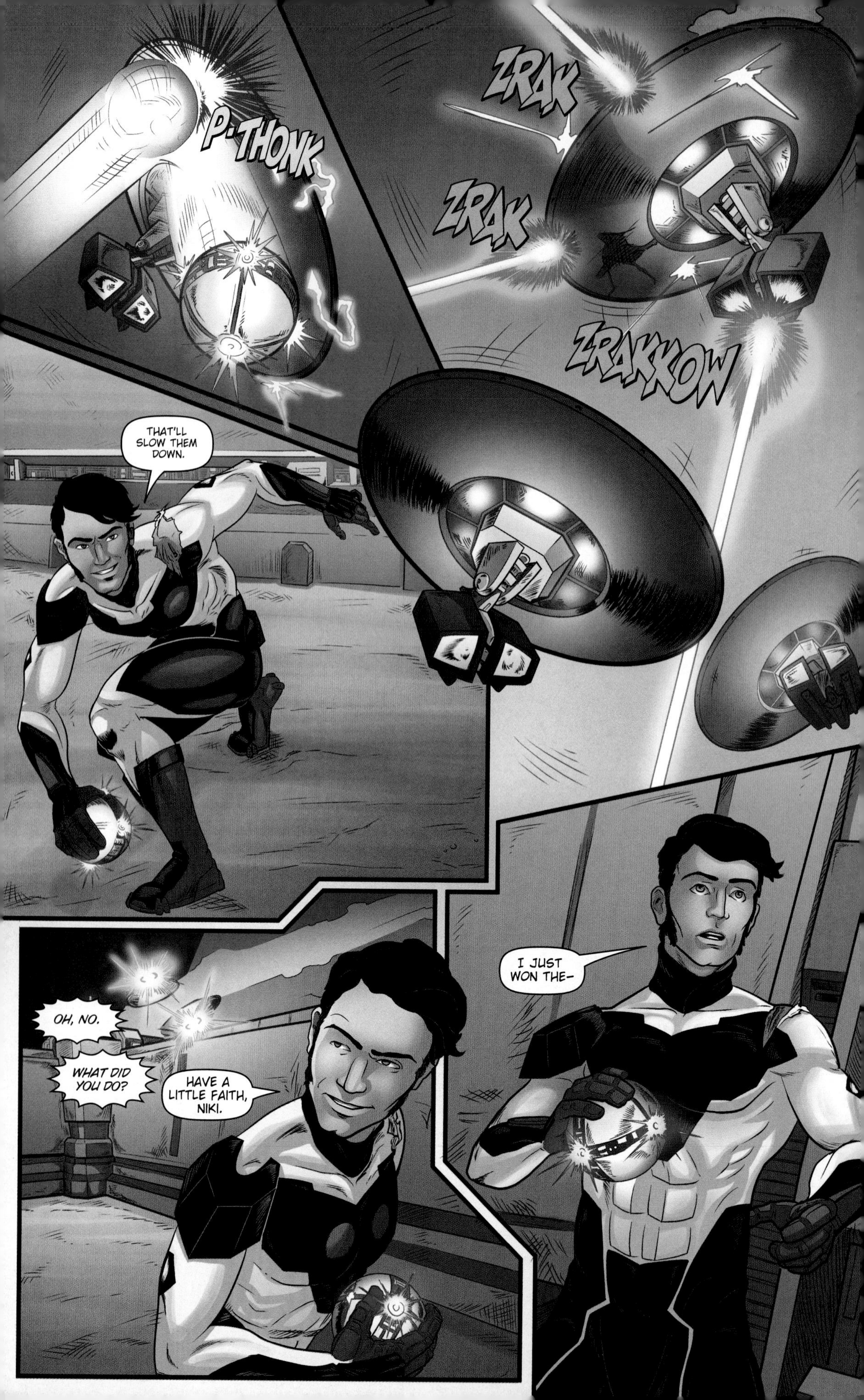
P-THONK
ZRAK
ZRAK
ZRAKKOW
THAT'LL SLOW THEM DOWN.
OH, NO.
WHAT DID YOU DO?
HAVE A LITTLE FAITH, NIKI.
I JUST WON THE-

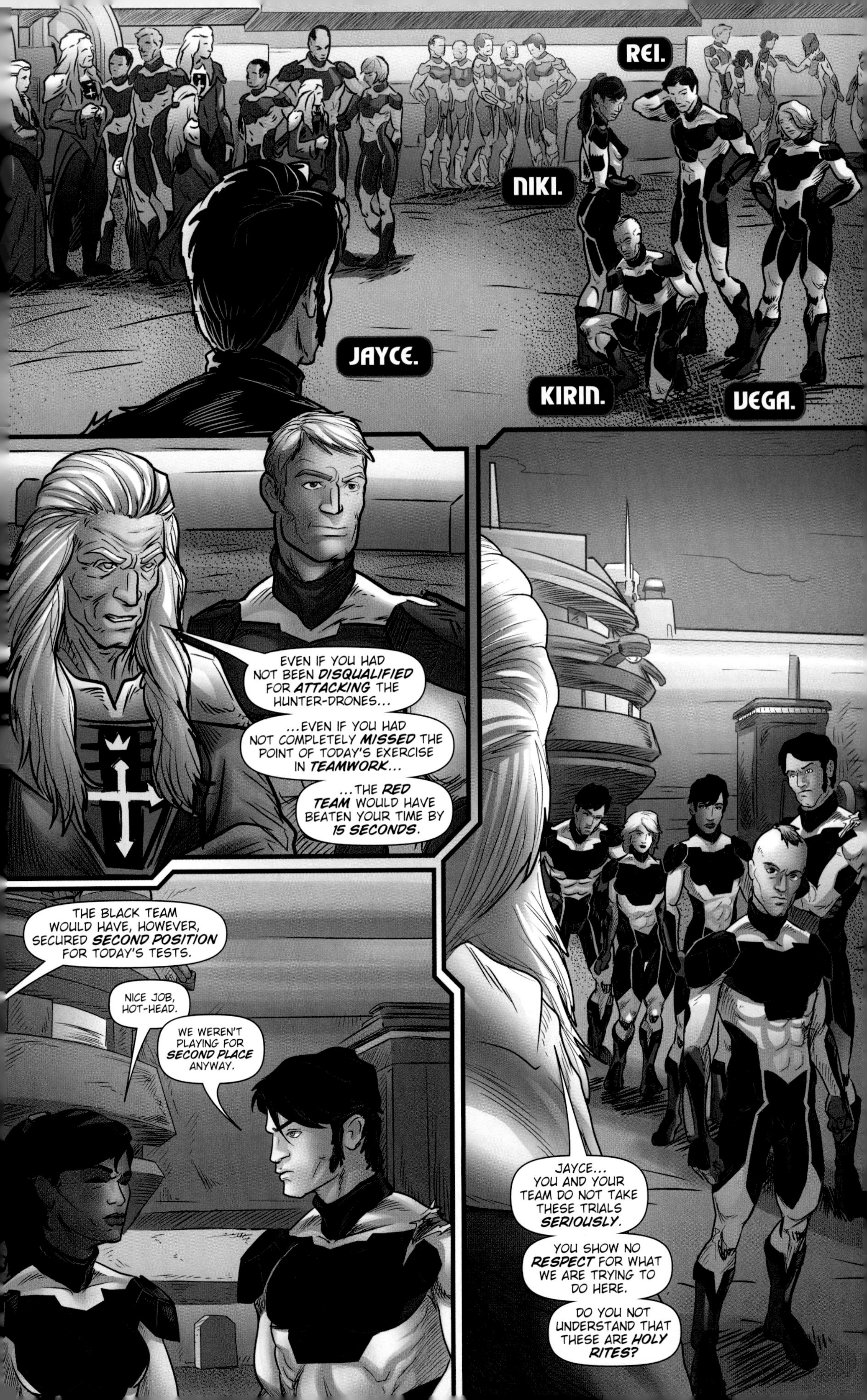
REI.
NIKI.
JAYCE.
KIRIN.
VEGA.
EVEN IF YOU HAD NOT BEEN DISQUALIFIED FOR ATTACKING THE HUNTER-DRONES...
...EVEN IF YOU HAD NOT COMPLETELY MISSED THE POINT OF TODAY'S EXERCISE IN TEAMWORK...
...THE RED TEAM WOULD HAVE BEATEN YOUR TIME BY 15 SECONDS.
THE BLACK TEAM WOULD HAVE, HOWEVER, SECURED SECOND POSITION FOR TODAY'S TESTS.
NICE JOB, HOT-HEAD.
WE WEREN'T PLAYING FOR SECOND PLACE ANYWAY.
JAYCE... YOU AND YOUR TEAM DO NOT TAKE THESE TRIALS SERIOUSLY.
YOU SHOW NO RESPECT FOR WHAT WE ARE TRYING TO DO HERE.
DO YOU NOT UNDERSTAND THAT THESE ARE HOLY RITES?

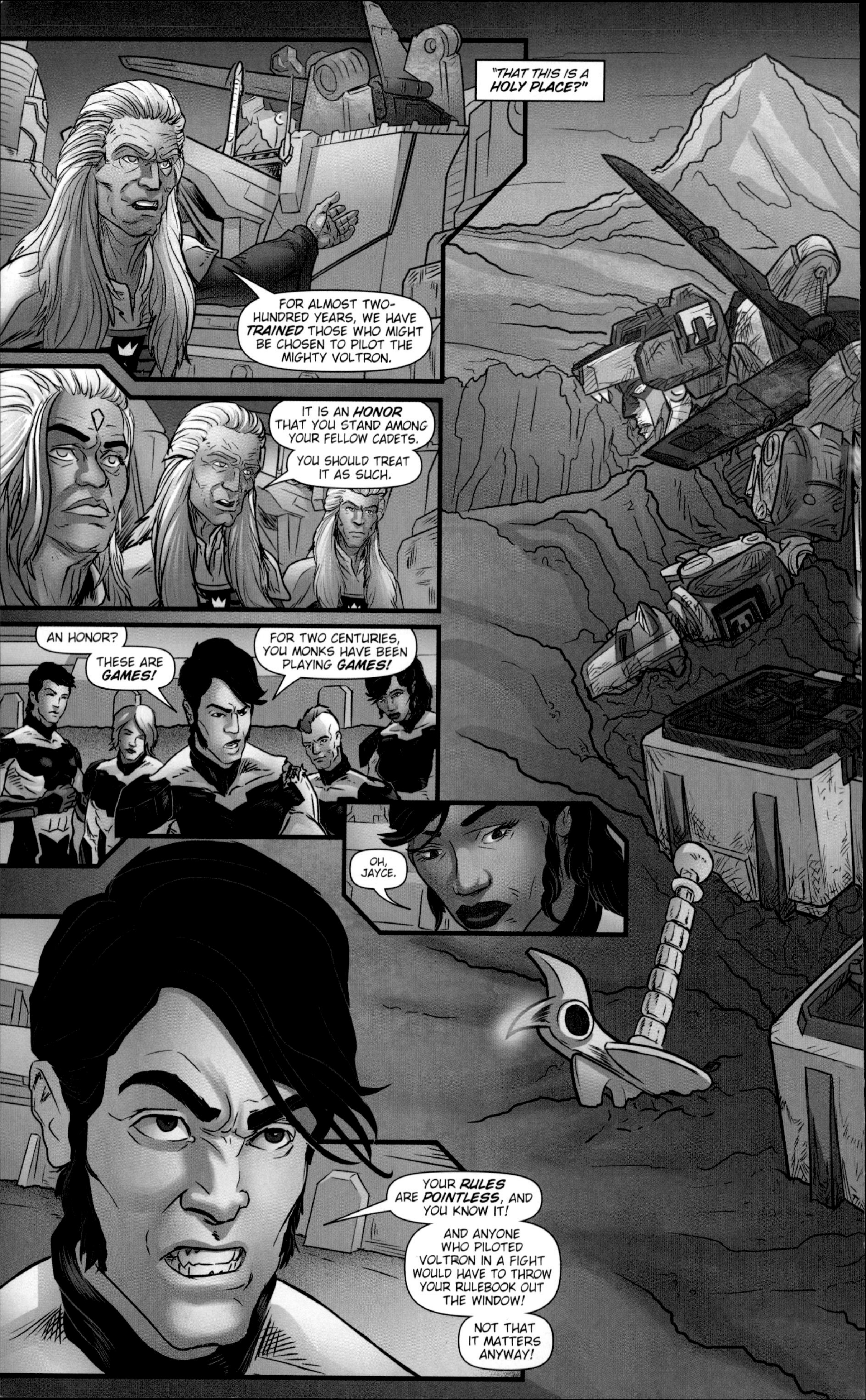
"THAT THIS IS A HOLY PLACE?"
FOR ALMOST TWO-HUNDRED YEARS, WE HAVE TRAINED THOSE WHO MIGHT BE CHOSEN TO PILOT THE MIGHTY VOLTRON.
IT IS AN HONOR THAT YOU STAND AMONG YOUR FELLOW CADETS.
YOU SHOULD TREAT IT AS SUCH.
AN HONOR?
THESE ARE GAMES!
FOR TWO CENTURIES, YOU MONKS HAVE BEEN PLAYING GAMES!
OH, JAYCE.
YOUR RULES ARE POINTLESS, AND YOU KNOW IT!
AND ANYONE WHO PILOTED VOLTRON IN A FIGHT WOULD HAVE TO THROW YOUR RULEBOOK OUT THE WINDOW!
NOT THAT IT MATTERS ANYWAY!

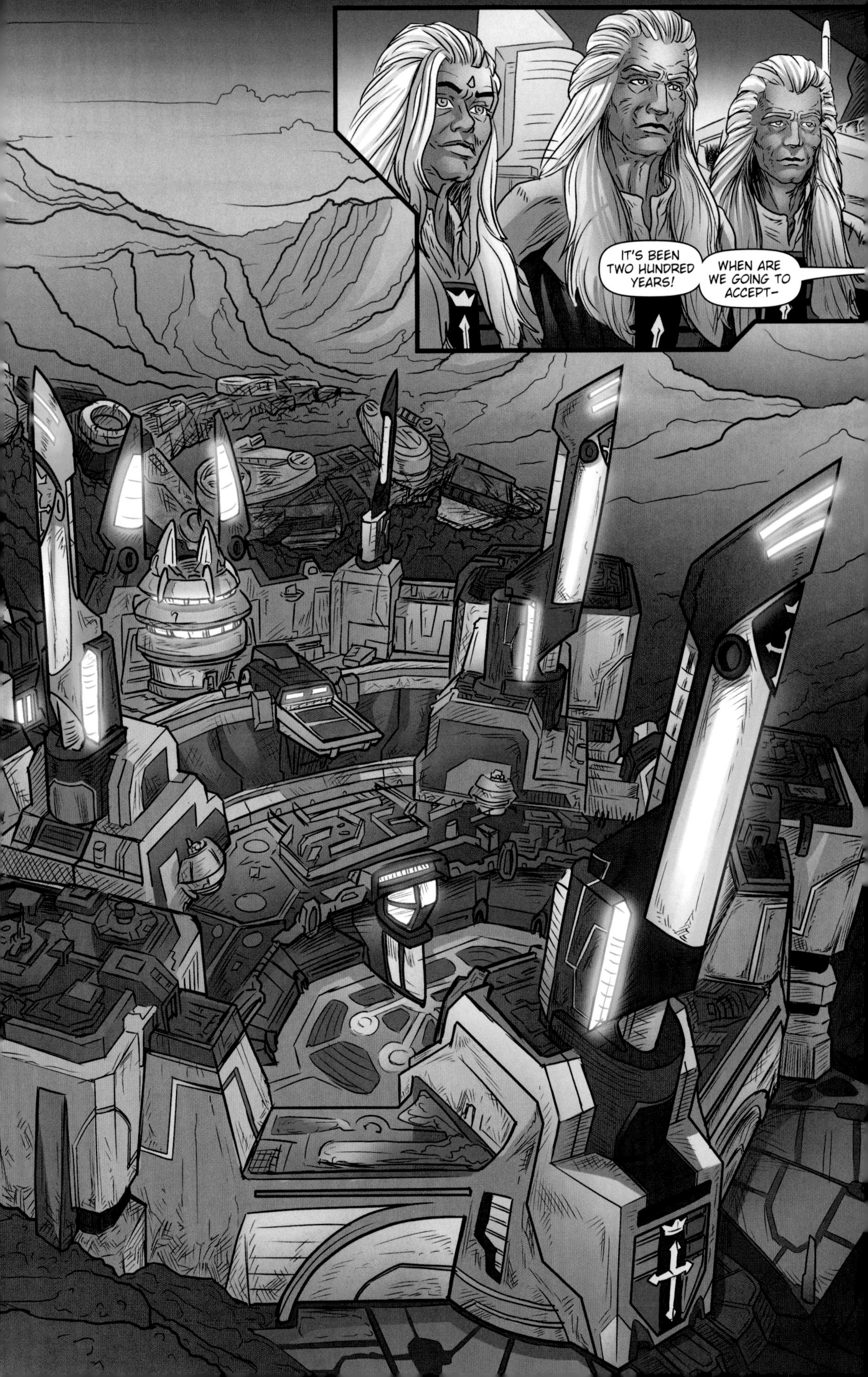
IT'S BEEN TWO HUNDRED YEARS!
WHEN ARE WE GOING TO ACCEPT-

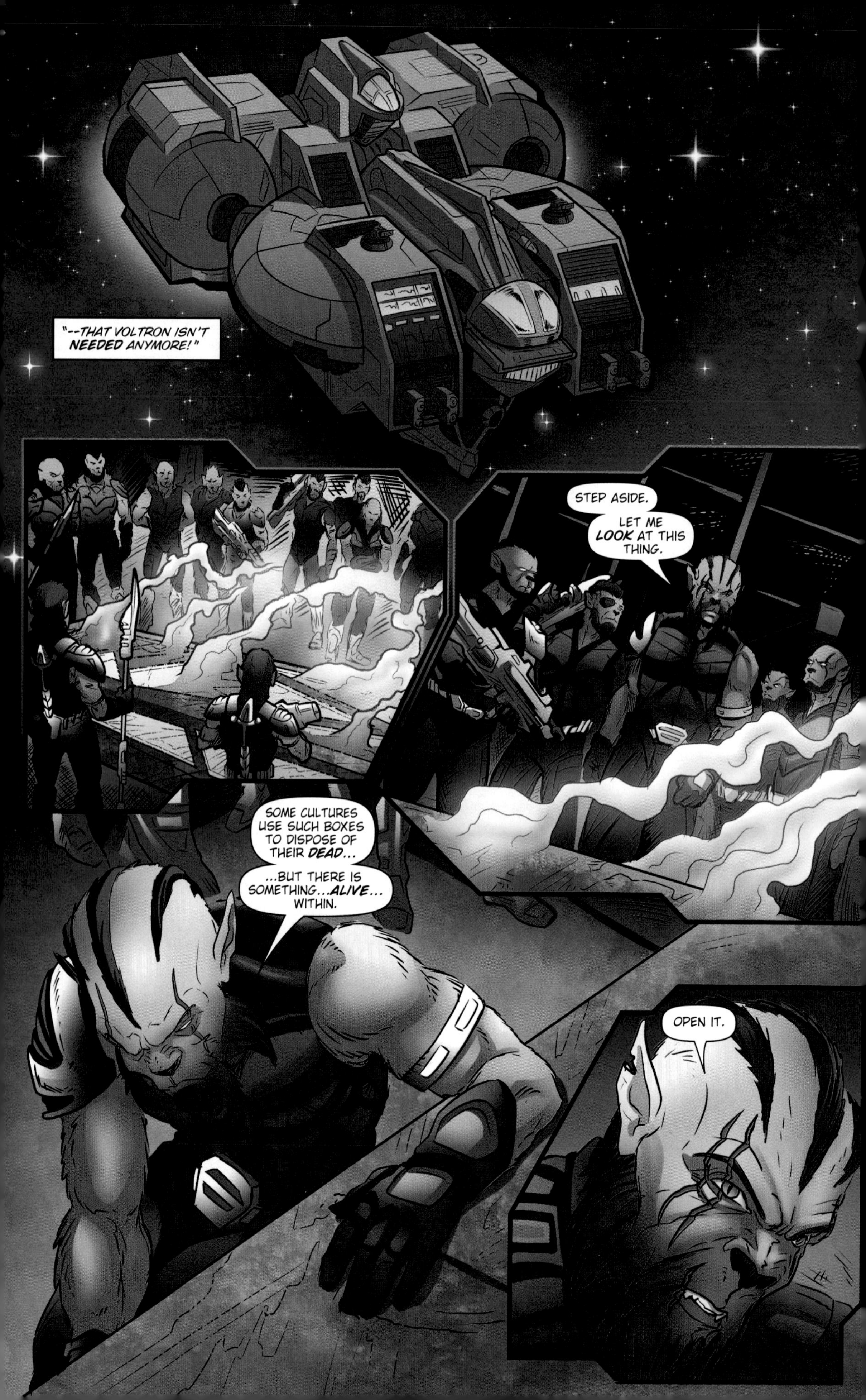
"--THAT VOLTRON ISN'T NEEDED ANYMORE!"
STEP ASIDE.
LET ME LOOK AT THIS THING.
SOME CULTURES USE SUCH BOXES TO DISPOSE OF THEIR DEAD...
...BUT THERE IS SOMETHING...ALIVE... WITHIN.
OPEN IT.

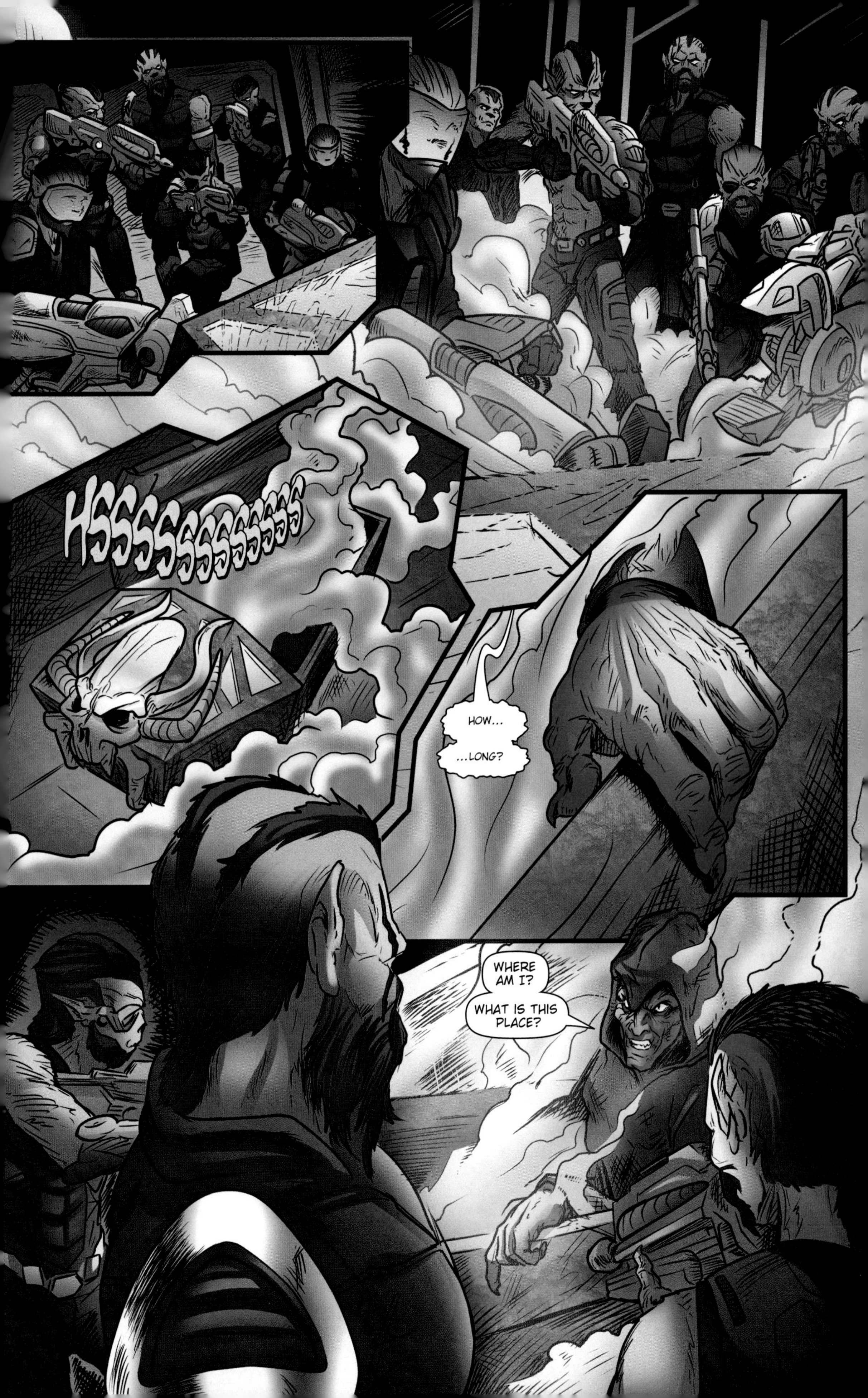
HSSSSSSSSSSSSS
HOW...
...LONG?
WHERE AM I?
WHAT IS THIS PLACE?

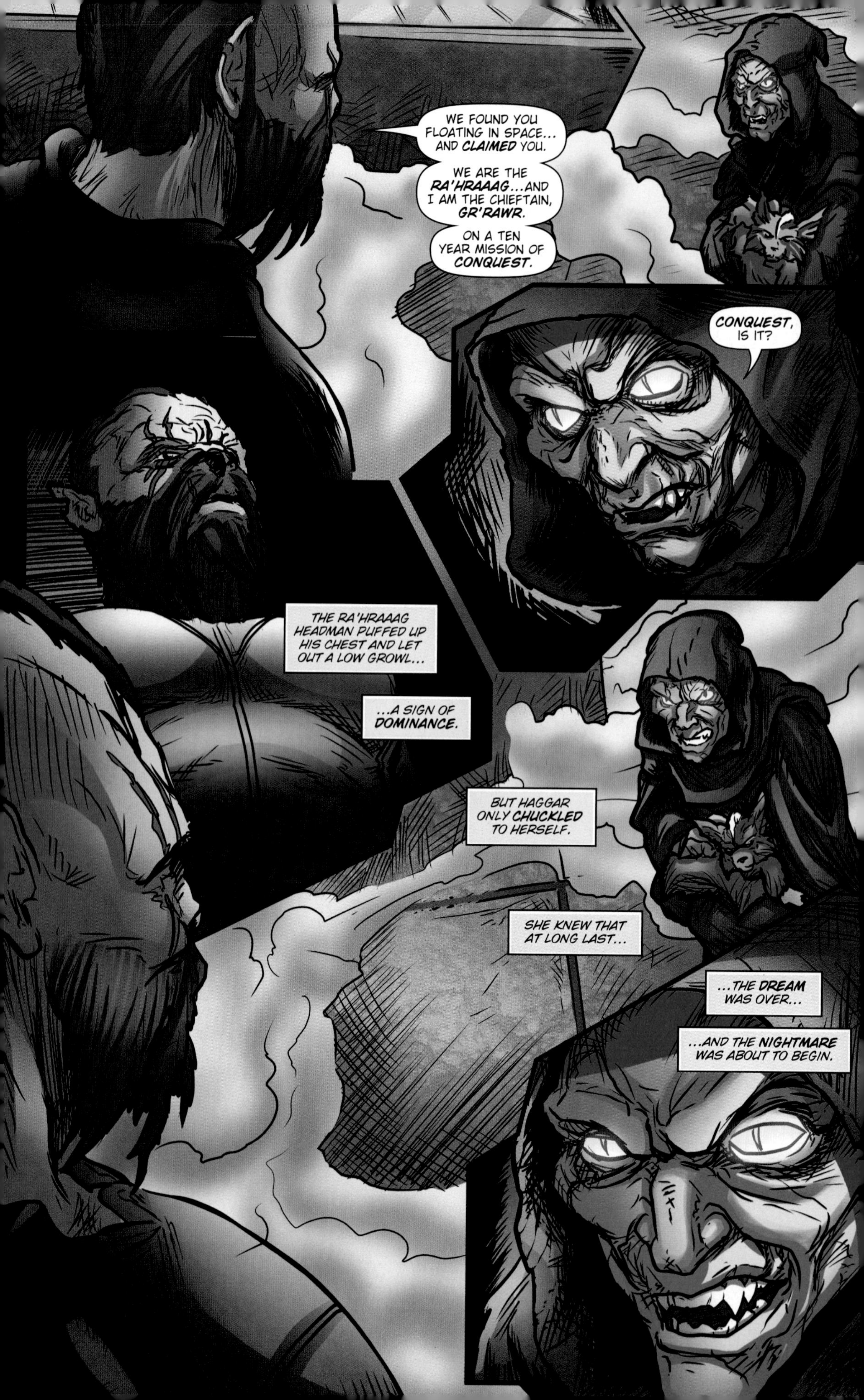

WE FOUND YOU FLOATING IN SPACE... AND CLAIMED YOU.
WE ARE THE RA'HRAAAG...AND I AM THE CHIEFTAIN, GR'RAWR.
ON A TEN YEAR MISSION OF CONQUEST.
CONQUEST, IS IT?
THE RA'HRAAAG HEADMAN PUFFED UP HIS CHEST AND LET OUT A LOW GROWL...
...A SIGN OF DOMINANCE.
BUT HAGGAR ONLY CHUCKLED TO HERSELF.
SHE KNEW THAT AT LONG LAST...
...THE DREAM WAS OVER...
...AND THE NIGHTMARE WAS ABOUT TO BEGIN.

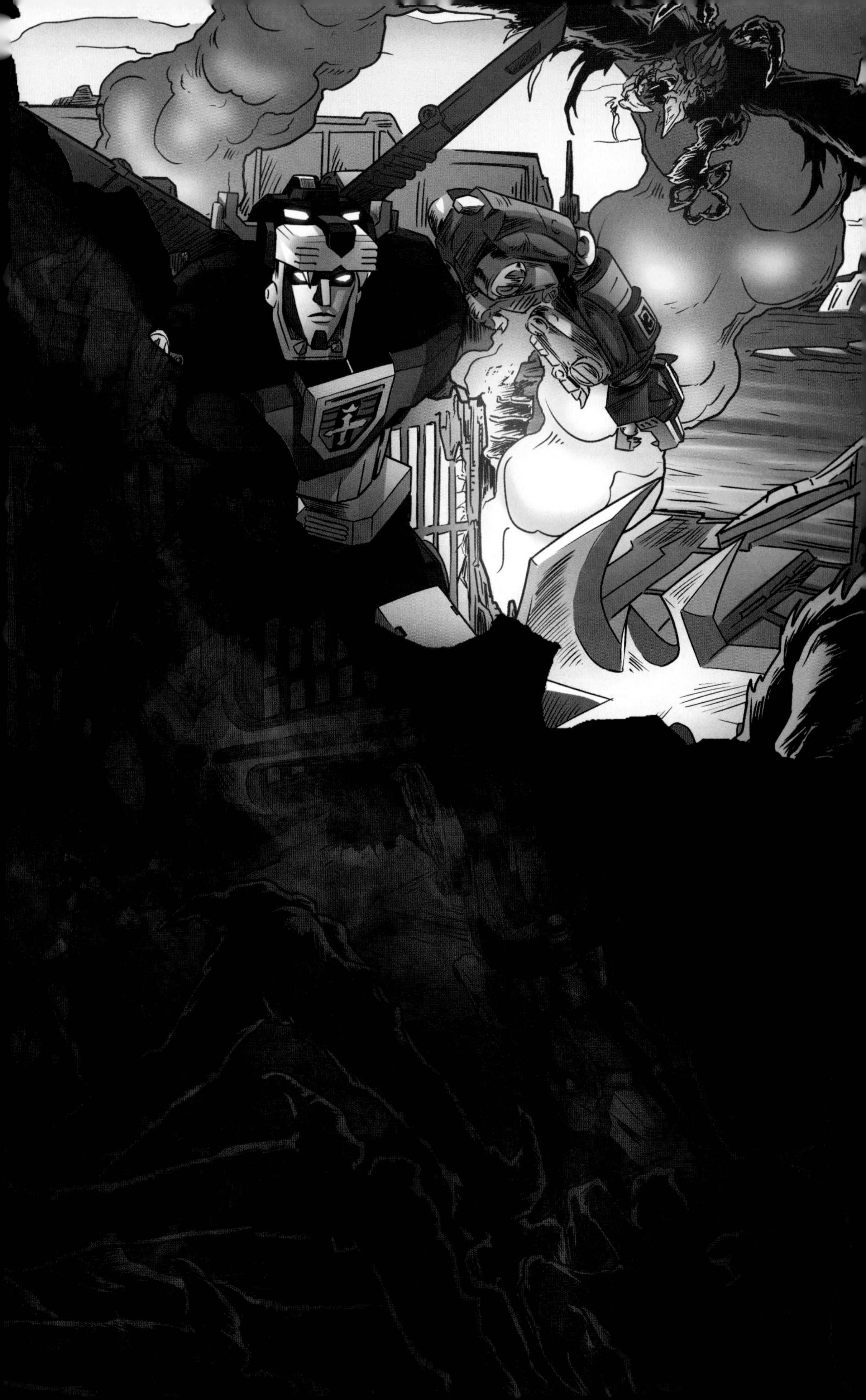

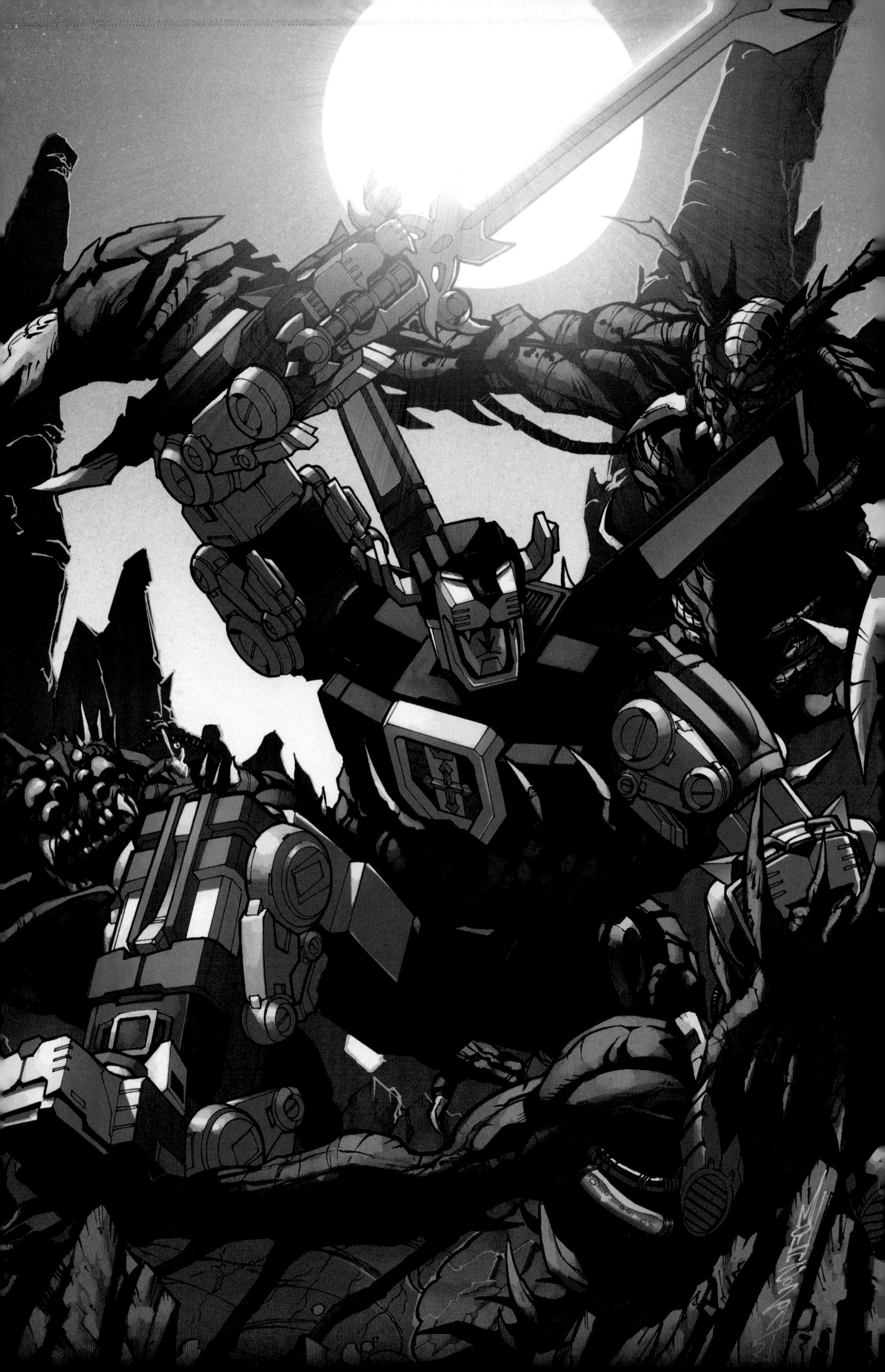

ISSUE 2 Cover by ALEX MILNE Colors by JOSH PEREZ

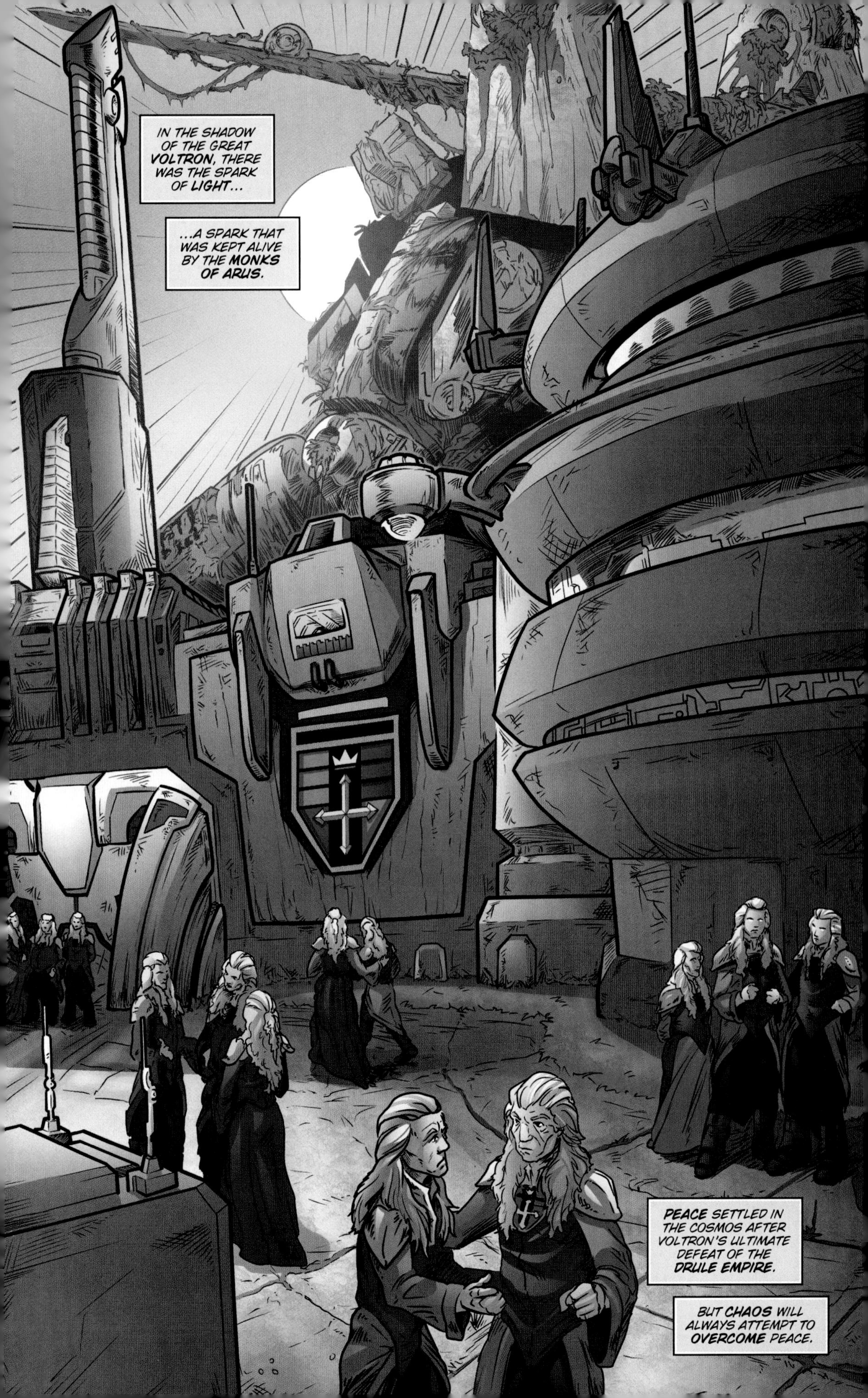
IN THE SHADOW OF THE GREAT VOLTRON, THERE WAS THE SPARK OF LIGHT...
...A SPARK THAT WAS KEPT ALIVE BY THE MONKS OF ARUS.
PEACE SETTLED IN THE COSMOS AFTER VOLTRON'S ULTIMATE DEFEAT OF THE DRULE EMPIRE.
BUT CHAOS WILL ALWAYS ATTEMPT TO OVERCOME PEACE.

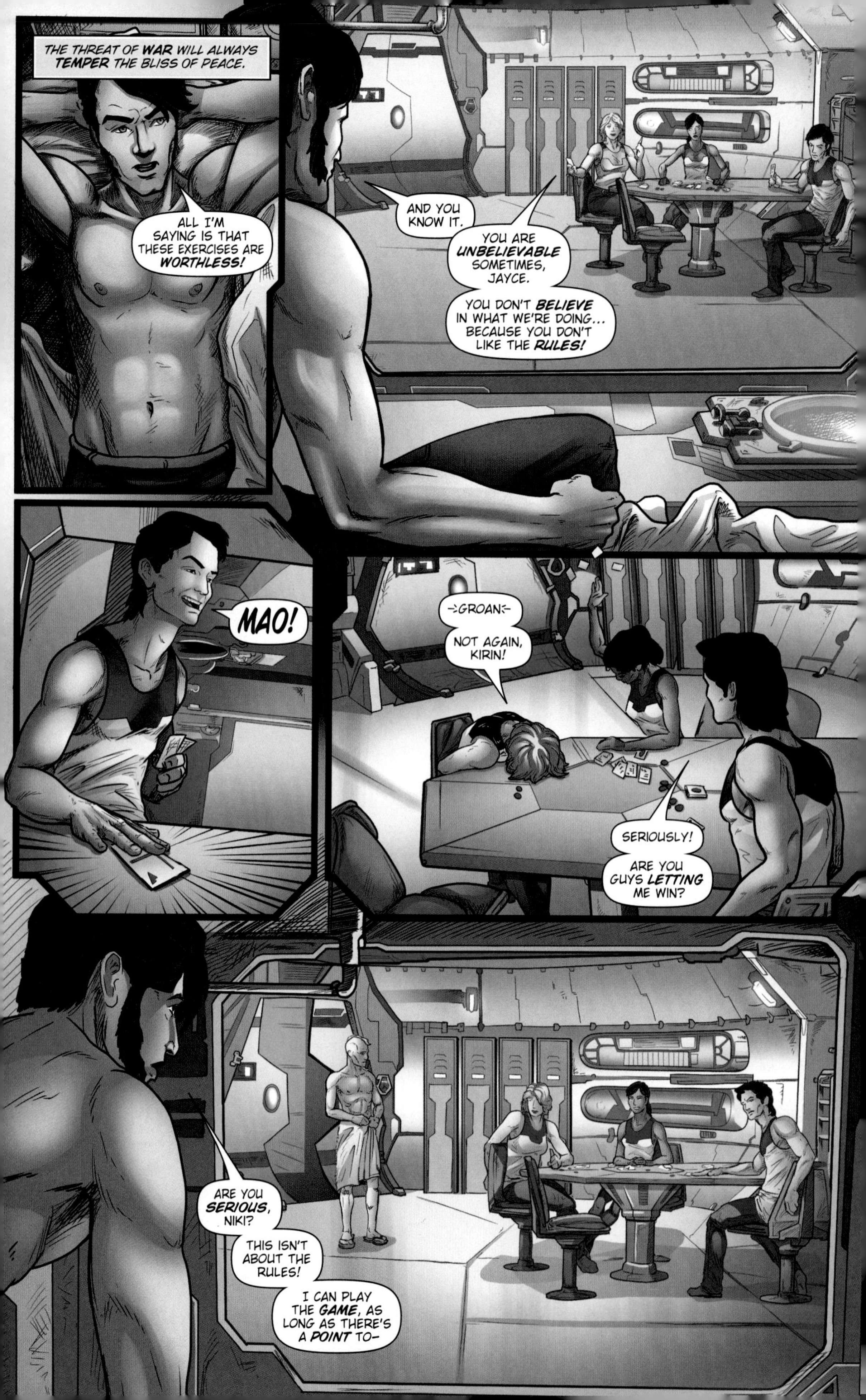
THE THREAT OF WAR WILL ALWAYS TEMPER THE BLISS OF PEACE.
ALL I'M SAYING IS THAT THESE EXERCISES ARE WORTHLESS!
AND YOU KNOW IT.
YOU ARE UNBELIEVABLE SOMETIMES, JAYCE.
YOU DON'T BELIEVE IN WHAT WE'RE DOING... BECAUSE YOU DON'T LIKE THE RULES!
MAO!
GROAN
NOT AGAIN, KIRIN!
SERIOUSLY!
ARE YOU GUYS LETTING ME WIN?
ARE YOU SERIOUS, NIKI?
THIS ISN'T ABOUT THE RULES!
I CAN PLAY THE GAME, AS LONG AS THERE'S A POINT TO-

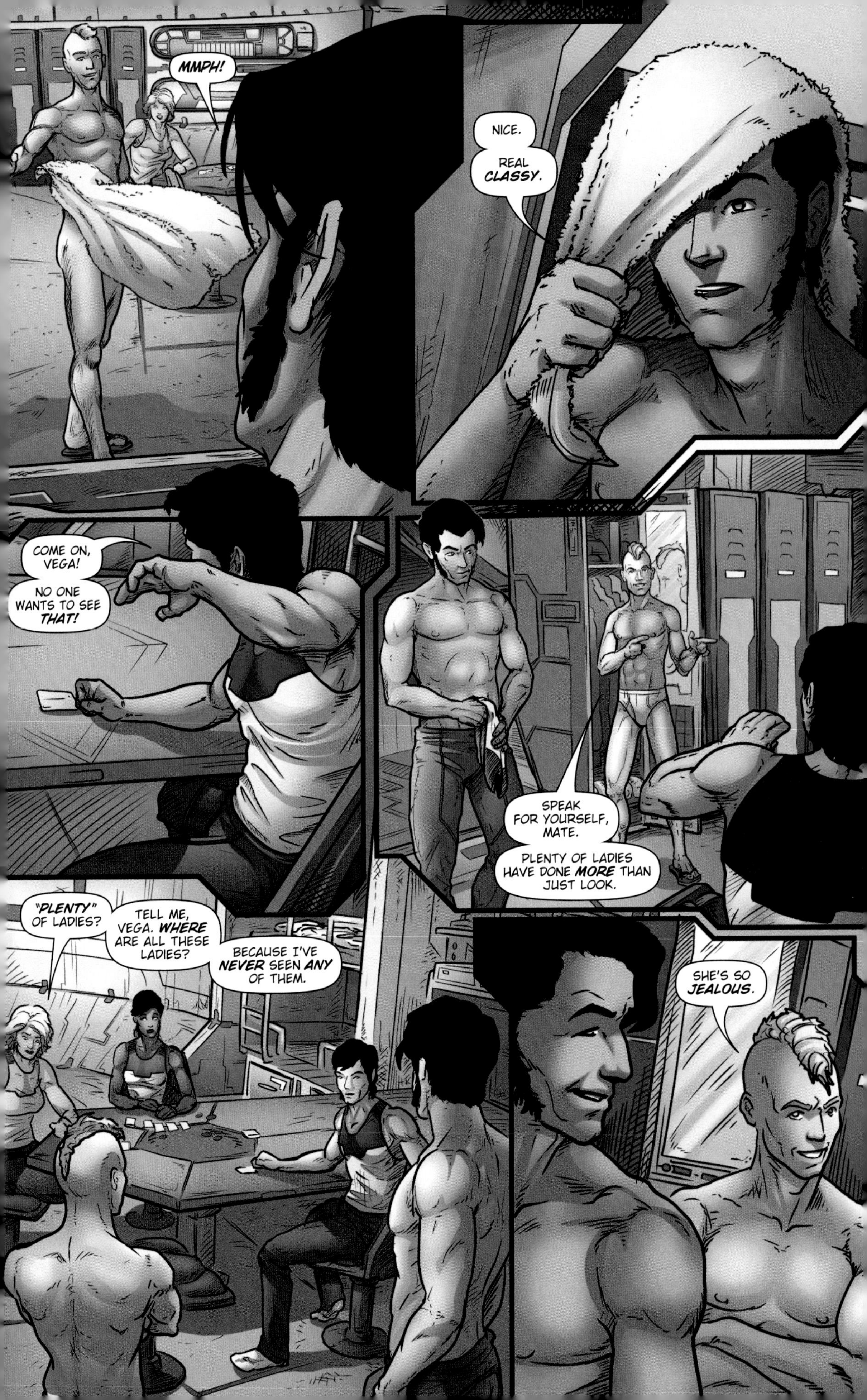
MMPH!
NICE.
REAL CLASSY.
COME ON, VEGA!
NO ONE WANTS TO SEE THAT!
SPEAK FOR YOURSELF, MATE.
PLENTY OF LADIES HAVE DONE MORE THAN JUST LOOK.
"PLENTY" OF LADIES?
TELL ME, VEGA. WHERE ARE ALL THESE LADIES?
BECAUSE I'VE NEVER SEEN ANY OF THEM.
SHE'S SO JEALOUS.

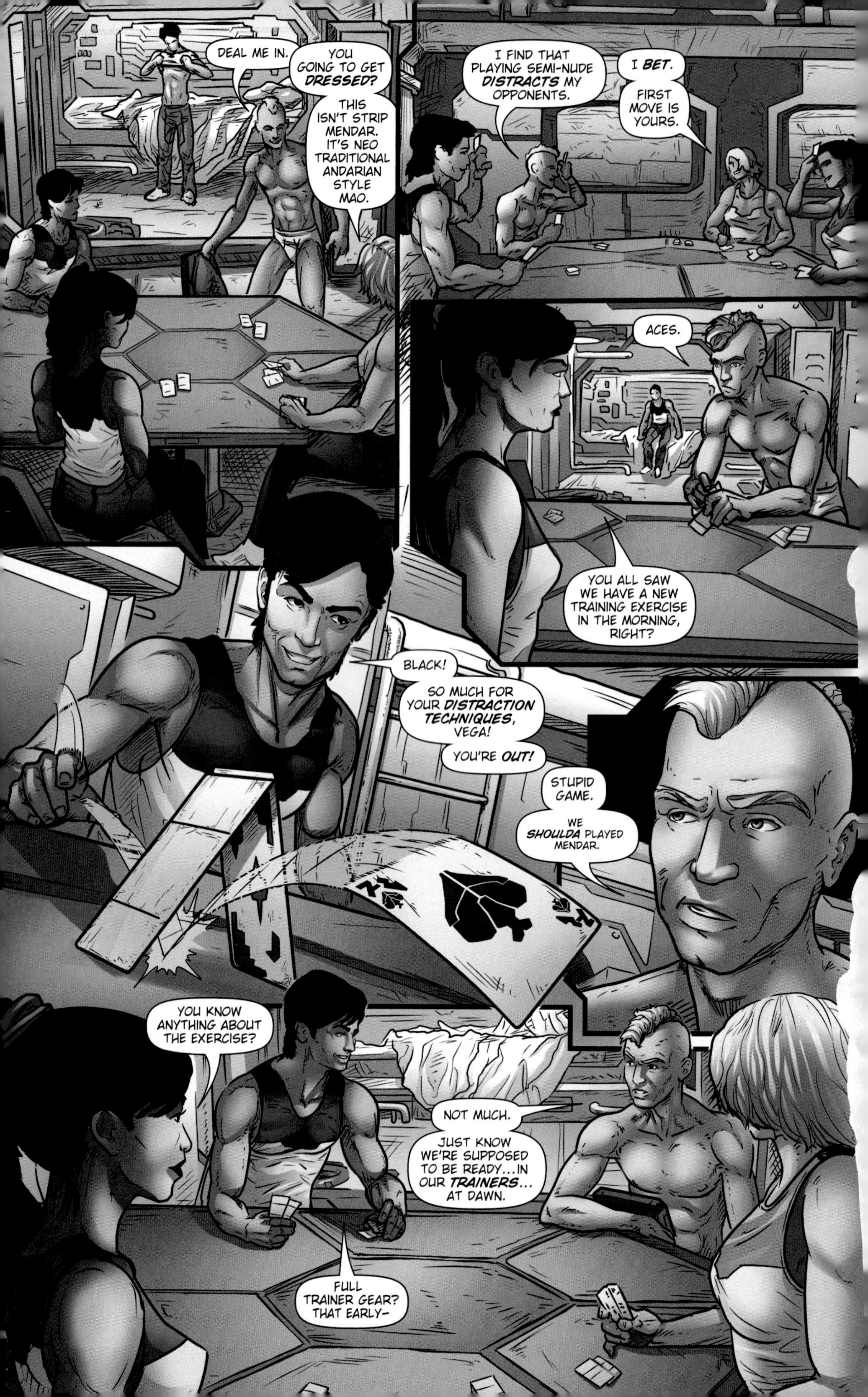
DEAL ME IN.
YOU GOING TO GET DRESSED?
THIS ISN'T STRIP MENDAR. IT'S NEO TRADITIONAL ANDARIAN STYLE MAO.
I FIND THAT PLAYING SEMI-NUDE DISTRACTS MY OPPONENTS.
I BET.
FIRST MOVE IS YOURS.
ACES.
YOU ALL SAW WE HAVE A NEW TRAINING EXERCISE IN THE MORNING, RIGHT?
BLACK!
SO MUCH FOR YOUR DISTRACTION TECHNIQUES, VEGA!
YOU'RE OUT!
STUPID GAME.
WE SHOULDA PLAYED MENDAR.
YOU KNOW ANYTHING ABOUT THE EXERCISE?
NOT MUCH.
JUST KNOW WE'RE SUPPOSED TO BE READY...IN OUR TRAINERS... AT DAWN.
FULL TRAINER GEAR? THAT EARLY-

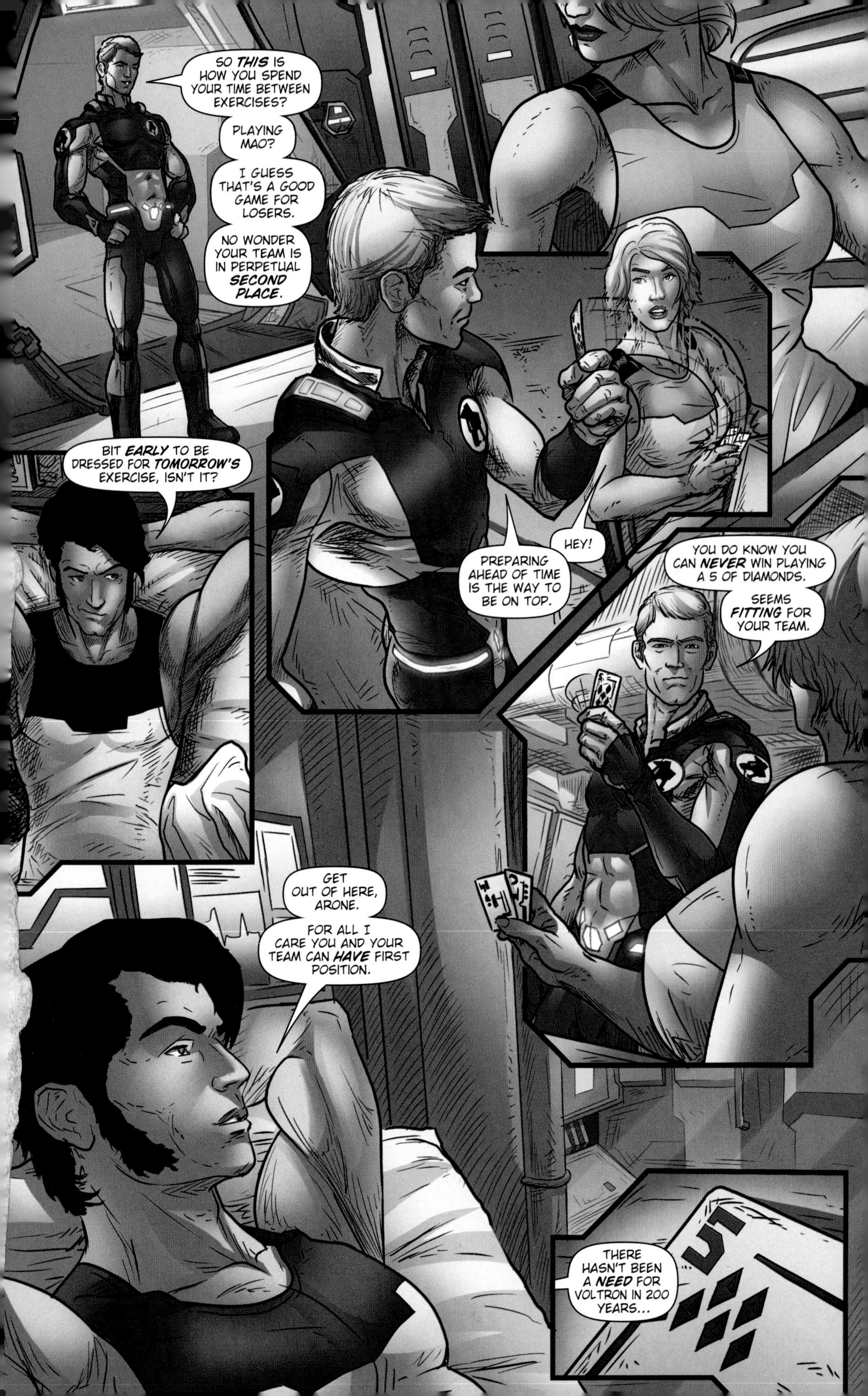
SO THIS IS HOW YOU SPEND YOUR TIME BETWEEN EXERCISES?
PLAYING MAO?
I GUESS THAT'S A GOOD GAME FOR LOSERS.
NO WONDER YOUR TEAM IS IN PERPETUAL SECOND PLACE.
BIT EARLY TO BE DRESSED FOR TOMORROW'S EXERCISE, ISN'T IT?
PREPARING AHEAD OF TIME IS THE WAY TO BE ON TOP.
HEY!
YOU DO KNOW YOU CAN NEVER WIN PLAYING A 5 OF DIAMONDS.
SEEMS FITTING FOR YOUR TEAM.
GET OUT OF HERE, ARONE.
FOR ALL I CARE YOU AND YOUR TEAM CAN HAVE FIRST POSITION.
THERE HASN'T BEEN A NEED FOR VOLTRON IN 200 YEARS...

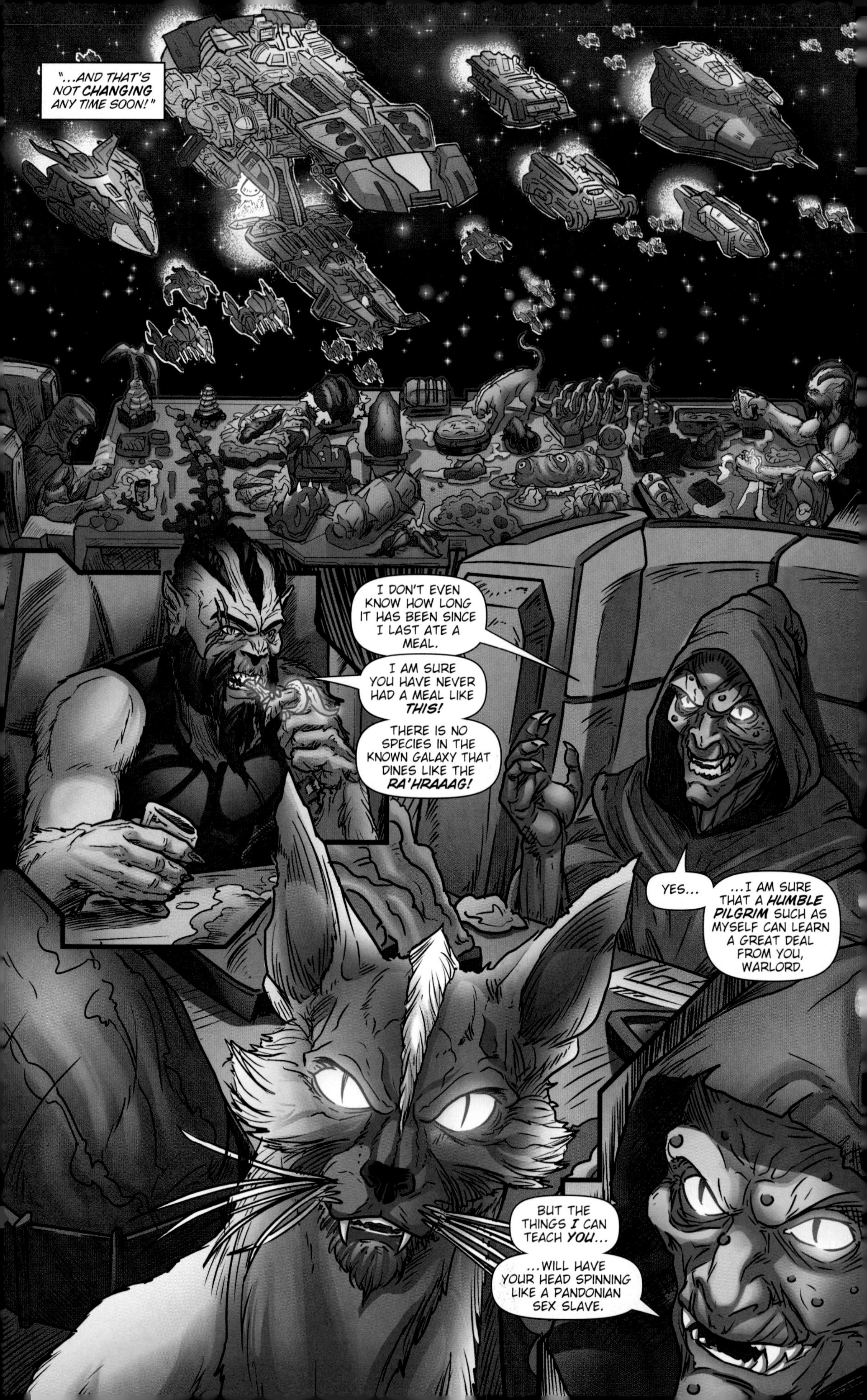
"...AND THAT'S NOT CHANGING ANY TIME SOON!"
I DON'T EVEN KNOW HOW LONG IT HAS BEEN SINCE I LAST ATE A MEAL.
I AM SURE YOU HAVE NEVER HAD A MEAL LIKE THIS!
THERE IS NO SPECIES IN THE KNOWN GALAXY THAT DINES LIKE THE RA'HRAAAG!
YES...
...I AM SURE THAT A HUMBLE PILGRIM SUCH AS MYSELF CAN LEARN A GREAT DEAL FROM YOU, WARLORD.
BUT THE THINGS I CAN TEACH YOU...
...WILL HAVE YOUR HEAD SPINNING LIKE A PANDONIAN SEX SLAVE.

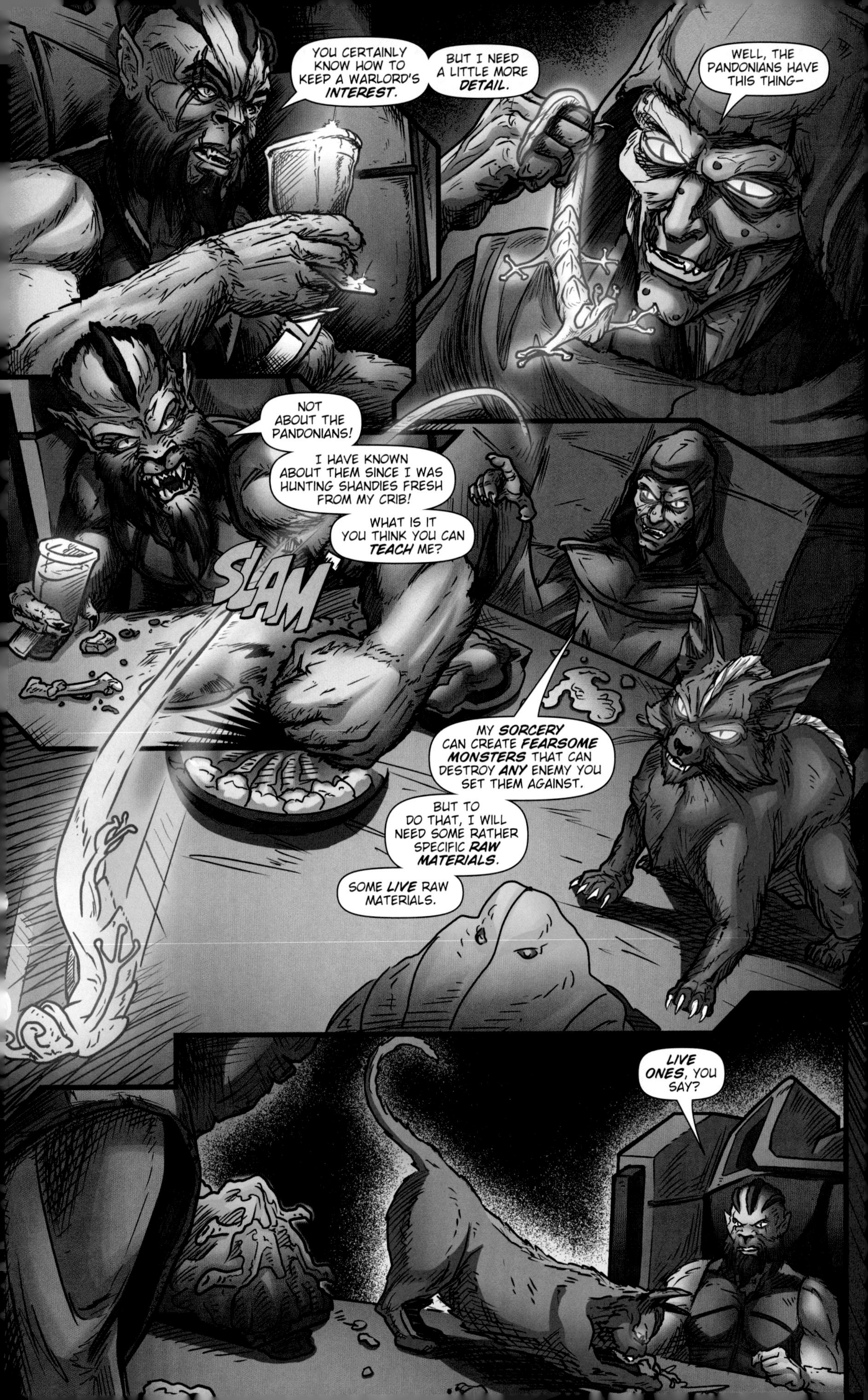
YOU CERTAINLY KNOW HOW TO KEEP A WARLORD'S INTEREST.
BUT I NEED A LITTLE MORE DETAIL.
WELL, THE PANDONIANS HAVE THIS THING–
NOT ABOUT THE PANDONIANS!
I HAVE KNOWN ABOUT THEM SINCE I WAS HUNTING SHANDIES FRESH FROM MY CRIB!
WHAT IS IT YOU THINK YOU CAN TEACH ME?
SLAM
MY SORCERY CAN CREATE FEARSOME MONSTERS THAT CAN DESTROY ANY ENEMY YOU SET THEM AGAINST.
BUT TO DO THAT, I WILL NEED SOME RATHER SPECIFIC RAW MATERIALS.
SOME LIVE RAW MATERIALS.
LIVE ONES, YOU SAY?

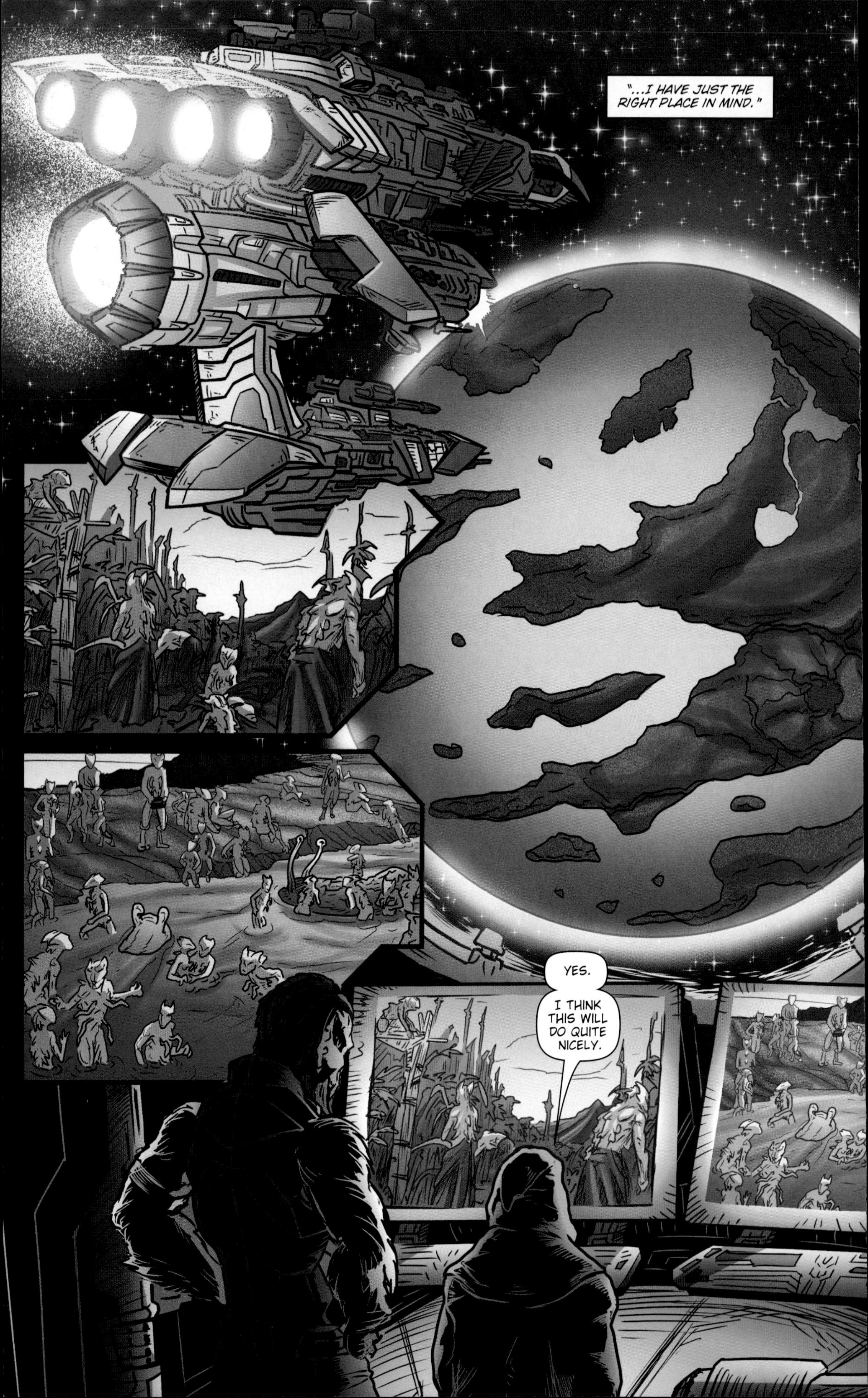
"...I HAVE JUST THE RIGHT PLACE IN MIND."
YES.
I THINK THIS WILL DO QUITE NICELY.

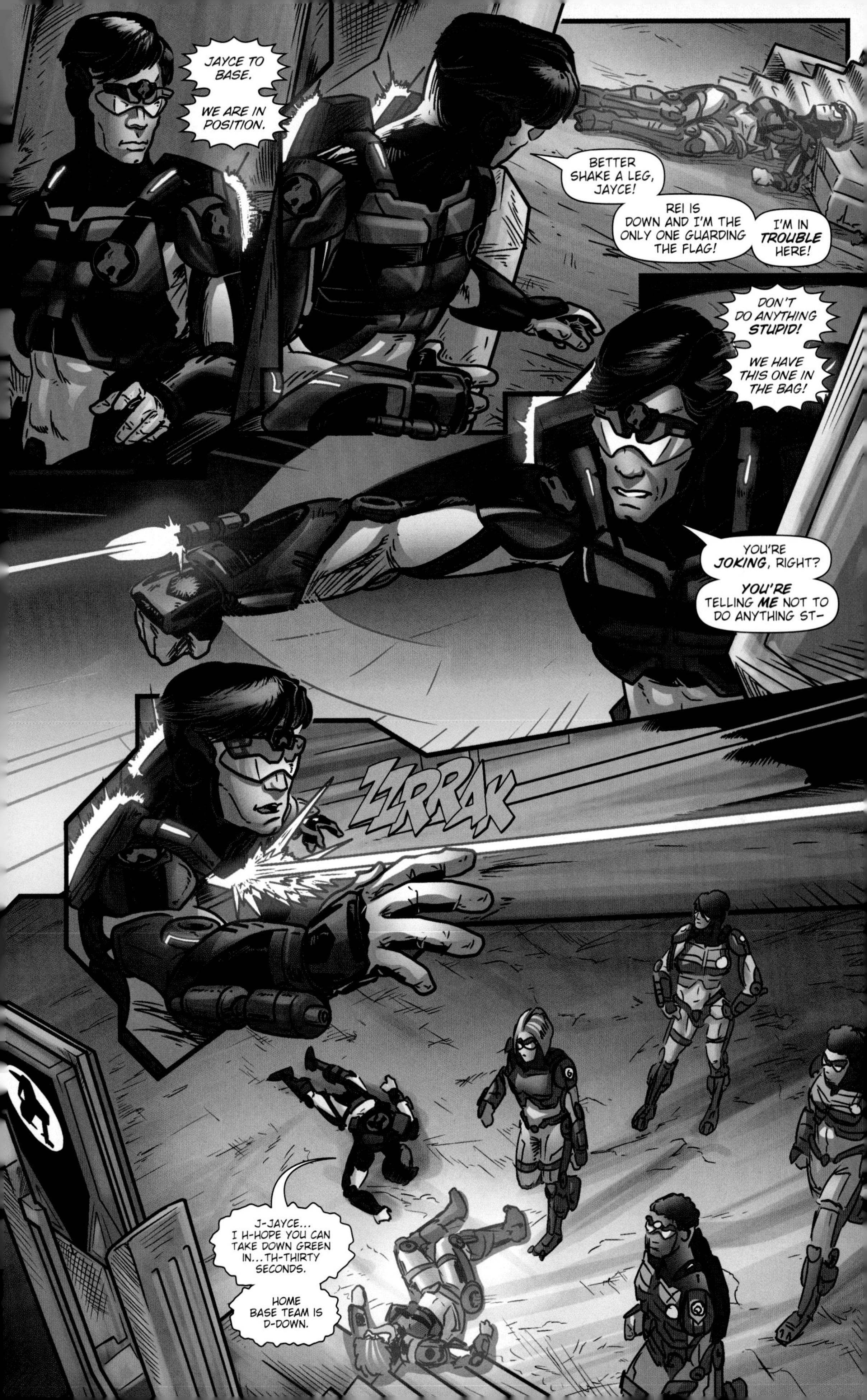
JAYCE TO BASE.
WE ARE IN POSITION.
BETTER SHAKE A LEG, JAYCE!
REI IS DOWN AND I'M THE ONLY ONE GUARDING THE FLAG!
I'M IN TROUBLE HERE!
DON'T DO ANYTHING STUPID!
WE HAVE THIS ONE IN THE BAG!
YOU'RE JOKING, RIGHT?
YOU'RE TELLING ME NOT TO DO ANYTHING ST-
ZZRRAK
J-JAYCE... I H-HOPE YOU CAN TAKE DOWN GREEN IN...TH-THIRTY SECONDS.
HOME BASE TEAM IS D-DOWN.

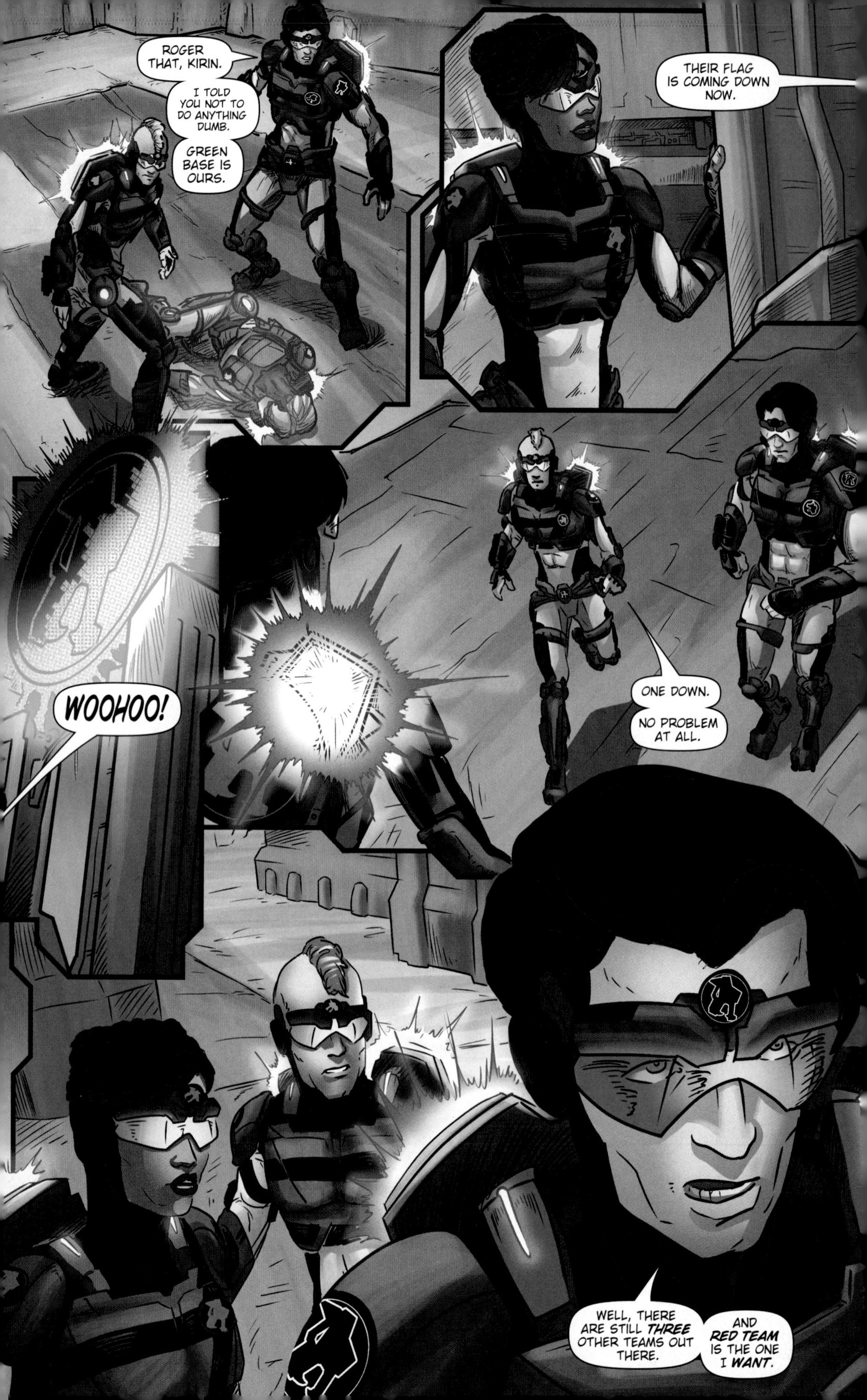
ROGER THAT, KIRIN.
I TOLD YOU NOT TO DO ANYTHING DUMB.
GREEN BASE IS OURS.
THEIR FLAG IS COMING DOWN NOW.
WOOHOO!
ONE DOWN.
NO PROBLEM AT ALL.
WELL, THERE ARE STILL THREE OTHER TEAMS OUT THERE.
AND RED TEAM IS THE ONE I WANT.

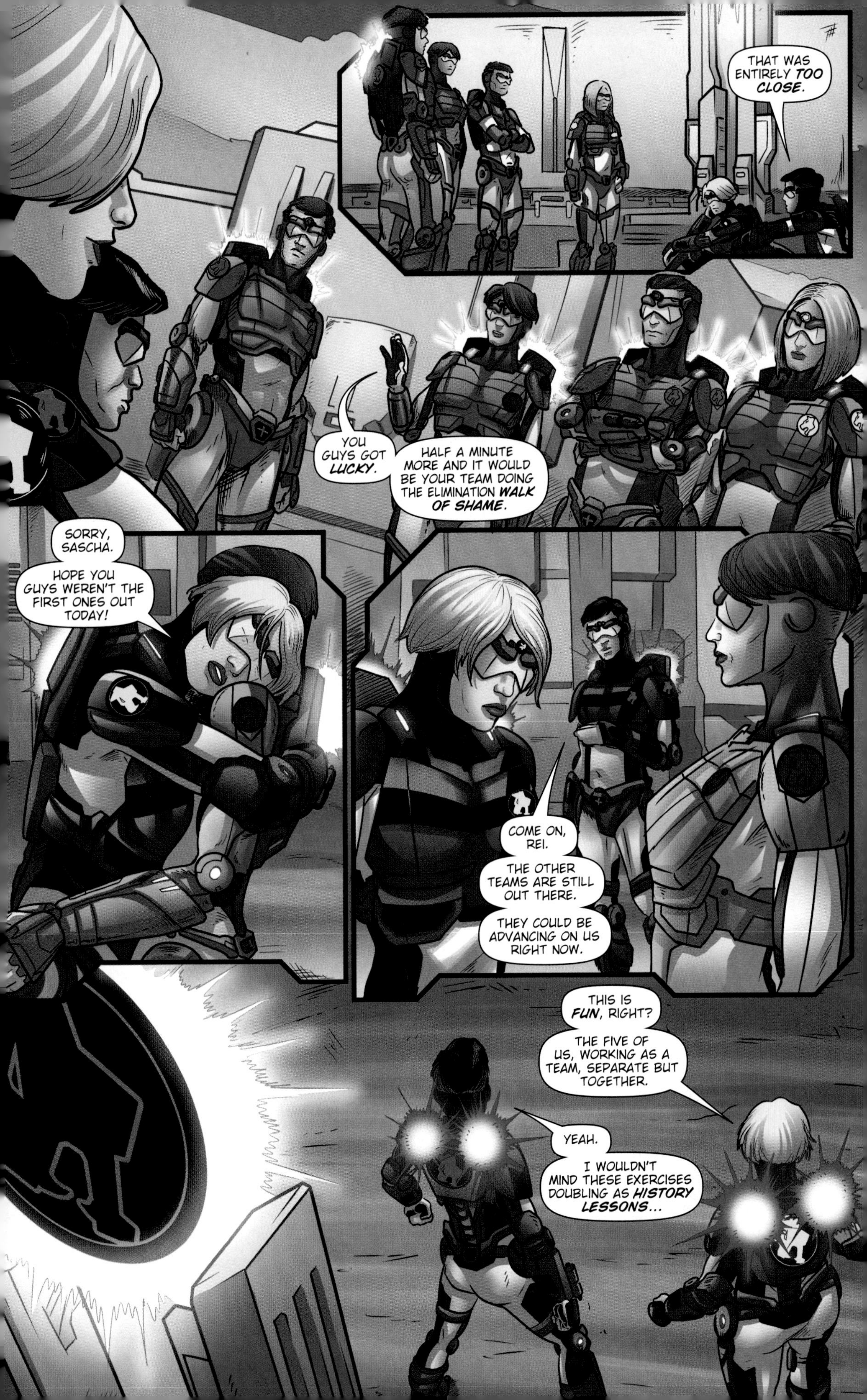
THAT WAS ENTIRELY TOO CLOSE.
YOU GUYS GOT LUCKY.
HALF A MINUTE MORE AND IT WOULD BE YOUR TEAM DOING THE ELIMINATION WALK OF SHAME.
SORRY, SASCHA.
HOPE YOU GUYS WEREN'T THE FIRST ONES OUT TODAY!
COME ON, REI.
THE OTHER TEAMS ARE STILL OUT THERE.
THEY COULD BE ADVANCING ON US RIGHT NOW.
THIS IS FUN, RIGHT?
THE FIVE OF US, WORKING AS A TEAM, SEPARATE BUT TOGETHER.
YEAH.
I WOULDN'T MIND THESE EXERCISES DOUBLING AS HISTORY LESSONS...

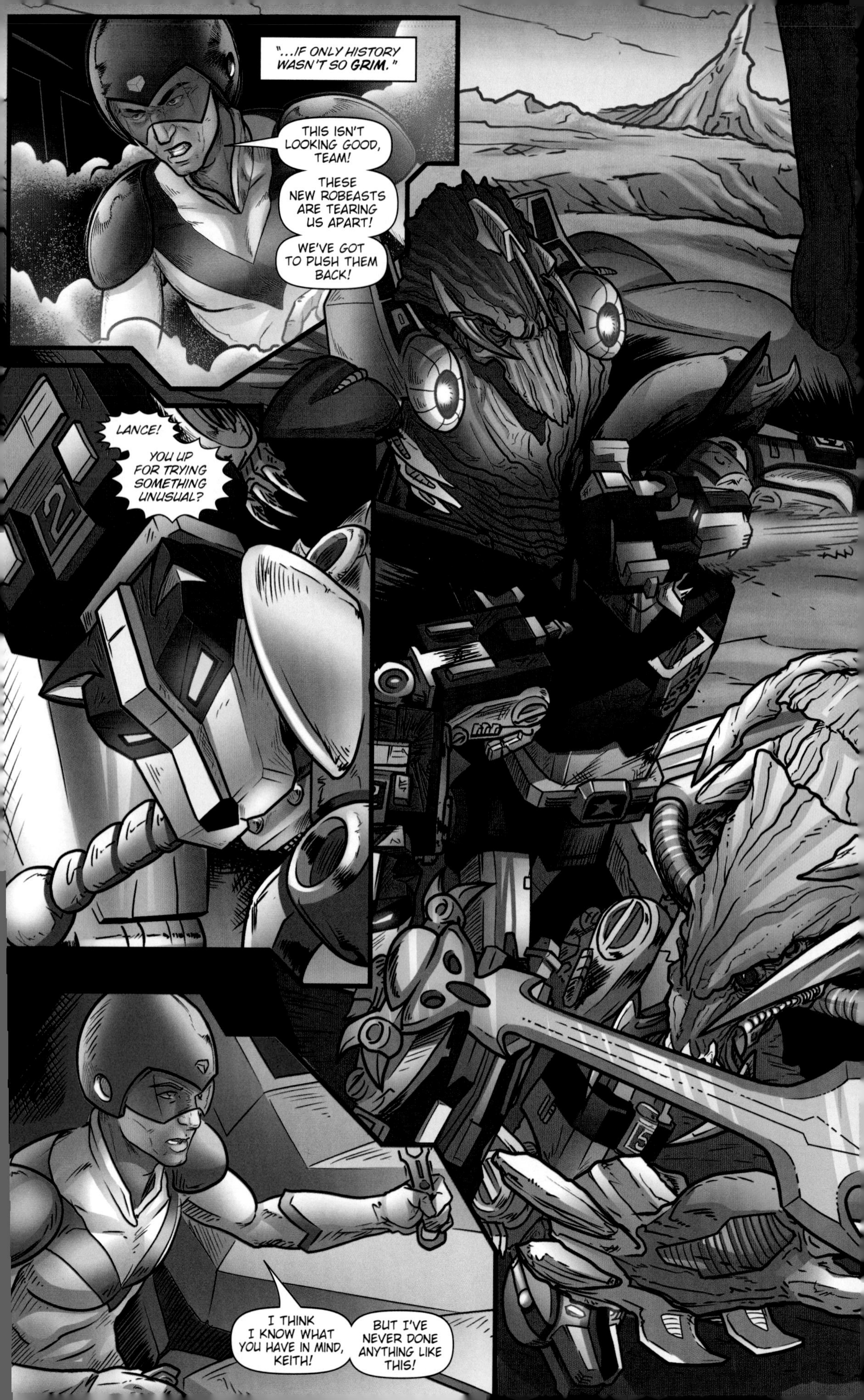
"...IF ONLY HISTORY WASN'T SO GRIM."
THIS ISN'T LOOKING GOOD, TEAM!
THESE NEW ROBEASTS ARE TEARING US APART!
WE'VE GOT TO PUSH THEM BACK!
LANCE!
YOU UP FOR TRYING SOMETHING UNUSUAL?
I THINK I KNOW WHAT YOU HAVE IN MIND, KEITH!
BUT I'VE NEVER DONE ANYTHING LIKE THIS!

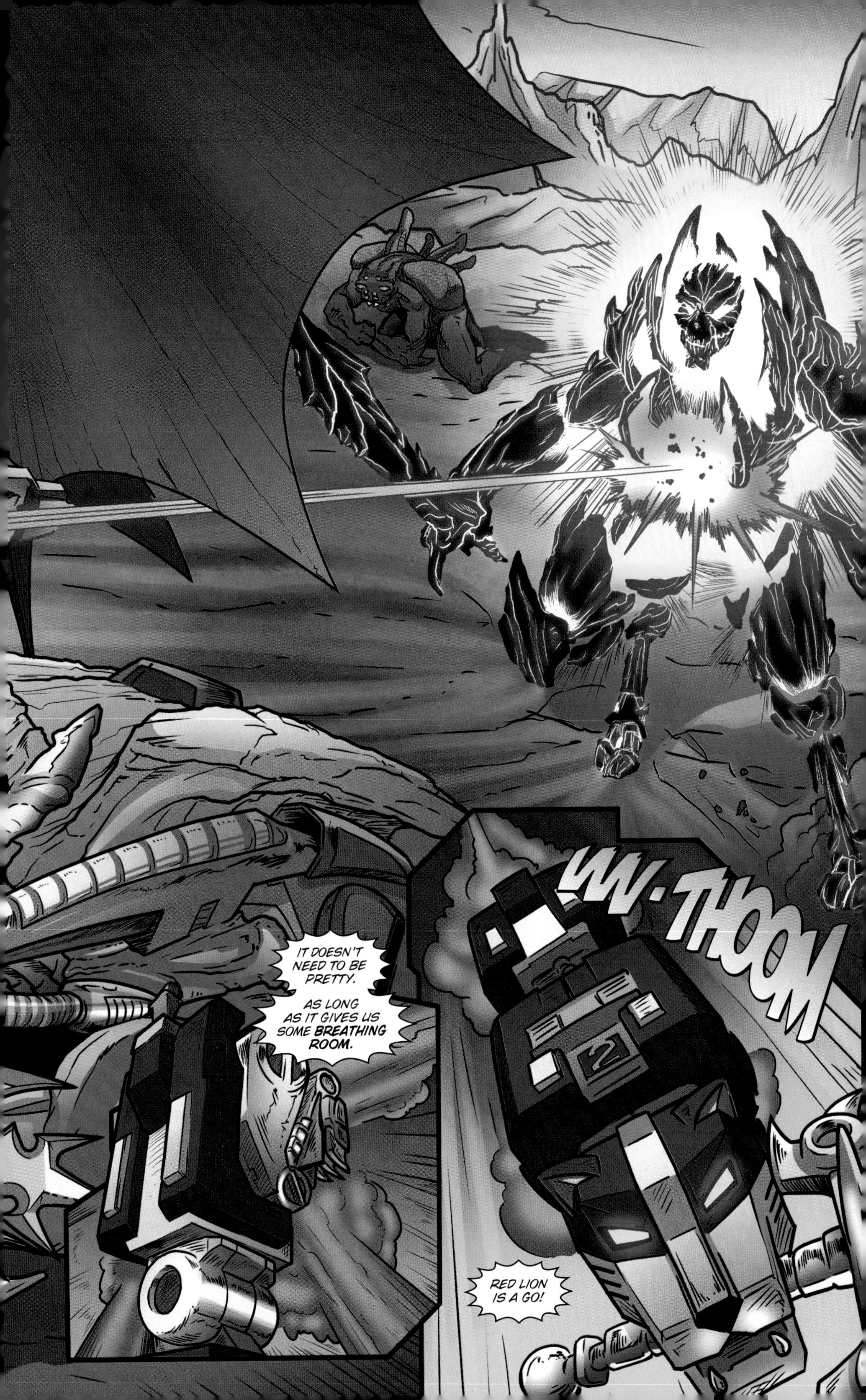
IT DOESN'T NEED TO BE PRETTY.
AS LONG AS IT GIVES US SOME **BREATHING ROOM.**
VVV-THOOM
RED LION IS A GO!

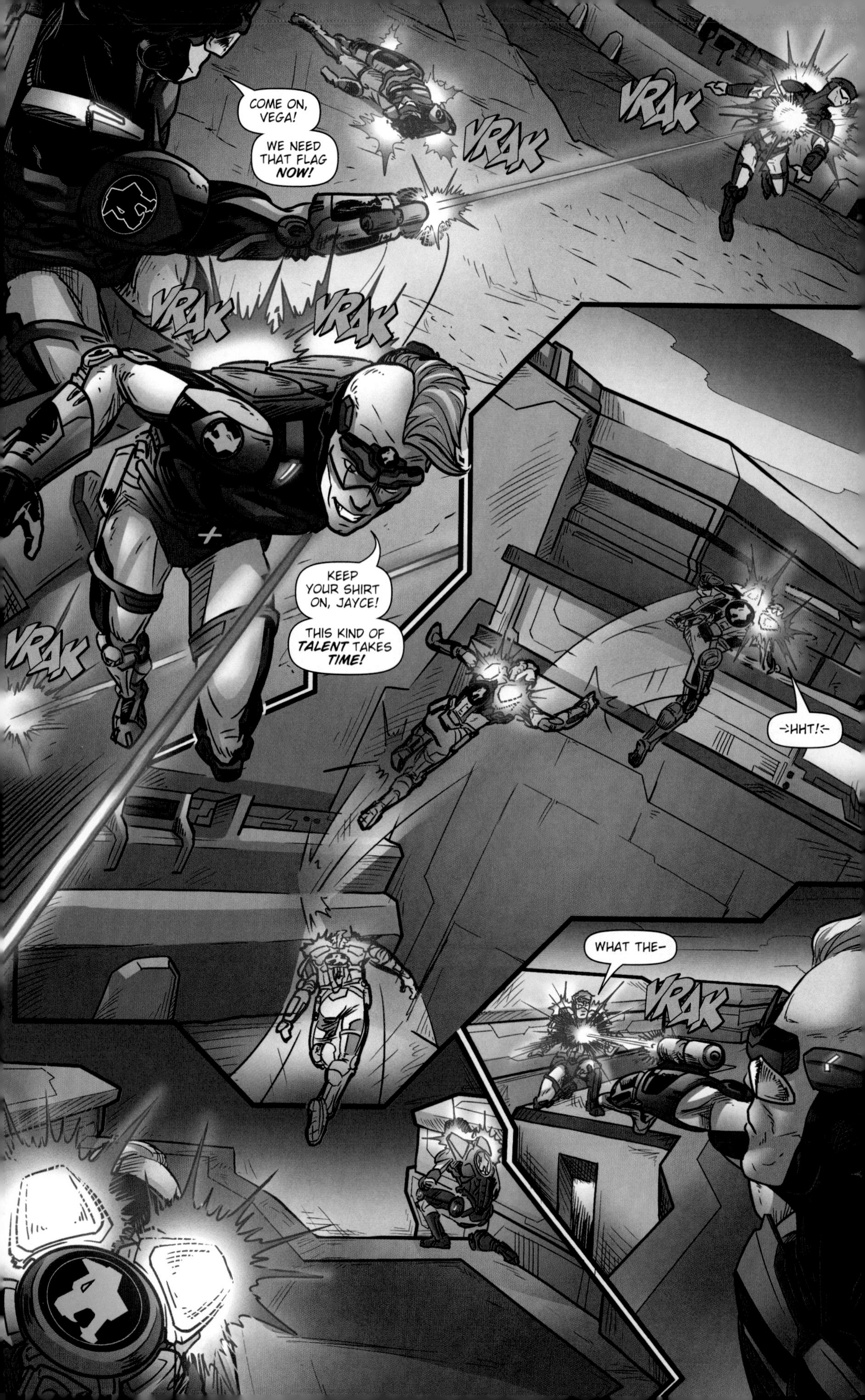
COME ON, VEGA!
WE NEED THAT FLAG NOW!
VRAK
VRAK
VRAK
VRAK
KEEP YOUR SHIRT ON, JAYCE!
THIS KIND OF TALENT TAKES TIME!
VRAK
-HHT!-
WHAT THE-
VRAK

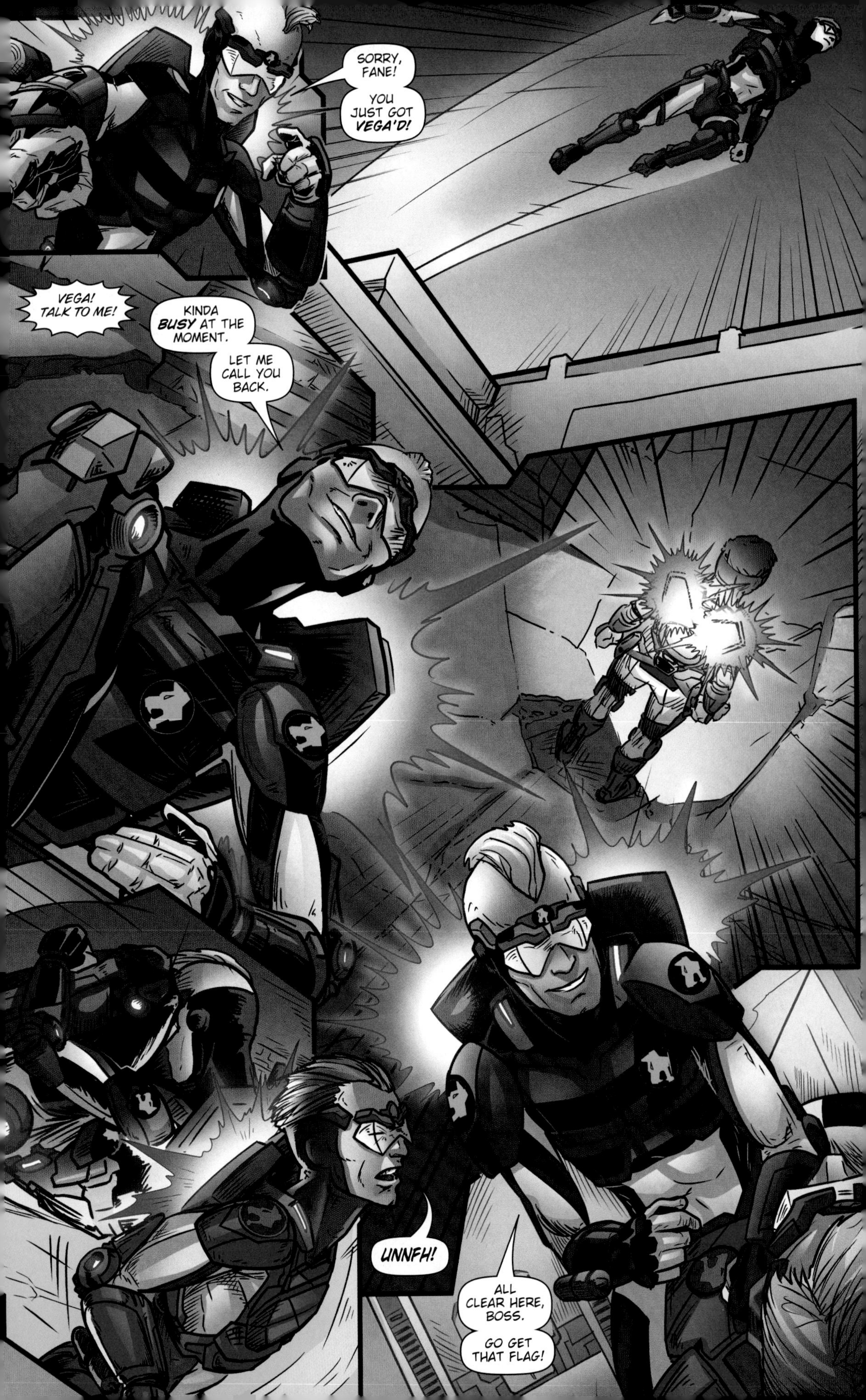
SORRY, FANE!
YOU JUST GOT VEGA'D!
VEGA! TALK TO ME!
KINDA BUSY AT THE MOMENT.
LET ME CALL YOU BACK.
UNNFH!
ALL CLEAR HERE, BOSS.
GO GET THAT FLAG!

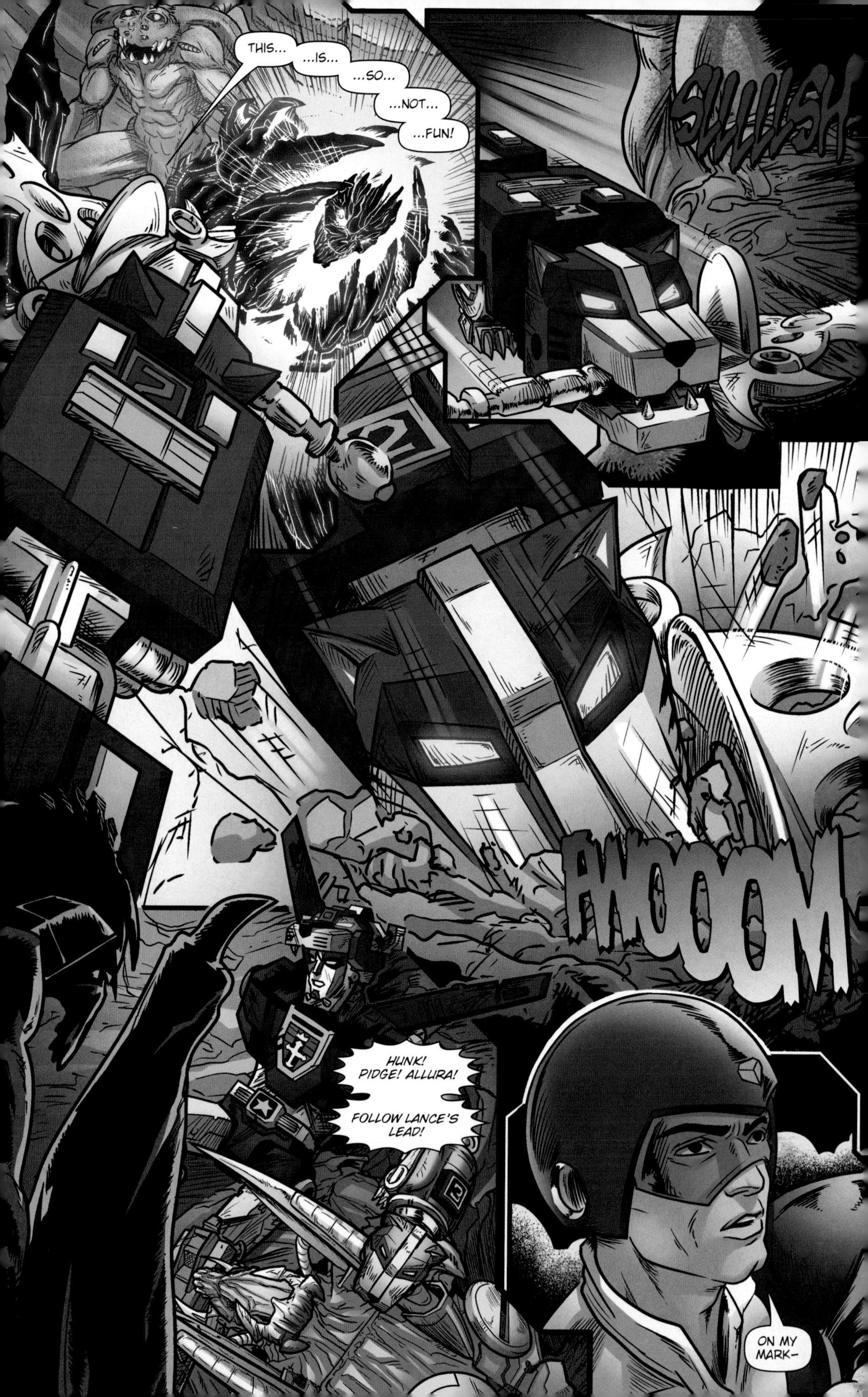
THIS...
...IS...
...SO...
...NOT...
...FUN!
SLLLLISH
FWOOOM
HUNK! PIDGE! ALLURA!
FOLLOW LANCE'S LEAD!
ON MY MARK–

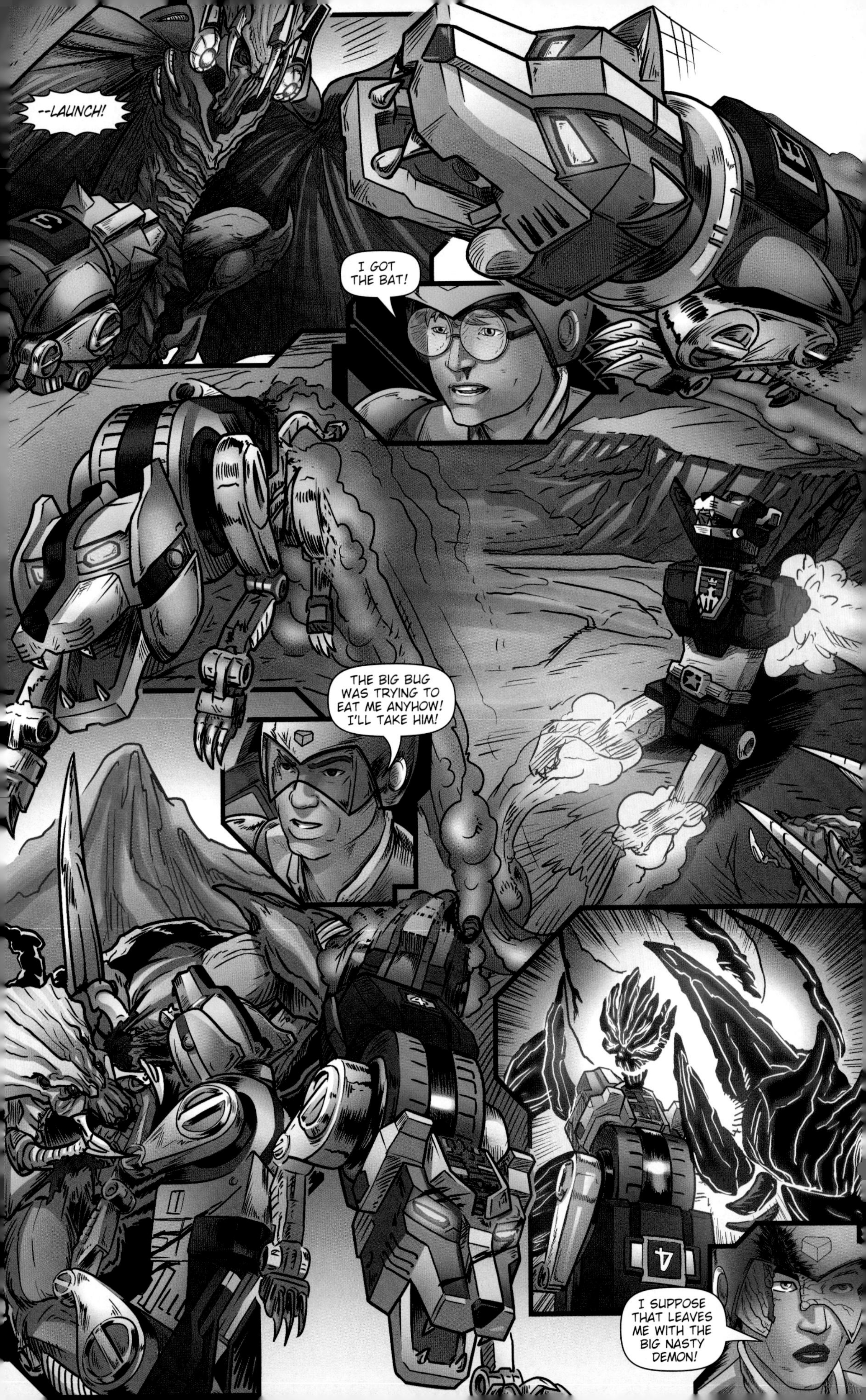
--LAUNCH!
I GOT THE BAT!
THE BIG BUG WAS TRYING TO EAT ME ANYHOW! I'LL TAKE HIM!
I SUPPOSE THAT LEAVES ME WITH THE BIG NASTY DEMON!

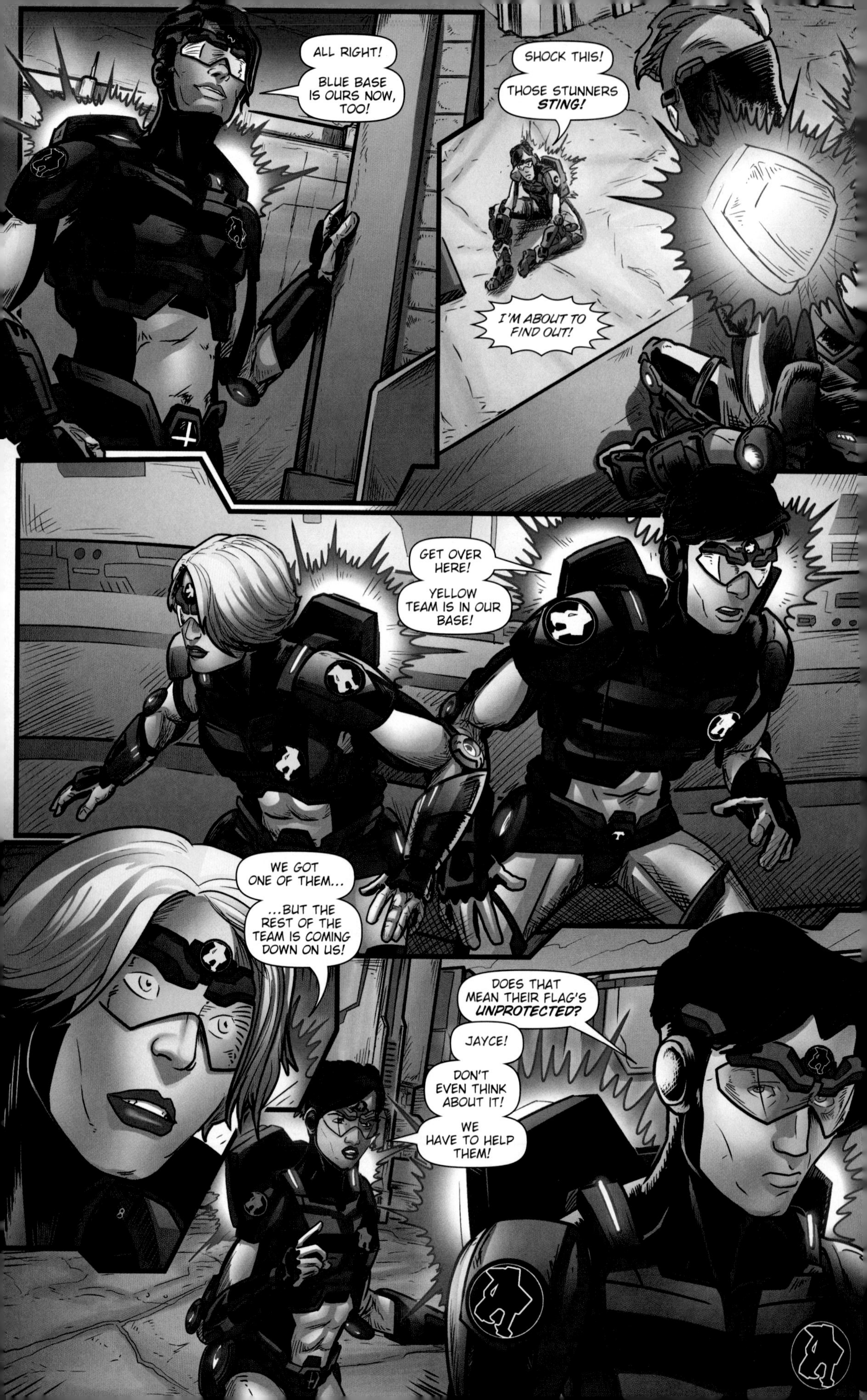
ALL RIGHT!
BLUE BASE IS OURS NOW, TOO!
SHOCK THIS!
THOSE STUNNERS **STING!**
I'M ABOUT TO FIND OUT!
GET OVER HERE!
YELLOW TEAM IS IN OUR BASE!
WE GOT ONE OF THEM...
...BUT THE REST OF THE TEAM IS COMING DOWN ON US!
DOES THAT MEAN THEIR FLAG'S **UNPROTECTED?**
JAYCE!
DON'T EVEN THINK ABOUT IT!
WE HAVE TO HELP THEM!

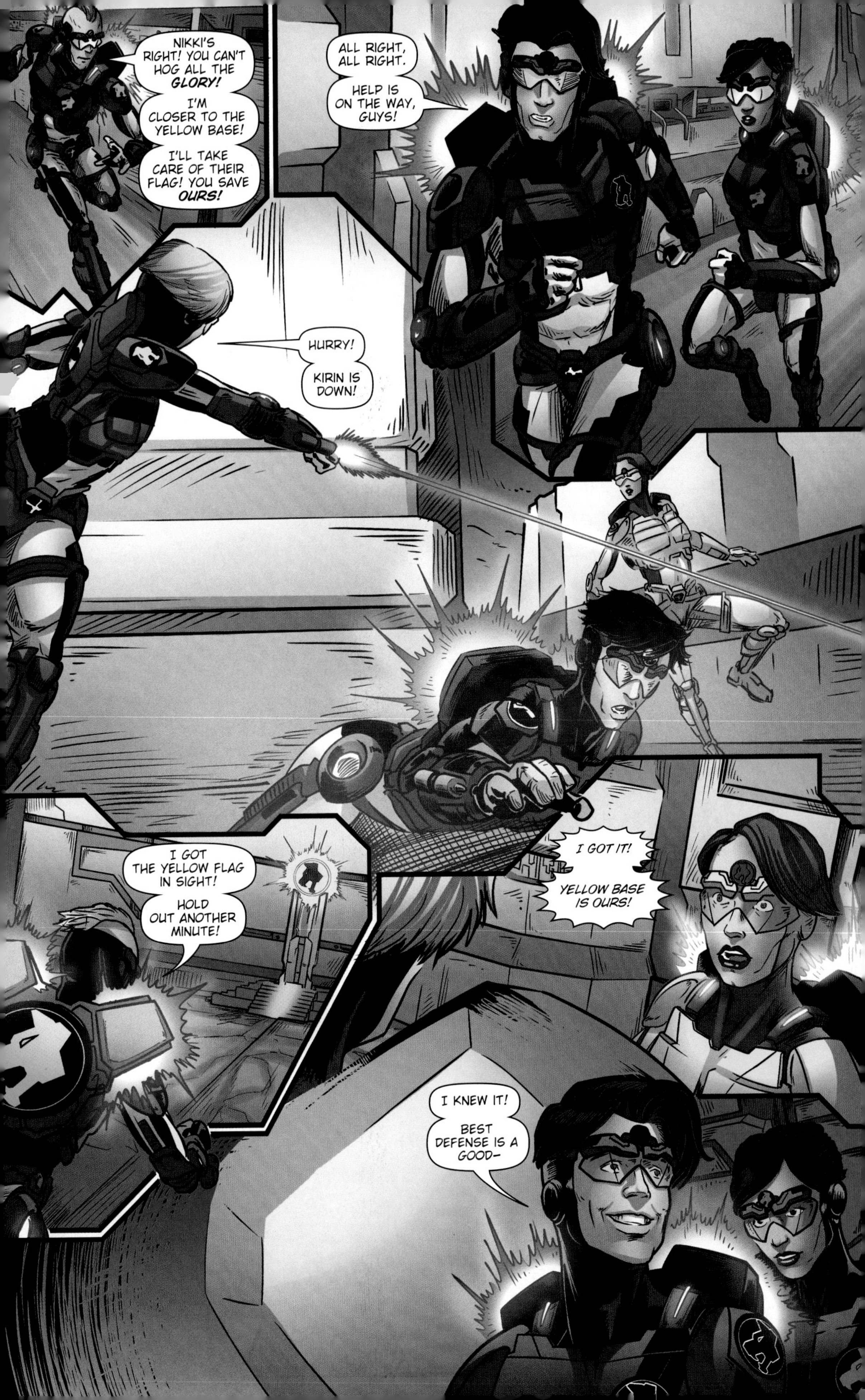
NIKKI'S RIGHT! YOU CAN'T HOG ALL THE GLORY!
I'M CLOSER TO THE YELLOW BASE!
I'LL TAKE CARE OF THEIR FLAG! YOU SAVE OURS!
ALL RIGHT, ALL RIGHT.
HELP IS ON THE WAY, GUYS!
HURRY!
KIRIN IS DOWN!
I GOT THE YELLOW FLAG IN SIGHT!
HOLD OUT ANOTHER MINUTE!
I GOT IT!
YELLOW BASE IS OURS!
I KNEW IT!
BEST DEFENSE IS A GOOD-

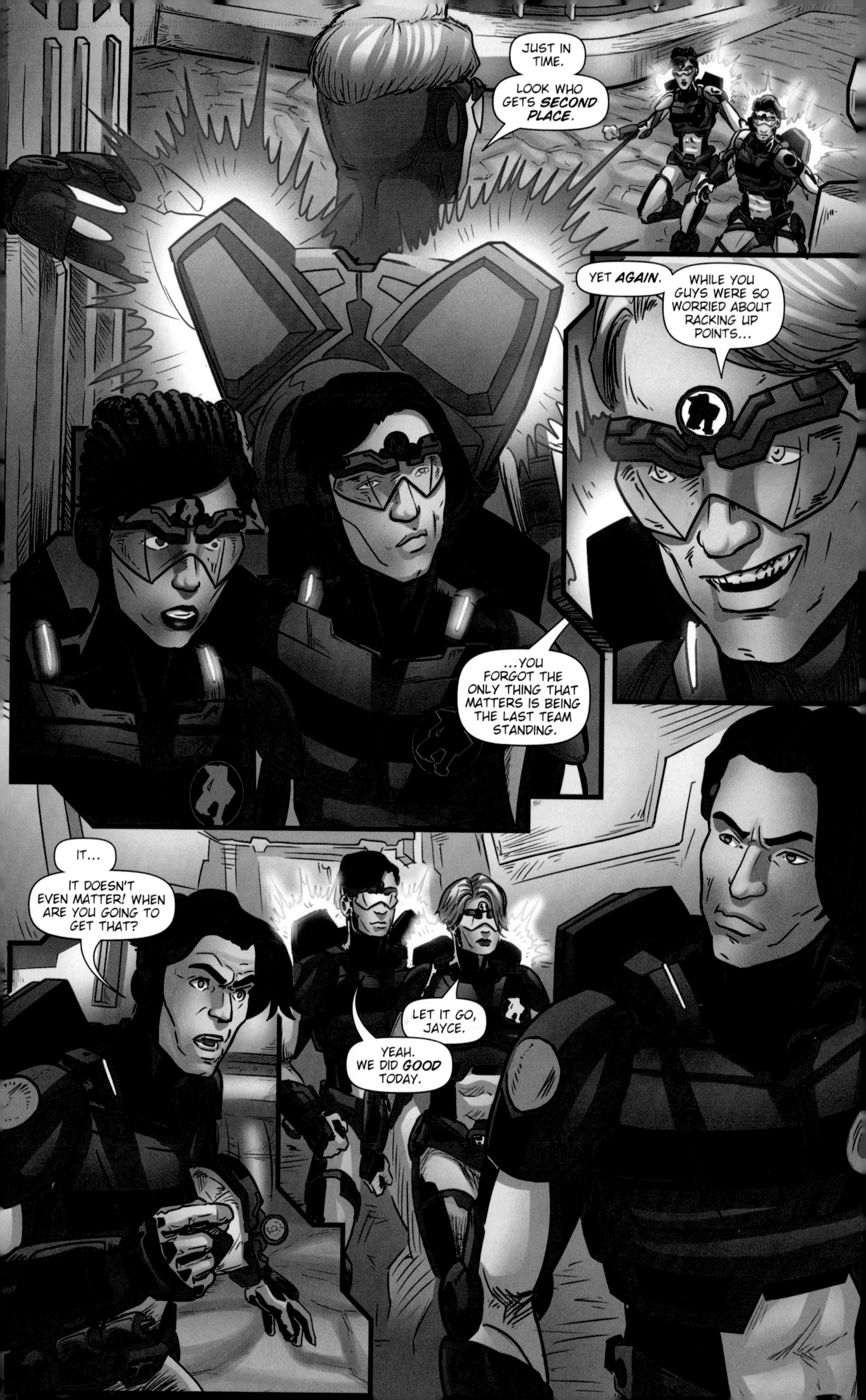
JUST IN TIME.
LOOK WHO GETS **SECOND PLACE**.
YET **AGAIN**.
WHILE YOU GUYS WERE SO WORRIED ABOUT RACKING UP POINTS...
...YOU FORGOT THE ONLY THING THAT MATTERS IS BEING THE LAST TEAM STANDING.
IT...
IT DOESN'T EVEN MATTER! WHEN ARE YOU GOING TO GET THAT?
LET IT GO, JAYCE.
YEAH. WE DID **GOOD** TODAY.

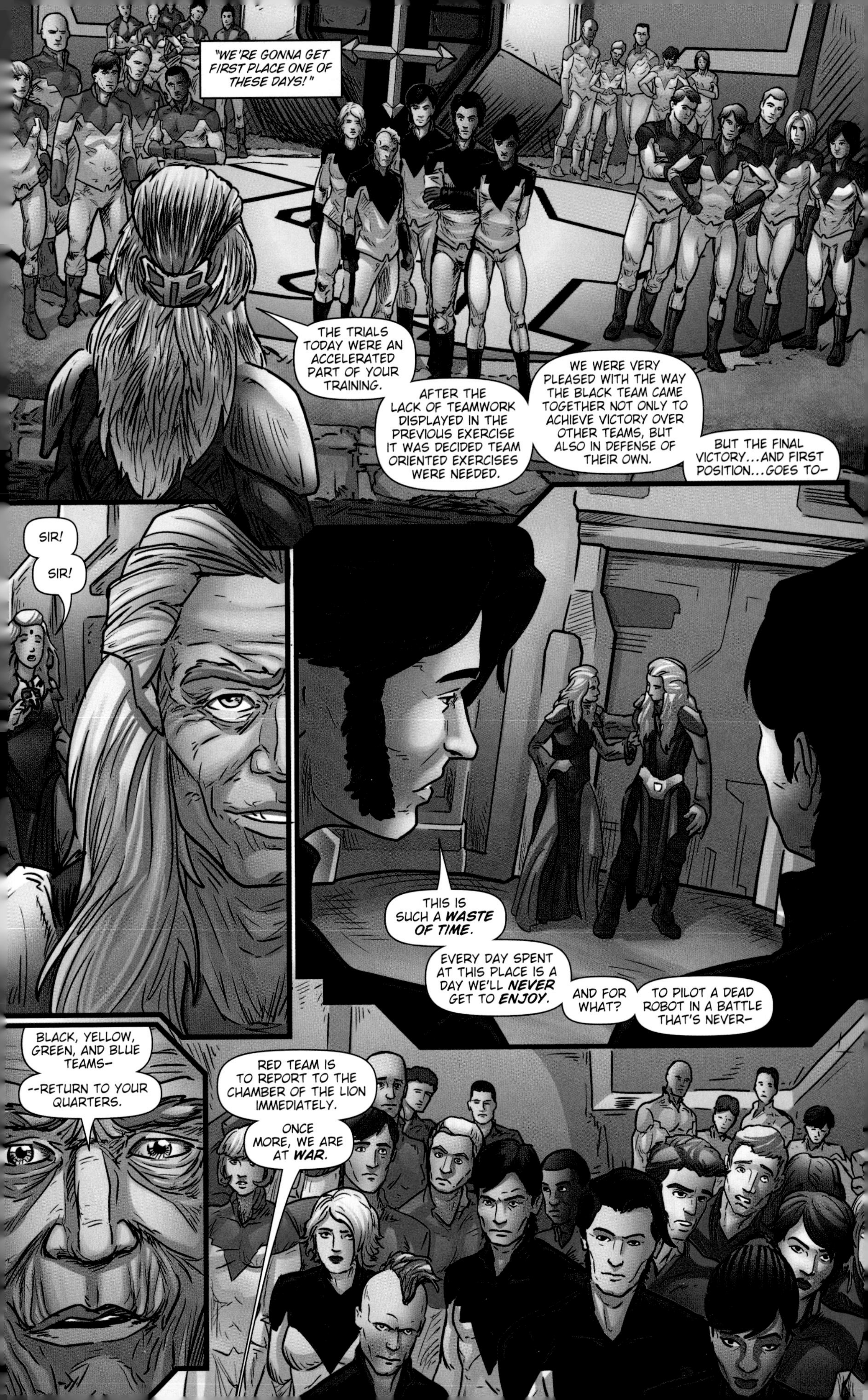
"WE'RE GONNA GET FIRST PLACE ONE OF THESE DAYS!"
THE TRIALS TODAY WERE AN ACCELERATED PART OF YOUR TRAINING.
AFTER THE LACK OF TEAMWORK DISPLAYED IN THE PREVIOUS EXERCISE IT WAS DECIDED TEAM ORIENTED EXERCISES WERE NEEDED.
WE WERE VERY PLEASED WITH THE WAY THE BLACK TEAM CAME TOGETHER NOT ONLY TO ACHIEVE VICTORY OVER OTHER TEAMS, BUT ALSO IN DEFENSE OF THEIR OWN.
BUT THE FINAL VICTORY...AND FIRST POSITION...GOES TO–
SIR!
SIR!
THIS IS SUCH A WASTE OF TIME.
EVERY DAY SPENT AT THIS PLACE IS A DAY WE'LL NEVER GET TO ENJOY.
AND FOR WHAT?
TO PILOT A DEAD ROBOT IN A BATTLE THAT'S NEVER–
BLACK, YELLOW, GREEN, AND BLUE TEAMS–
--RETURN TO YOUR QUARTERS.
RED TEAM IS TO REPORT TO THE CHAMBER OF THE LION IMMEDIATELY.
ONCE MORE, WE ARE AT WAR.

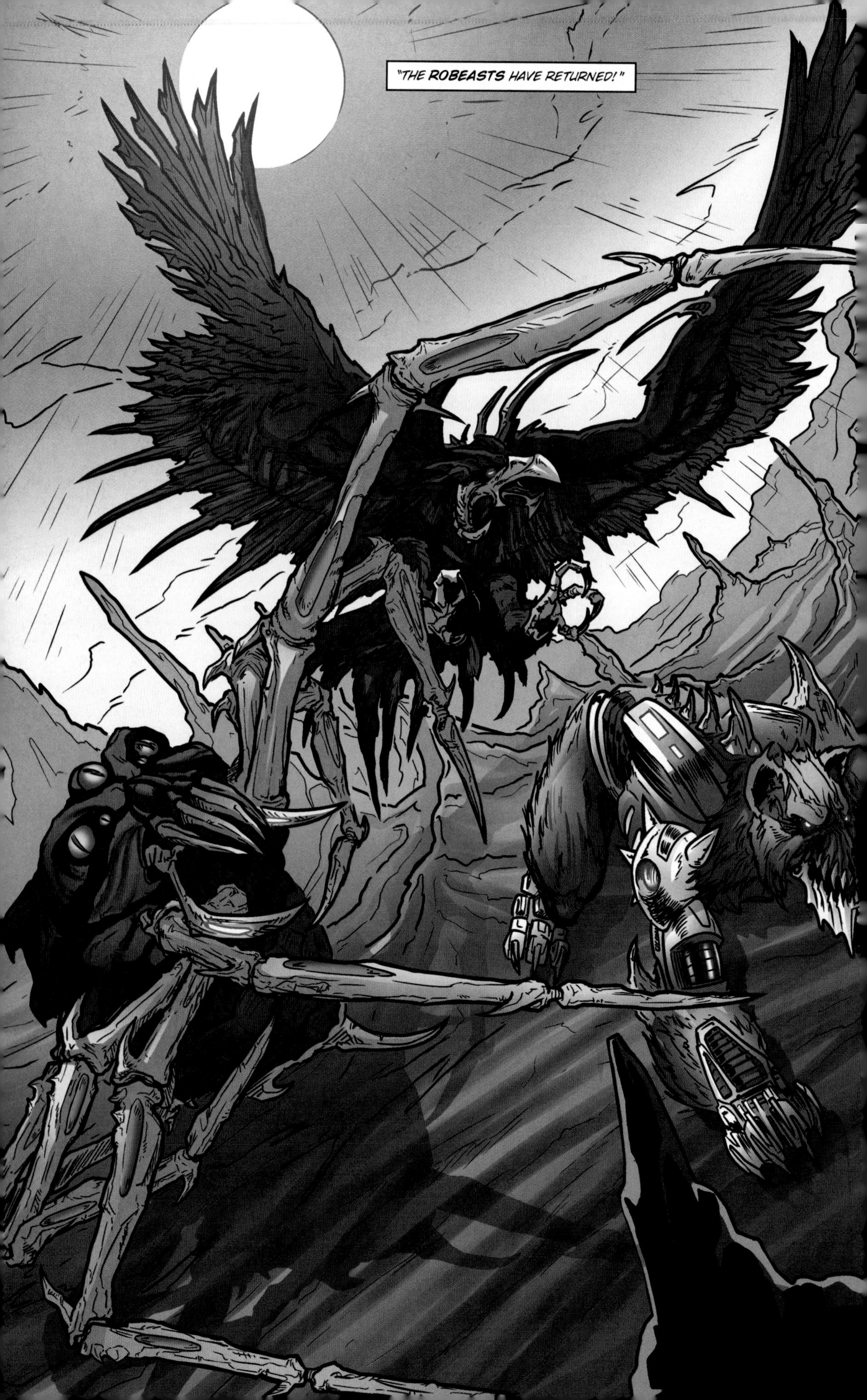
"THE ROBEASTS HAVE RETURNED!"

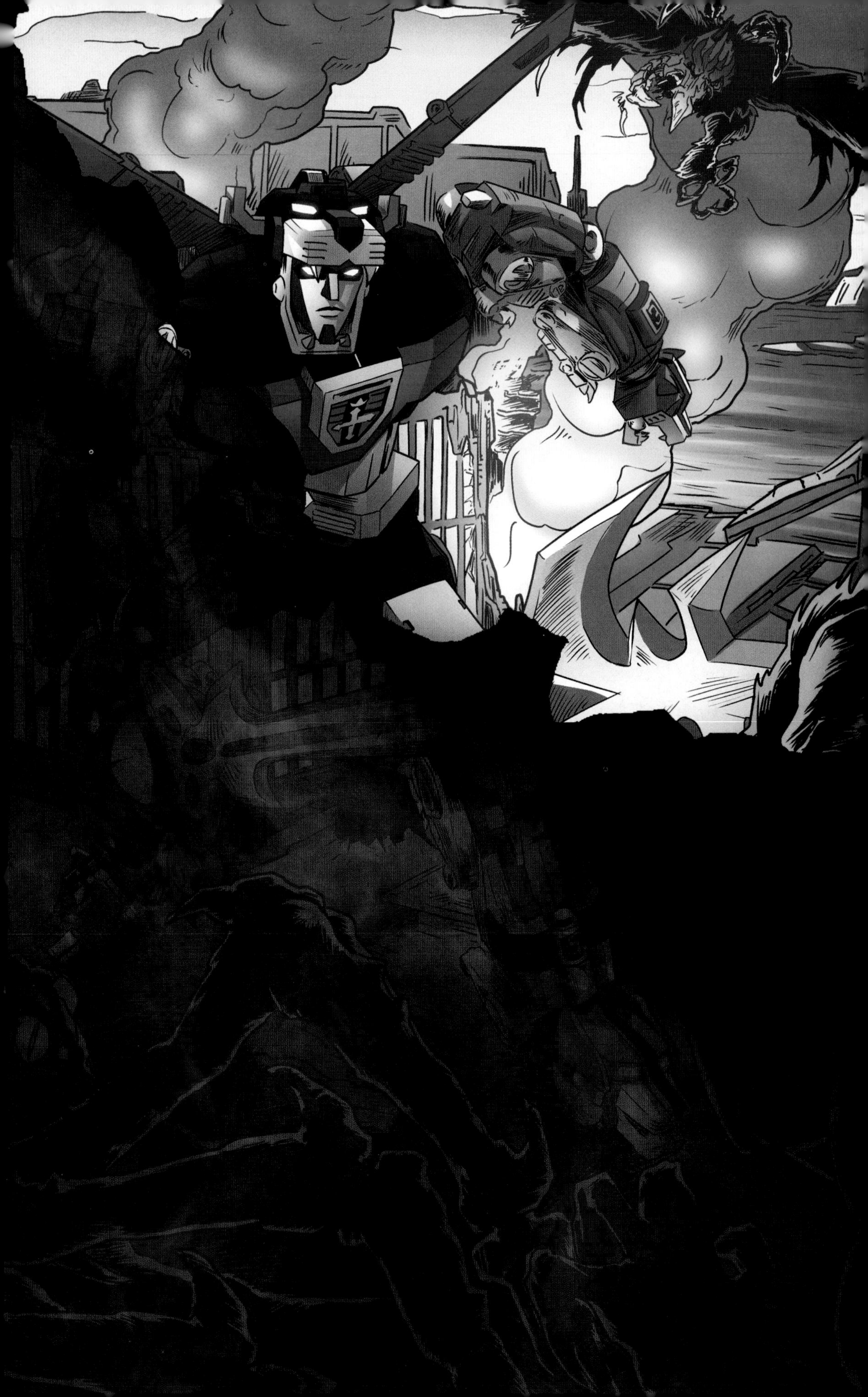

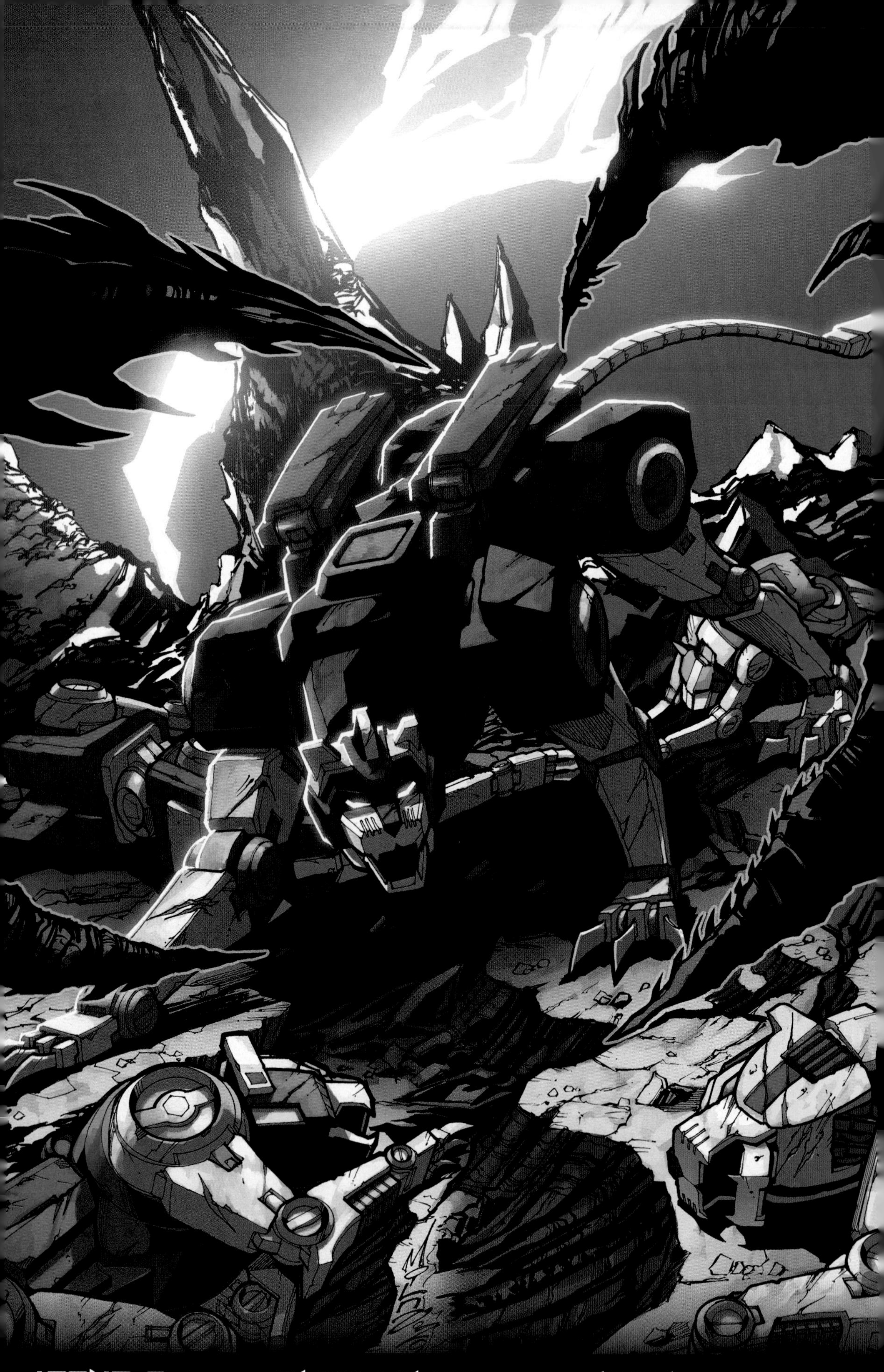

ISSUE 3 Cover by ALEX MILNE Colors by JOSH PEREZ

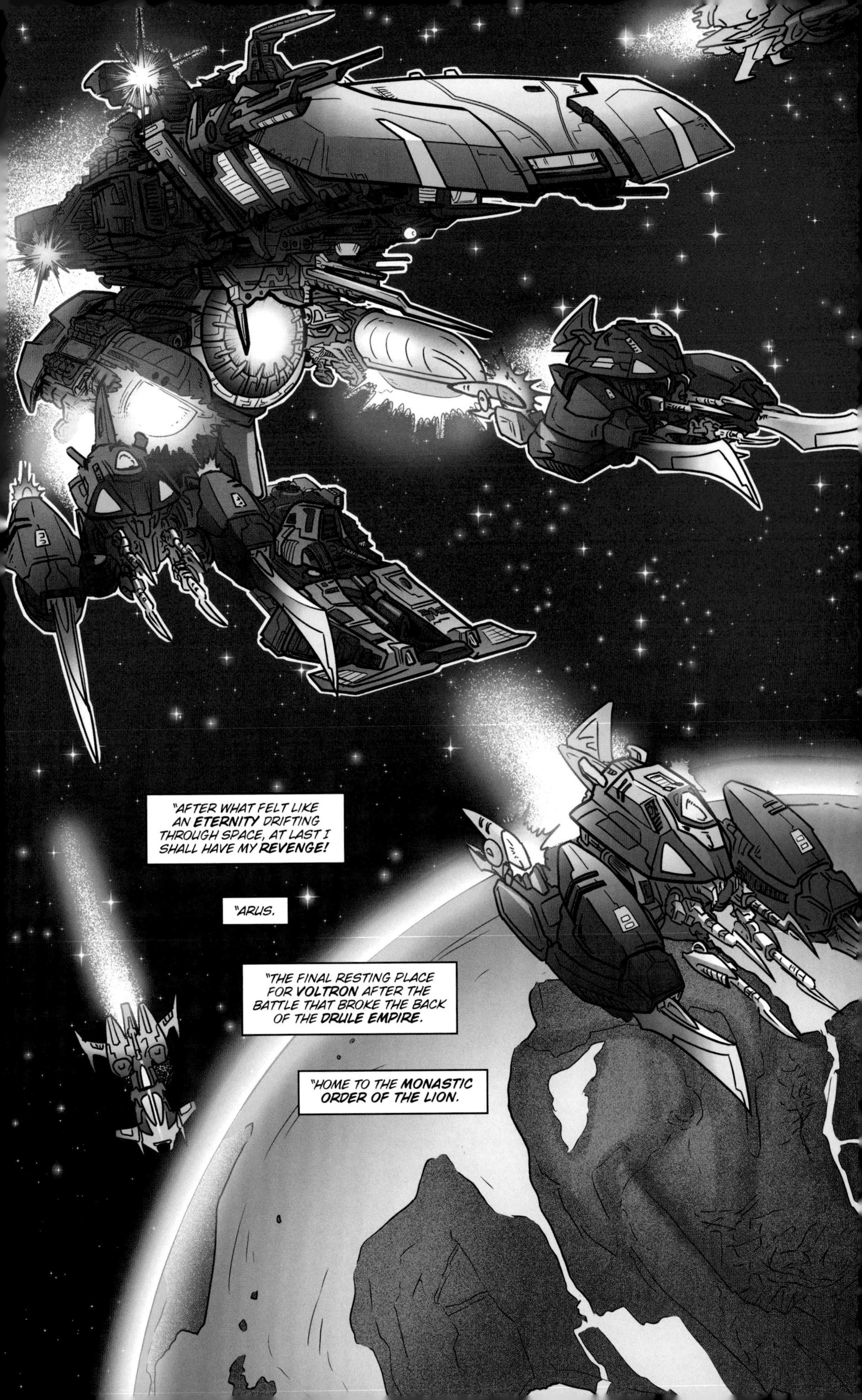
"AFTER WHAT FELT LIKE AN ETERNITY DRIFTING THROUGH SPACE, AT LAST I SHALL HAVE MY REVENGE!
"ARUS.
"THE FINAL RESTING PLACE FOR VOLTRON AFTER THE BATTLE THAT BROKE THE BACK OF THE DRULE EMPIRE.
"HOME TO THE MONASTIC ORDER OF THE LION.

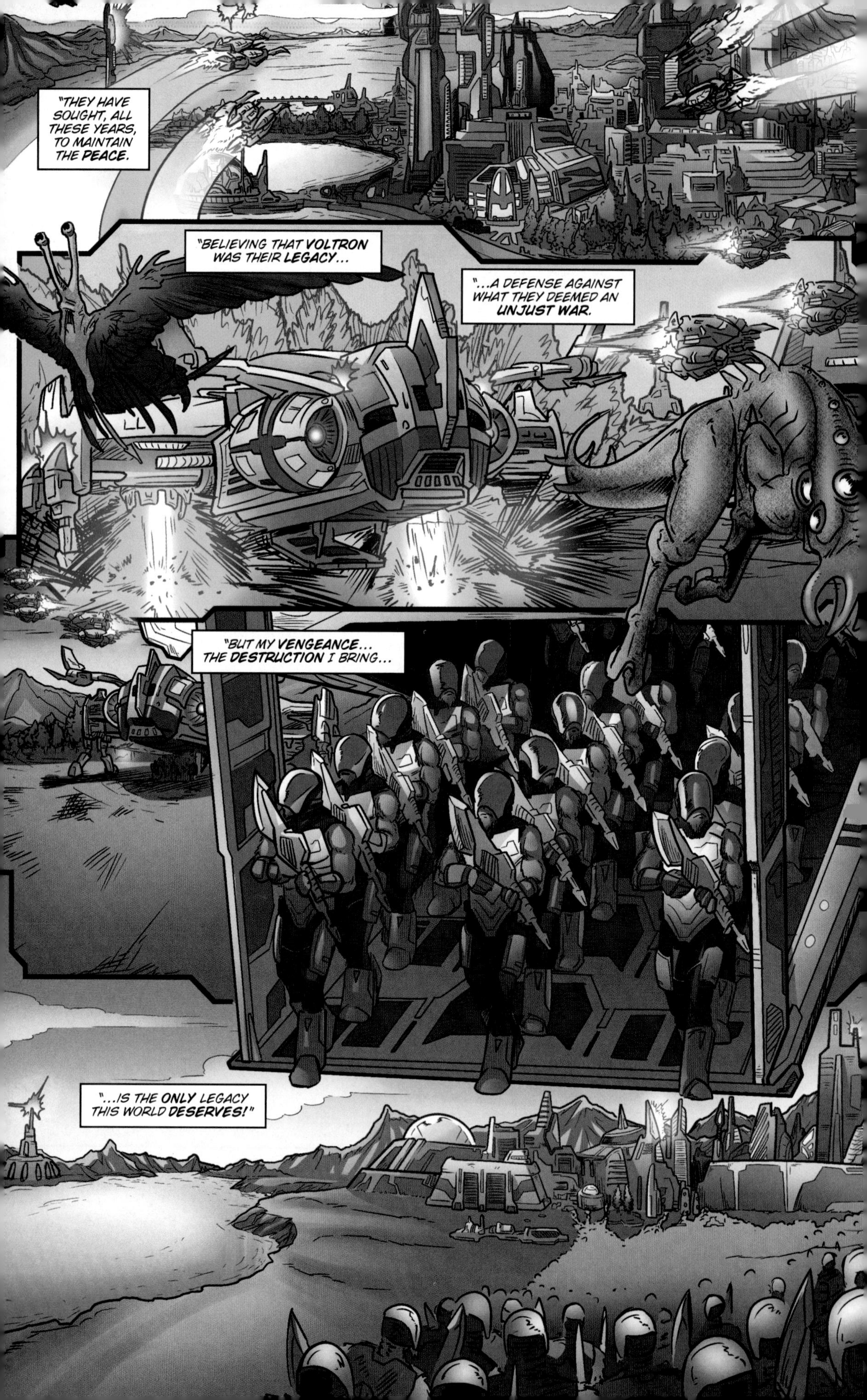
"THEY HAVE SOUGHT, ALL THESE YEARS, TO MAINTAIN THE PEACE.
"BELIEVING THAT VOLTRON WAS THEIR LEGACY...
"...A DEFENSE AGAINST WHAT THEY DEEMED AN UNJUST WAR.
"BUT MY VENGEANCE... THE DESTRUCTION I BRING...
"...IS THE ONLY LEGACY THIS WORLD DESERVES!"

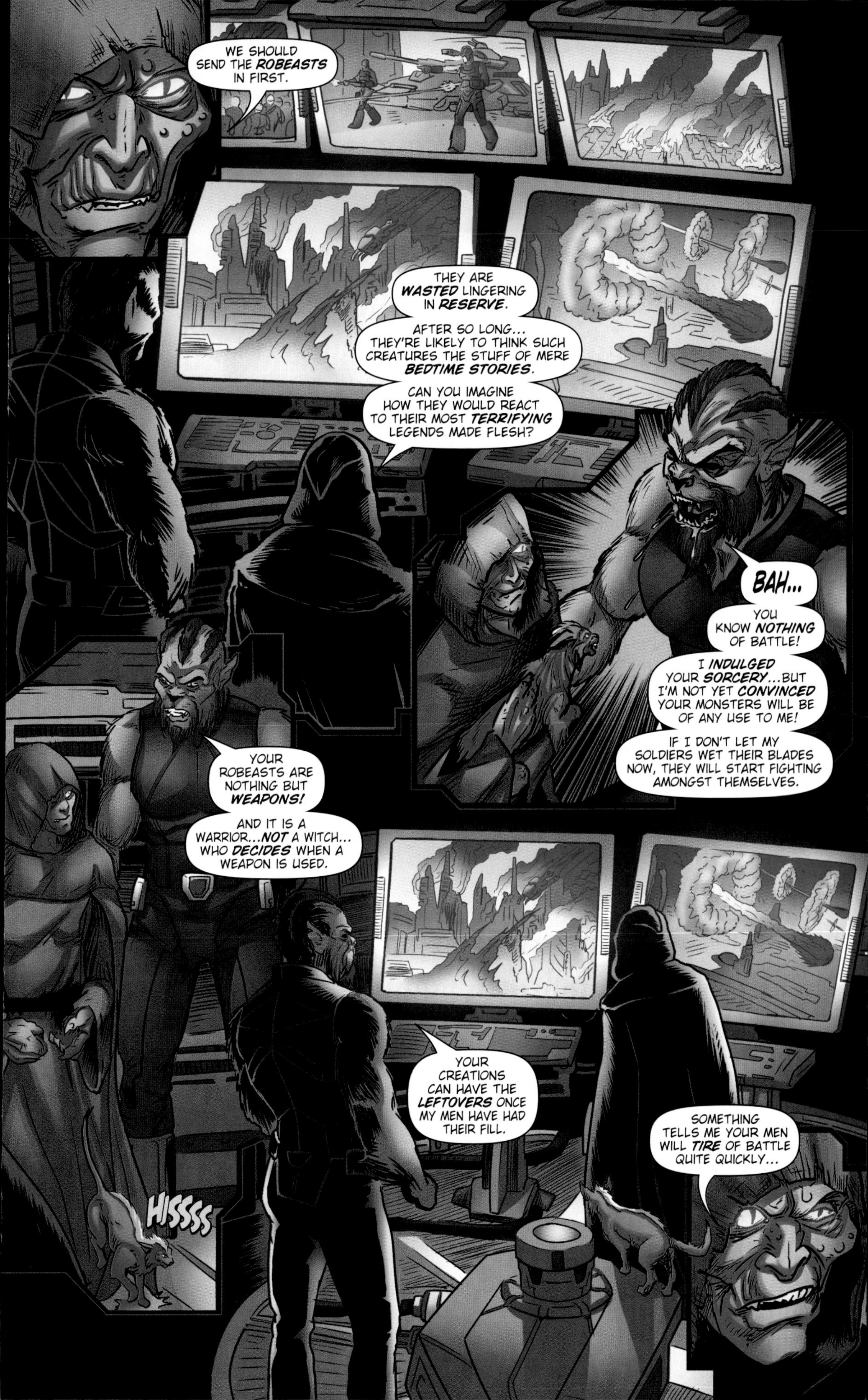
WE SHOULD SEND THE ROBEASTS IN FIRST.
THEY ARE WASTED LINGERING IN RESERVE.
AFTER SO LONG... THEY'RE LIKELY TO THINK SUCH CREATURES THE STUFF OF MERE BEDTIME STORIES.
CAN YOU IMAGINE HOW THEY WOULD REACT TO THEIR MOST TERRIFYING LEGENDS MADE FLESH?
BAH...
YOU KNOW NOTHING OF BATTLE!
I INDULGED YOUR SORCERY...BUT I'M NOT YET CONVINCED YOUR MONSTERS WILL BE OF ANY USE TO ME!
IF I DON'T LET MY SOLDIERS WET THEIR BLADES NOW, THEY WILL START FIGHTING AMONGST THEMSELVES.
YOUR ROBEASTS ARE NOTHING BUT WEAPONS!
AND IT IS A WARRIOR...NOT A WITCH... WHO DECIDES WHEN A WEAPON IS USED.
YOUR CREATIONS CAN HAVE THE LEFTOVERS ONCE MY MEN HAVE HAD THEIR FILL.
SOMETHING TELLS ME YOUR MEN WILL TIRE OF BATTLE QUITE QUICKLY...
HISSSS

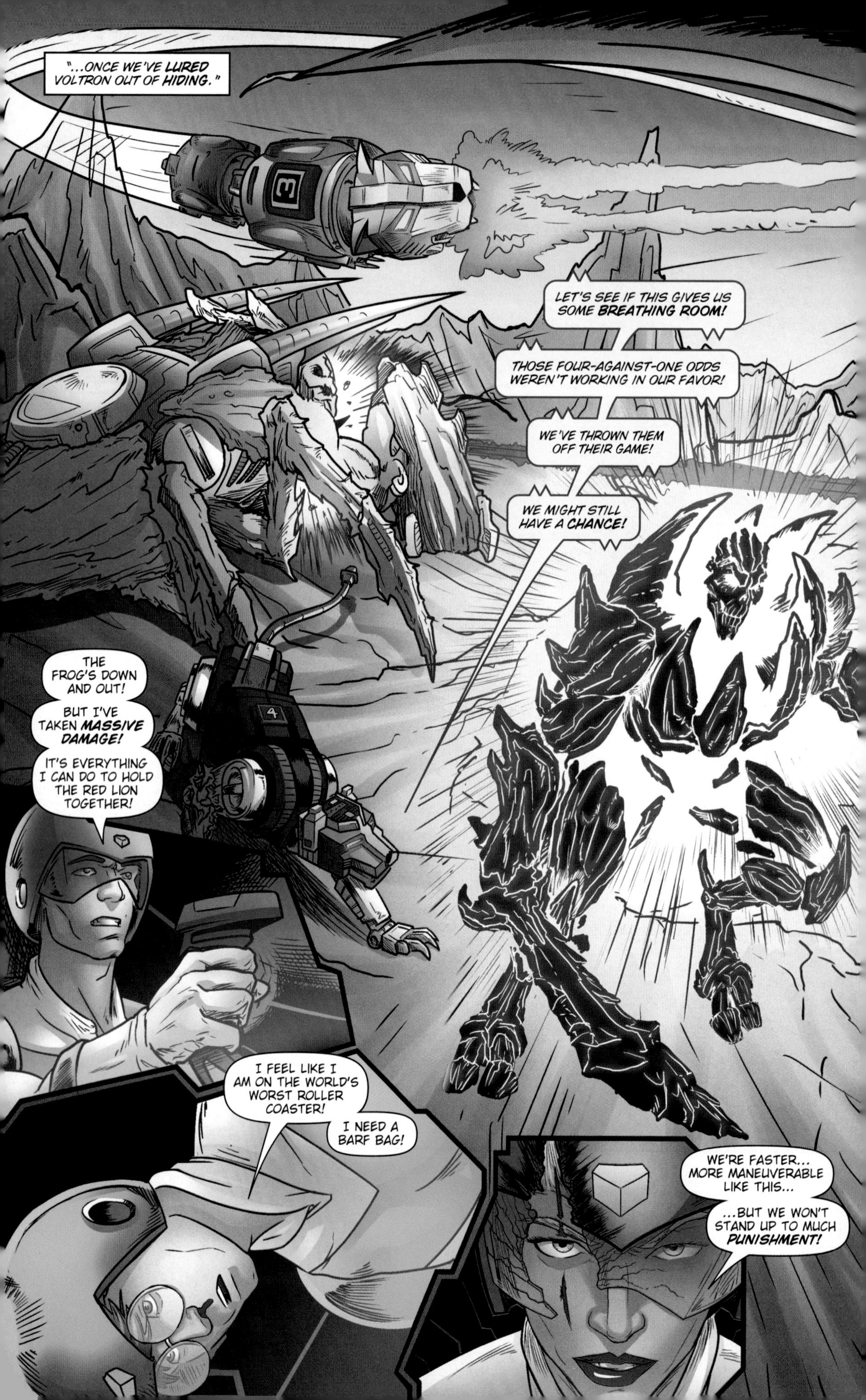
"...ONCE WE'VE LURED VOLTRON OUT OF HIDING."
LET'S SEE IF THIS GIVES US SOME BREATHING ROOM!
THOSE FOUR-AGAINST-ONE ODDS WEREN'T WORKING IN OUR FAVOR!
WE'VE THROWN THEM OFF THEIR GAME!
WE MIGHT STILL HAVE A CHANCE!
THE FROG'S DOWN AND OUT!
BUT I'VE TAKEN MASSIVE DAMAGE!
IT'S EVERYTHING I CAN DO TO HOLD THE RED LION TOGETHER!
I FEEL LIKE I AM ON THE WORLD'S WORST ROLLER COASTER!
I NEED A BARF BAG!
WE'RE FASTER... MORE MANEUVERABLE LIKE THIS...
...BUT WE WON'T STAND UP TO MUCH PUNISHMENT!

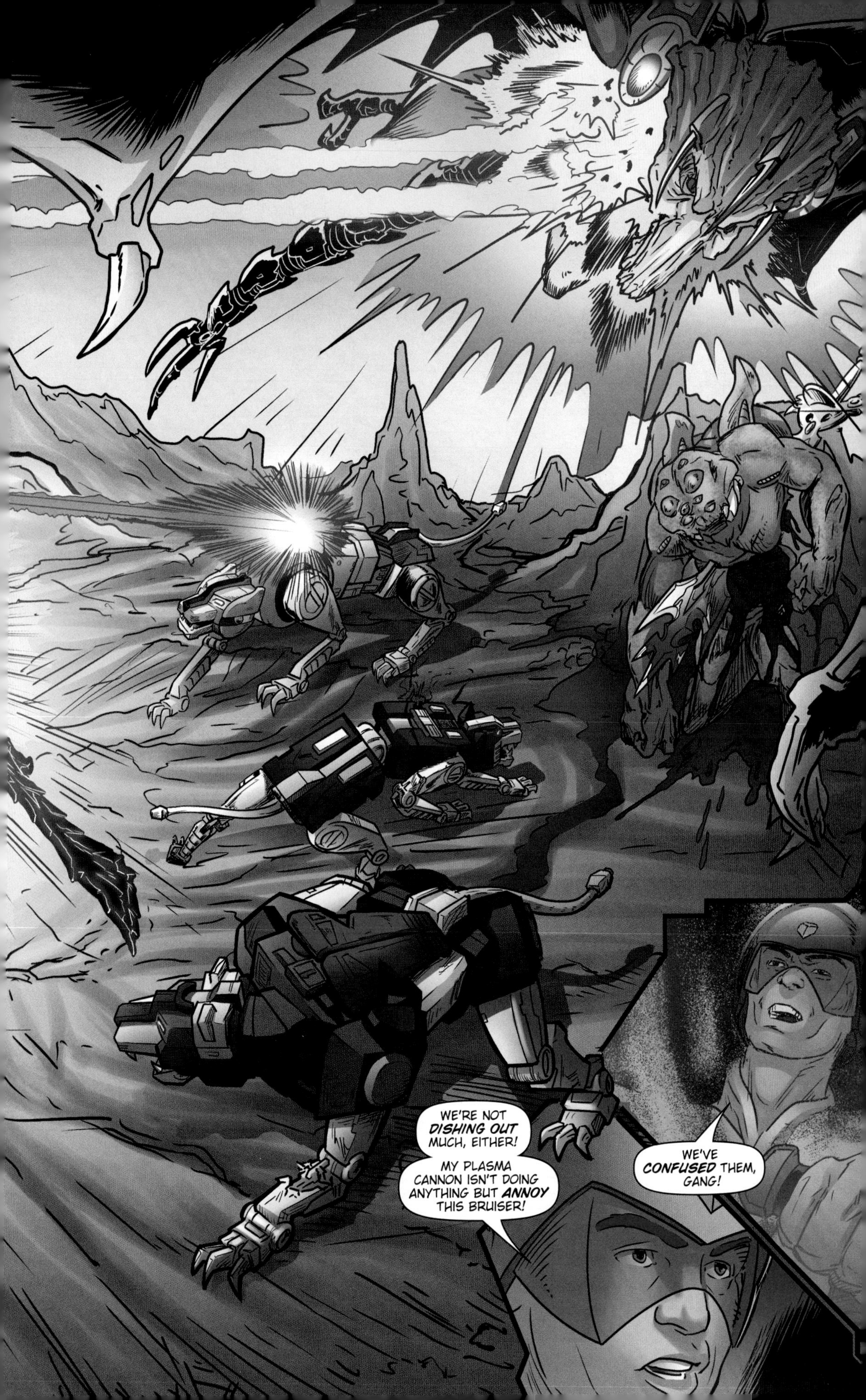
WE'VE *CONFUSED* THEM, GANG!
WE'RE NOT *DISHING OUT* MUCH, EITHER!
MY PLASMA CANNON ISN'T DOING ANYTHING BUT *ANNOY* THIS BRUISER!

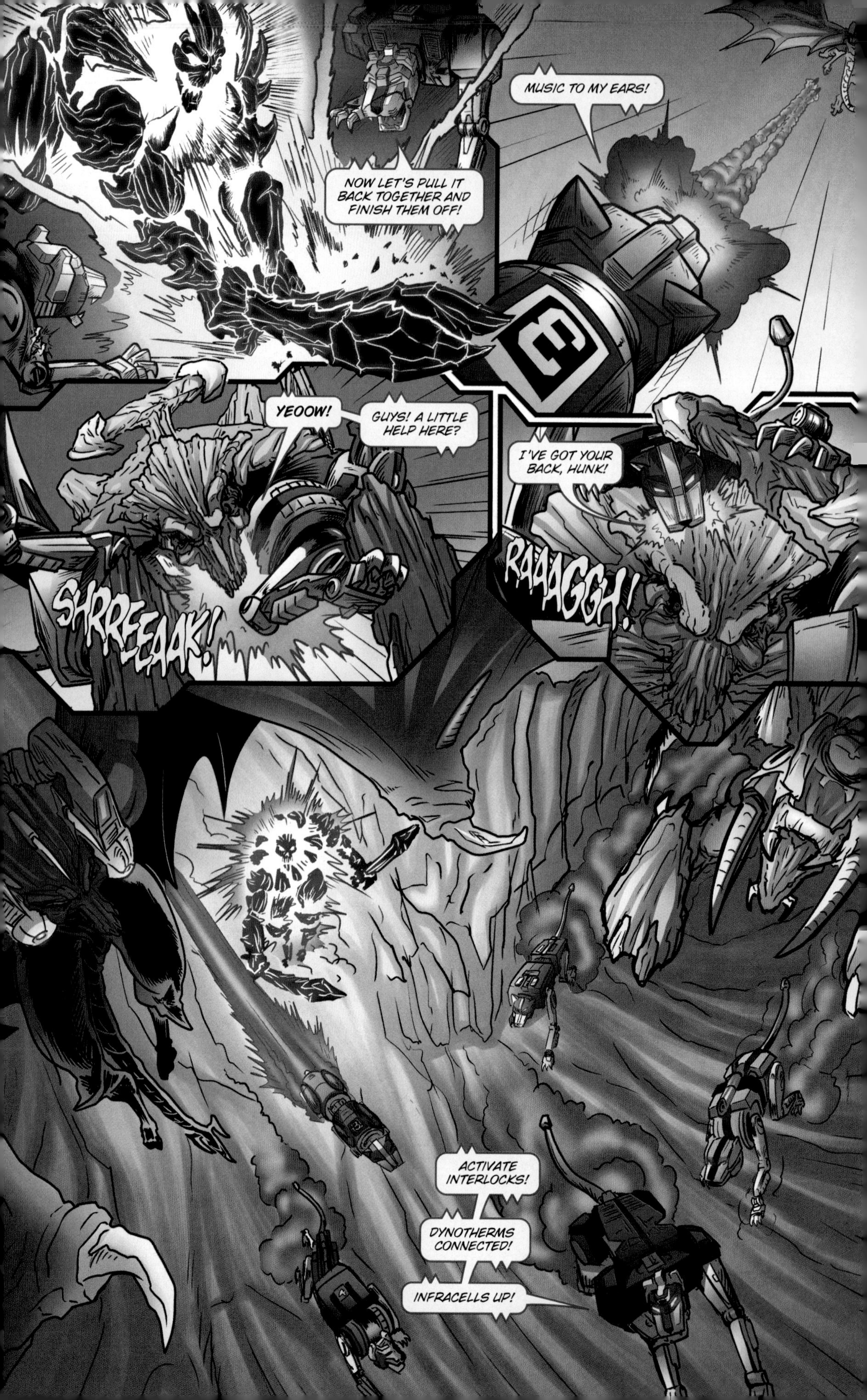
NOW LET'S PULL IT BACK TOGETHER AND FINISH THEM OFF!
MUSIC TO MY EARS!
YEOOW!
GUYS! A LITTLE HELP HERE?
SHRREEAAK!
I'VE GOT YOUR BACK, HUNK!
RAAAGGH!
ACTIVATE INTERLOCKS!
DYNOTHERMS CONNECTED!
INFRACELLS UP!

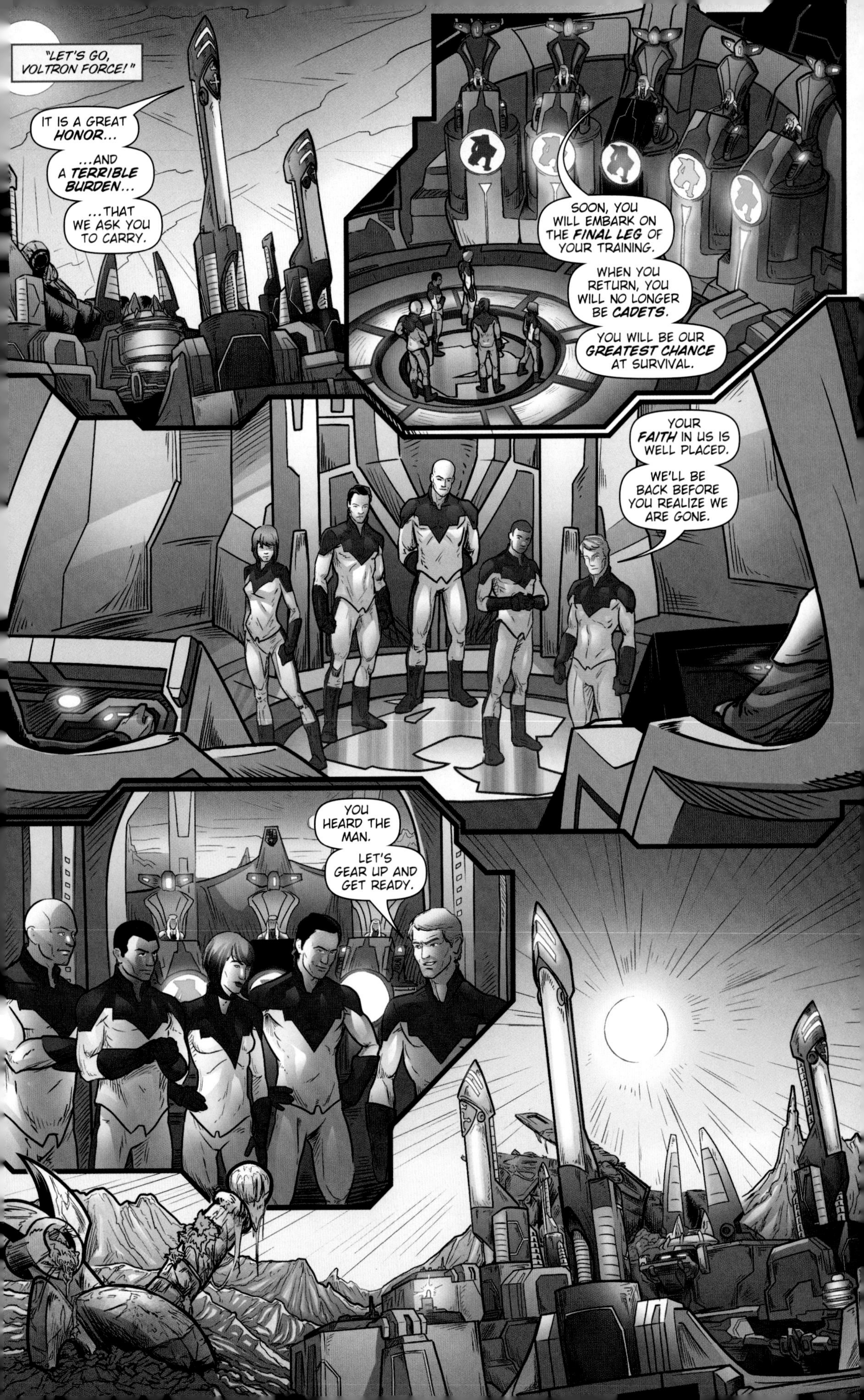
"LET'S GO, VOLTRON FORCE!"
IT IS A GREAT HONOR...
...AND A TERRIBLE BURDEN...
...THAT WE ASK YOU TO CARRY.
SOON, YOU WILL EMBARK ON THE FINAL LEG OF YOUR TRAINING.
WHEN YOU RETURN, YOU WILL NO LONGER BE CADETS.
YOU WILL BE OUR GREATEST CHANCE AT SURVIVAL.
YOUR FAITH IN US IS WELL PLACED.
WE'LL BE BACK BEFORE YOU REALIZE WE ARE GONE.
YOU HEARD THE MAN.
LET'S GEAR UP AND GET READY.

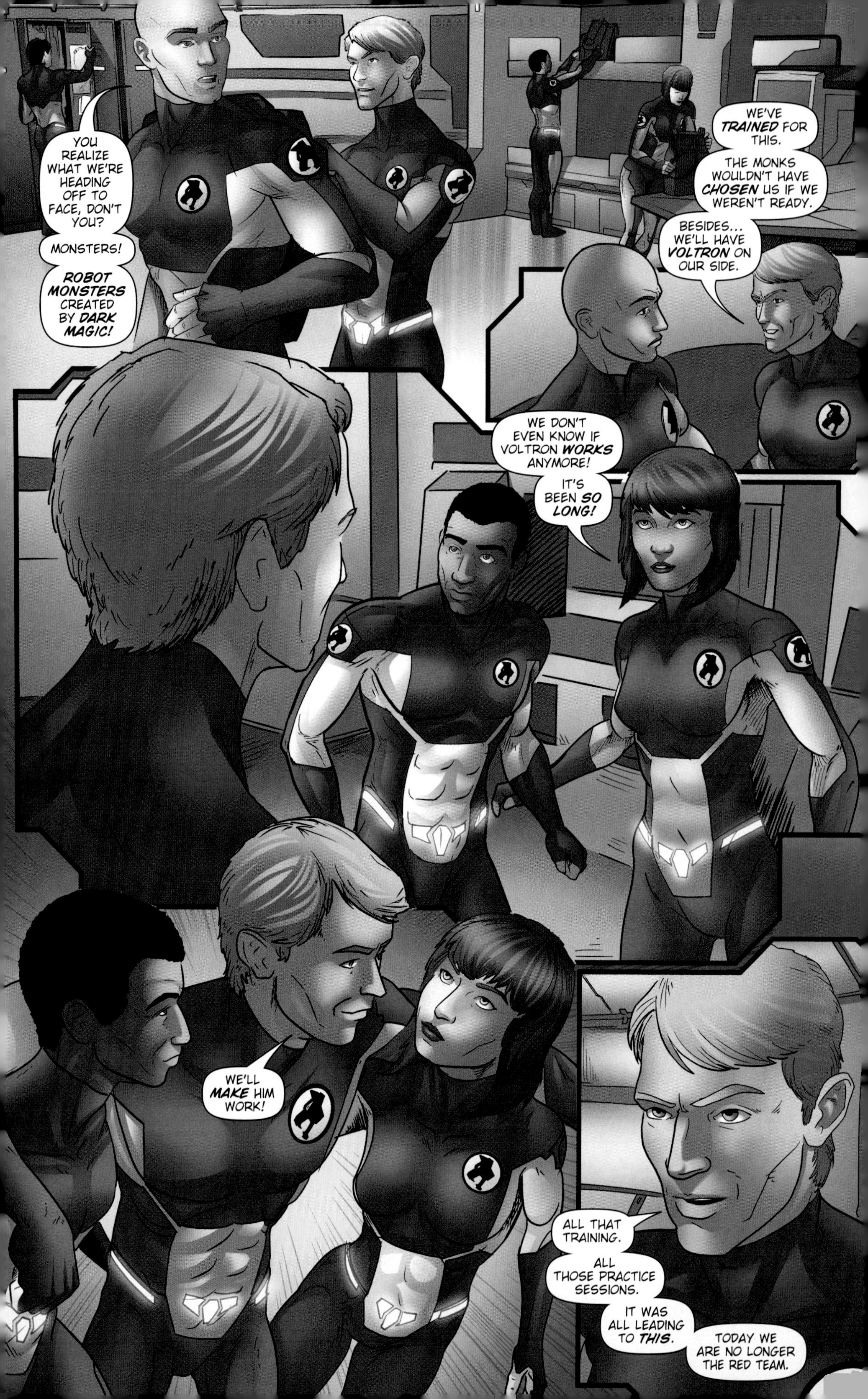
YOU REALIZE WHAT WE'RE HEADING OFF TO FACE, DON'T YOU?
MONSTERS!
ROBOT MONSTERS CREATED BY DARK MAGIC!
WE'VE TRAINED FOR THIS.
THE MONKS WOULDN'T HAVE CHOSEN US IF WE WEREN'T READY.
BESIDES... WE'LL HAVE VOLTRON ON OUR SIDE.
WE DON'T EVEN KNOW IF VOLTRON WORKS ANYMORE!
IT'S BEEN SO LONG!
WE'LL MAKE HIM WORK!
ALL THAT TRAINING.
ALL THOSE PRACTICE SESSIONS.
IT WAS ALL LEADING TO THIS.
TODAY WE ARE NO LONGER THE RED TEAM.

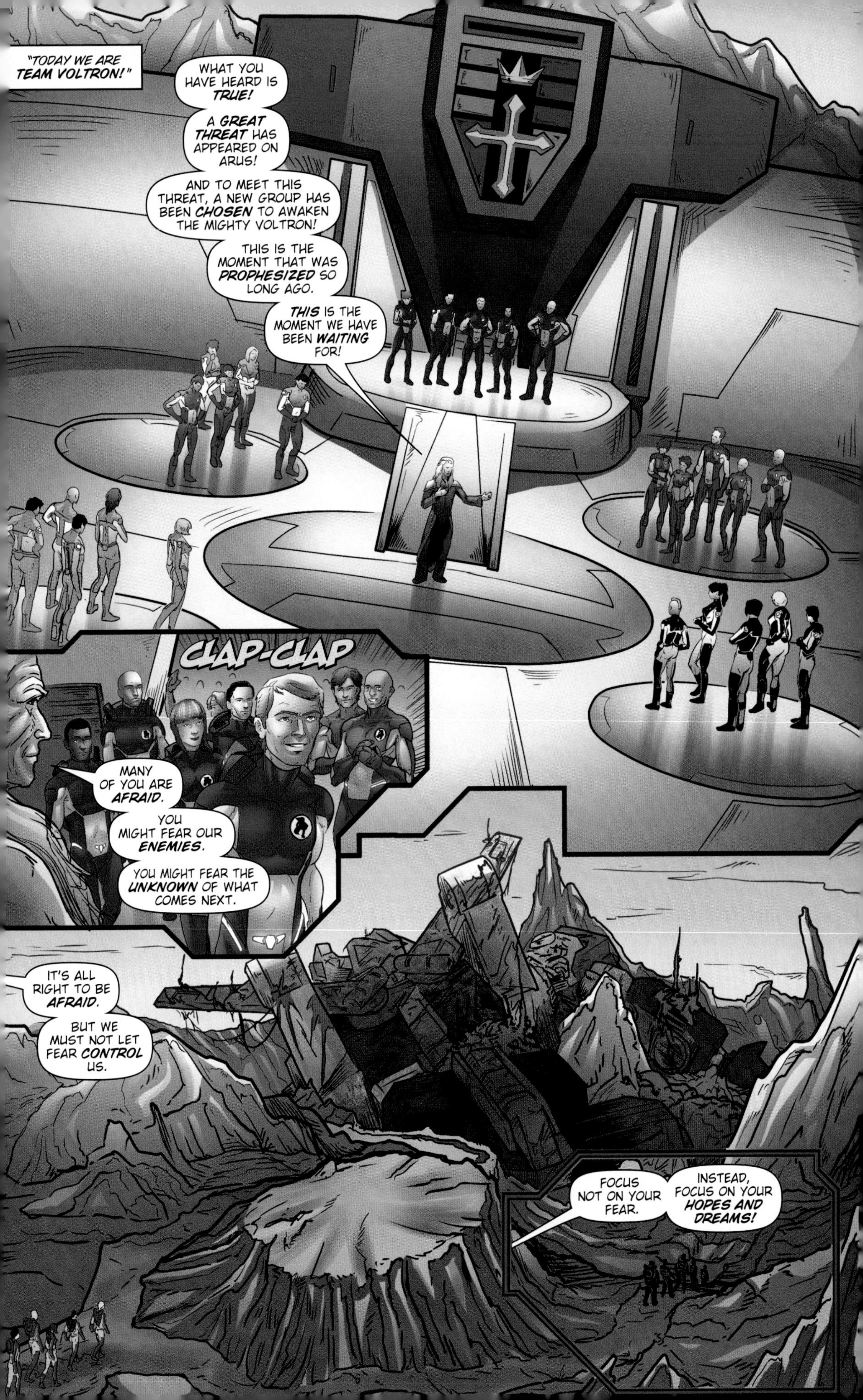
"TODAY WE ARE **TEAM VOLTRON!**"
WHAT YOU HAVE HEARD IS ***TRUE!***
A ***GREAT THREAT*** HAS APPEARED ON ARUS!
AND TO MEET THIS THREAT, A NEW GROUP HAS BEEN ***CHOSEN*** TO AWAKEN THE MIGHTY VOLTRON!
THIS IS THE MOMENT THAT WAS ***PROPHESIZED*** SO LONG AGO.
***THIS*** IS THE MOMENT WE HAVE BEEN ***WAITING*** FOR!
CLAP-CLAP
MANY OF YOU ARE ***AFRAID***.
YOU MIGHT FEAR OUR ***ENEMIES***.
YOU MIGHT FEAR THE ***UNKNOWN*** OF WHAT COMES NEXT.
IT'S ALL RIGHT TO BE ***AFRAID***.
BUT WE MUST NOT LET FEAR ***CONTROL*** US.
FOCUS NOT ON YOUR FEAR.
INSTEAD, FOCUS ON YOUR ***HOPES AND DREAMS!***

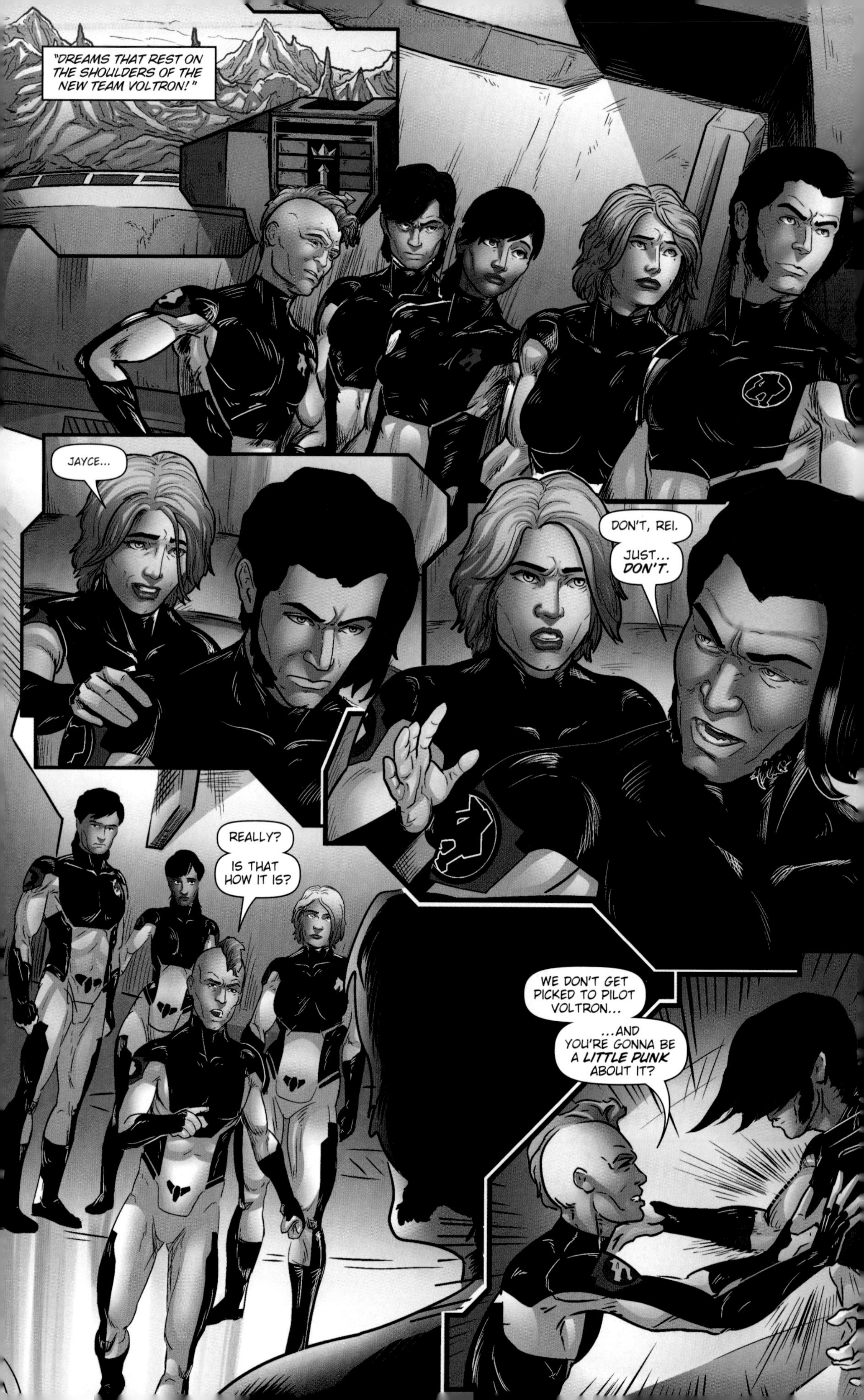
"DREAMS THAT REST ON THE SHOULDERS OF THE NEW TEAM VOLTRON!"
JAYCE...
DON'T, REI.
JUST... DON'T.
REALLY?
IS THAT HOW IT IS?
WE DON'T GET PICKED TO PILOT VOLTRON...
...AND YOU'RE GONNA BE A LITTLE PUNK ABOUT IT?

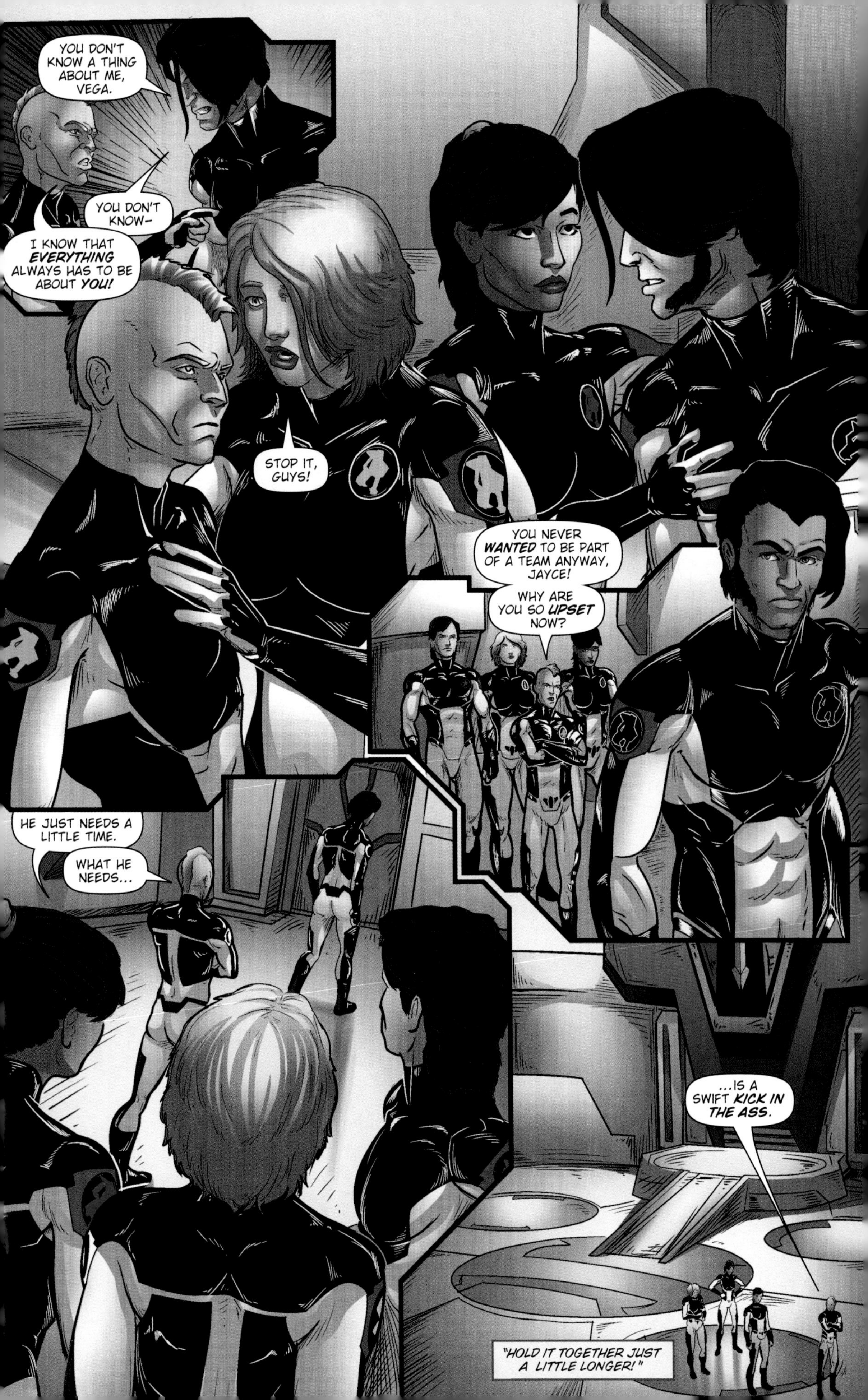
YOU DON'T KNOW A THING ABOUT ME, VEGA.
YOU DON'T KNOW-
I KNOW THAT **EVERYTHING** ALWAYS HAS TO BE ABOUT **YOU!**
STOP IT, GUYS!
YOU NEVER **WANTED** TO BE PART OF A TEAM ANYWAY, JAYCE!
WHY ARE YOU SO **UPSET** NOW?
HE JUST NEEDS A LITTLE TIME.
WHAT HE NEEDS...
...IS A SWIFT **KICK IN THE ASS**.
*"HOLD IT TOGETHER JUST A LITTLE LONGER!"*

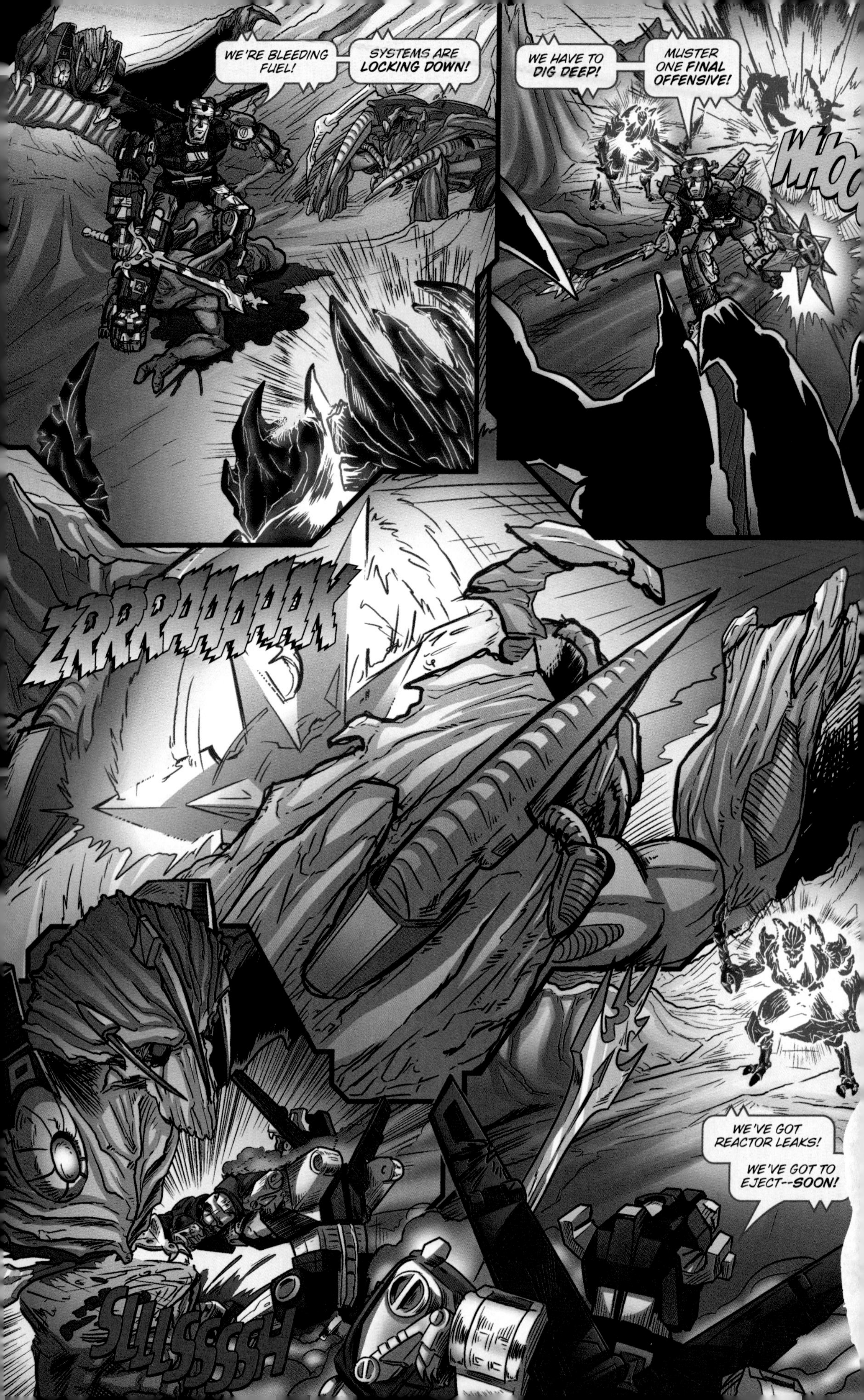
WE'RE BLEEDING FUEL!
SYSTEMS ARE LOCKING DOWN!
WE HAVE TO DIG DEEP!
MUSTER ONE FINAL OFFENSIVE!
WHOO
ZRRRAAAAAK
WE'VE GOT REACTOR LEAKS!
WE'VE GOT TO EJECT--SOON!
SLLLSSSSH

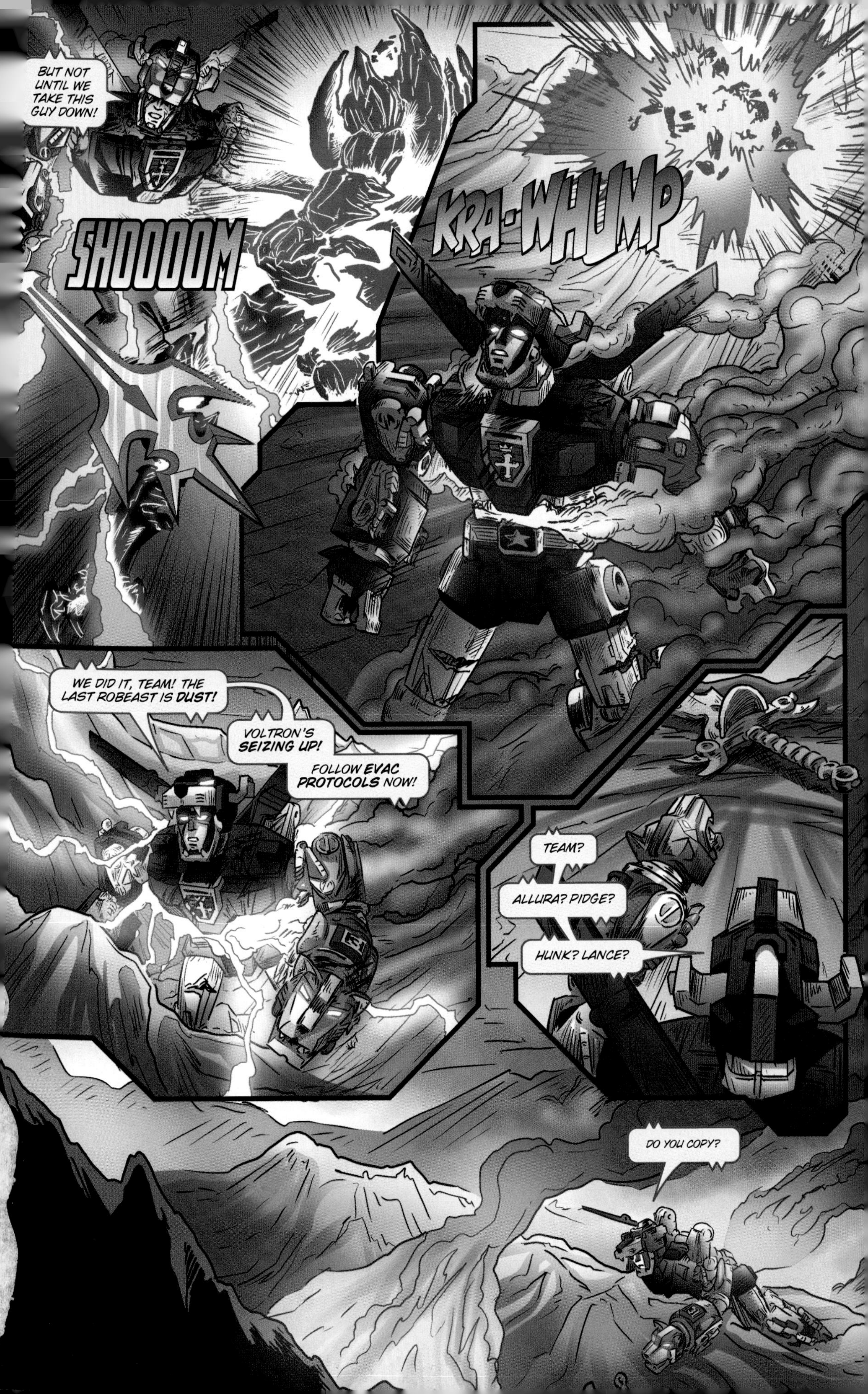
BUT NOT UNTIL WE TAKE THIS GUY DOWN!
SHOOOOM
KRA-WHUMP
WE DID IT, TEAM! THE LAST ROBEAST IS DUST!
VOLTRON'S SEIZING UP!
FOLLOW EVAC PROTOCOLS NOW!
TEAM?
ALLURA? PIDGE?
HUNK? LANCE?
DO YOU COPY?

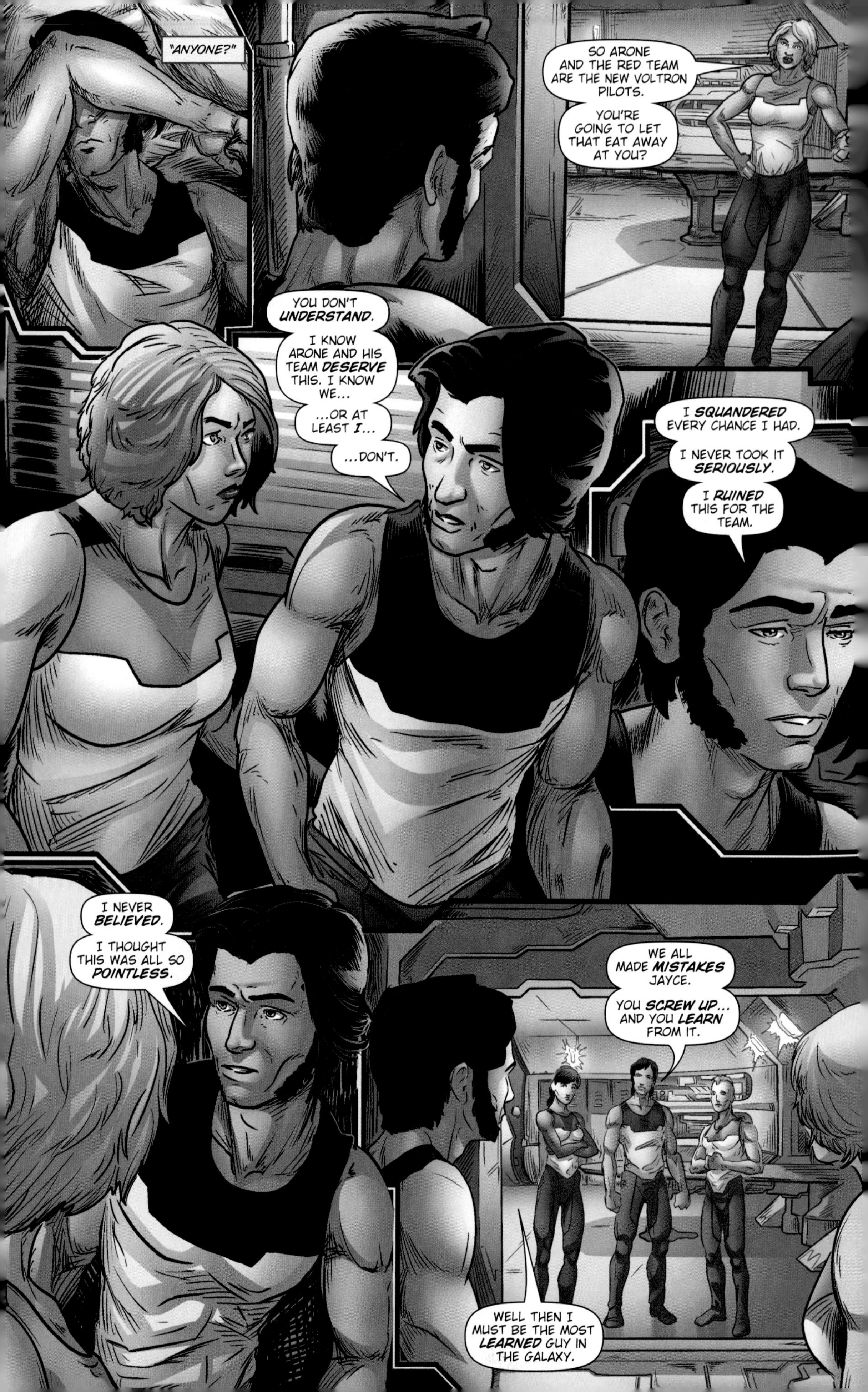
"ANYONE?"
SO ARONE AND THE RED TEAM ARE THE NEW VOLTRON PILOTS.
YOU'RE GOING TO LET THAT EAT AWAY AT YOU?
YOU DON'T UNDERSTAND.
I KNOW ARONE AND HIS TEAM DESERVE THIS. I KNOW WE...
...OR AT LEAST I...
...DON'T.
I SQUANDERED EVERY CHANCE I HAD.
I NEVER TOOK IT SERIOUSLY.
I RUINED THIS FOR THE TEAM.
I NEVER BELIEVED.
I THOUGHT THIS WAS ALL SO POINTLESS.
WE ALL MADE MISTAKES JAYCE.
YOU SCREW UP... AND YOU LEARN FROM IT.
WELL THEN I MUST BE THE MOST LEARNED GUY IN THE GALAXY.

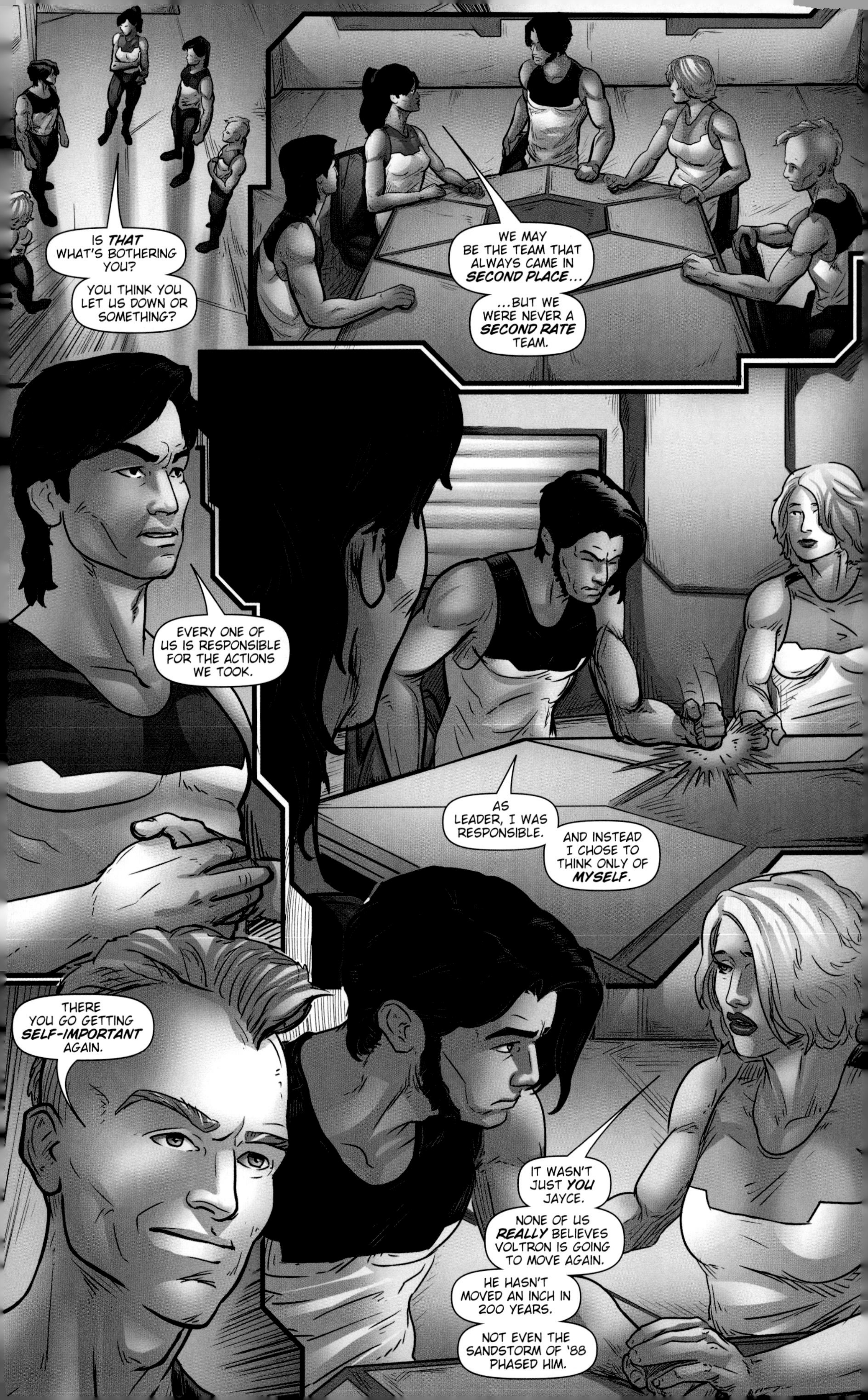
IS THAT WHAT'S BOTHERING YOU?
YOU THINK YOU LET US DOWN OR SOMETHING?
WE MAY BE THE TEAM THAT ALWAYS CAME IN SECOND PLACE...
...BUT WE WERE NEVER A SECOND RATE TEAM.
EVERY ONE OF US IS RESPONSIBLE FOR THE ACTIONS WE TOOK.
AS LEADER, I WAS RESPONSIBLE.
AND INSTEAD I CHOSE TO THINK ONLY OF MYSELF.
THERE YOU GO GETTING SELF-IMPORTANT AGAIN.
IT WASN'T JUST YOU JAYCE.
NONE OF US REALLY BELIEVES VOLTRON IS GOING TO MOVE AGAIN.
HE HASN'T MOVED AN INCH IN 200 YEARS.
NOT EVEN THE SANDSTORM OF '88 PHASED HIM.

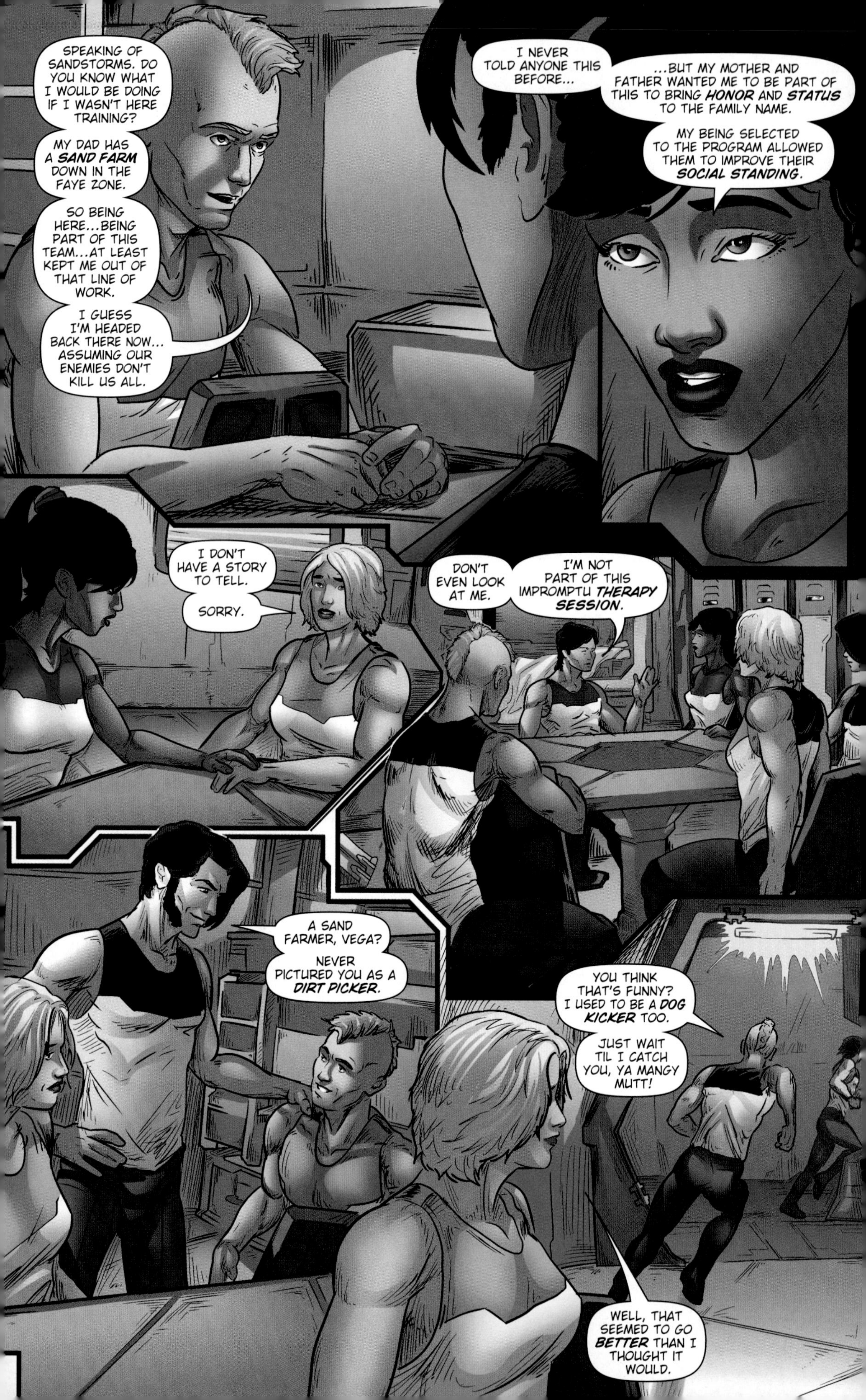
SPEAKING OF SANDSTORMS. DO YOU KNOW WHAT I WOULD BE DOING IF I WASN'T HERE TRAINING?
MY DAD HAS A SAND FARM DOWN IN THE FAYE ZONE.
SO BEING HERE...BEING PART OF THIS TEAM...AT LEAST KEPT ME OUT OF THAT LINE OF WORK.
I GUESS I'M HEADED BACK THERE NOW... ASSUMING OUR ENEMIES DON'T KILL US ALL.
I NEVER TOLD ANYONE THIS BEFORE...
...BUT MY MOTHER AND FATHER WANTED ME TO BE PART OF THIS TO BRING HONOR AND STATUS TO THE FAMILY NAME.
MY BEING SELECTED TO THE PROGRAM ALLOWED THEM TO IMPROVE THEIR SOCIAL STANDING.
I DON'T HAVE A STORY TO TELL.
SORRY.
DON'T EVEN LOOK AT ME.
I'M NOT PART OF THIS IMPROMPTU THERAPY SESSION.
A SAND FARMER, VEGA?
NEVER PICTURED YOU AS A DIRT PICKER.
YOU THINK THAT'S FUNNY? I USED TO BE A DOG KICKER TOO.
JUST WAIT TIL I CATCH YOU, YA MANGY MUTT!
WELL, THAT SEEMED TO GO BETTER THAN I THOUGHT IT WOULD.

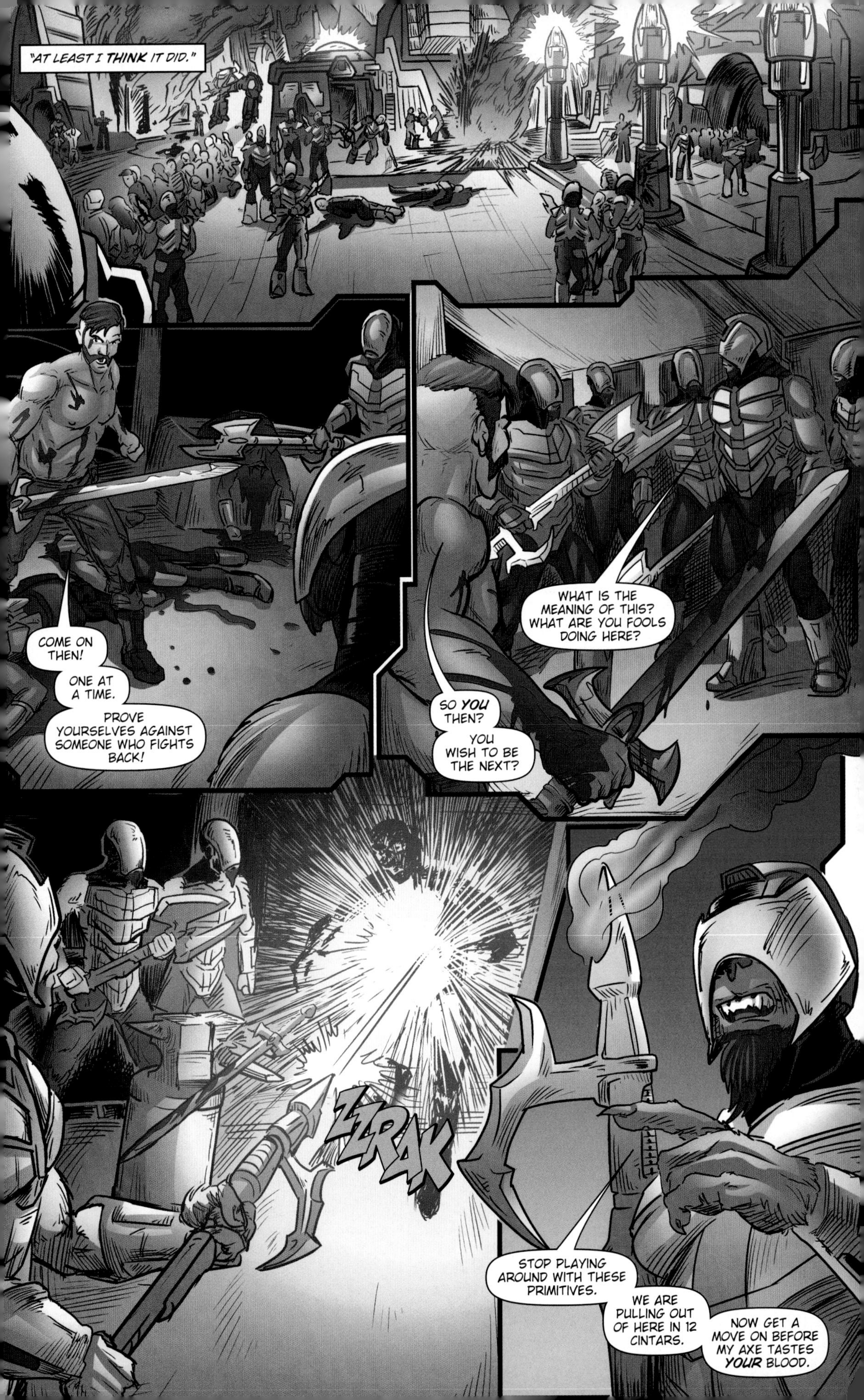
"AT LEAST I THINK IT DID."
COME ON THEN!
ONE AT A TIME.
PROVE YOURSELVES AGAINST SOMEONE WHO FIGHTS BACK!
WHAT IS THE MEANING OF THIS? WHAT ARE YOU FOOLS DOING HERE?
SO YOU THEN?
YOU WISH TO BE THE NEXT?
ZZRAK
STOP PLAYING AROUND WITH THESE PRIMITIVES.
WE ARE PULLING OUT OF HERE IN 12 CINTARS.
NOW GET A MOVE ON BEFORE MY AXE TASTES YOUR BLOOD.

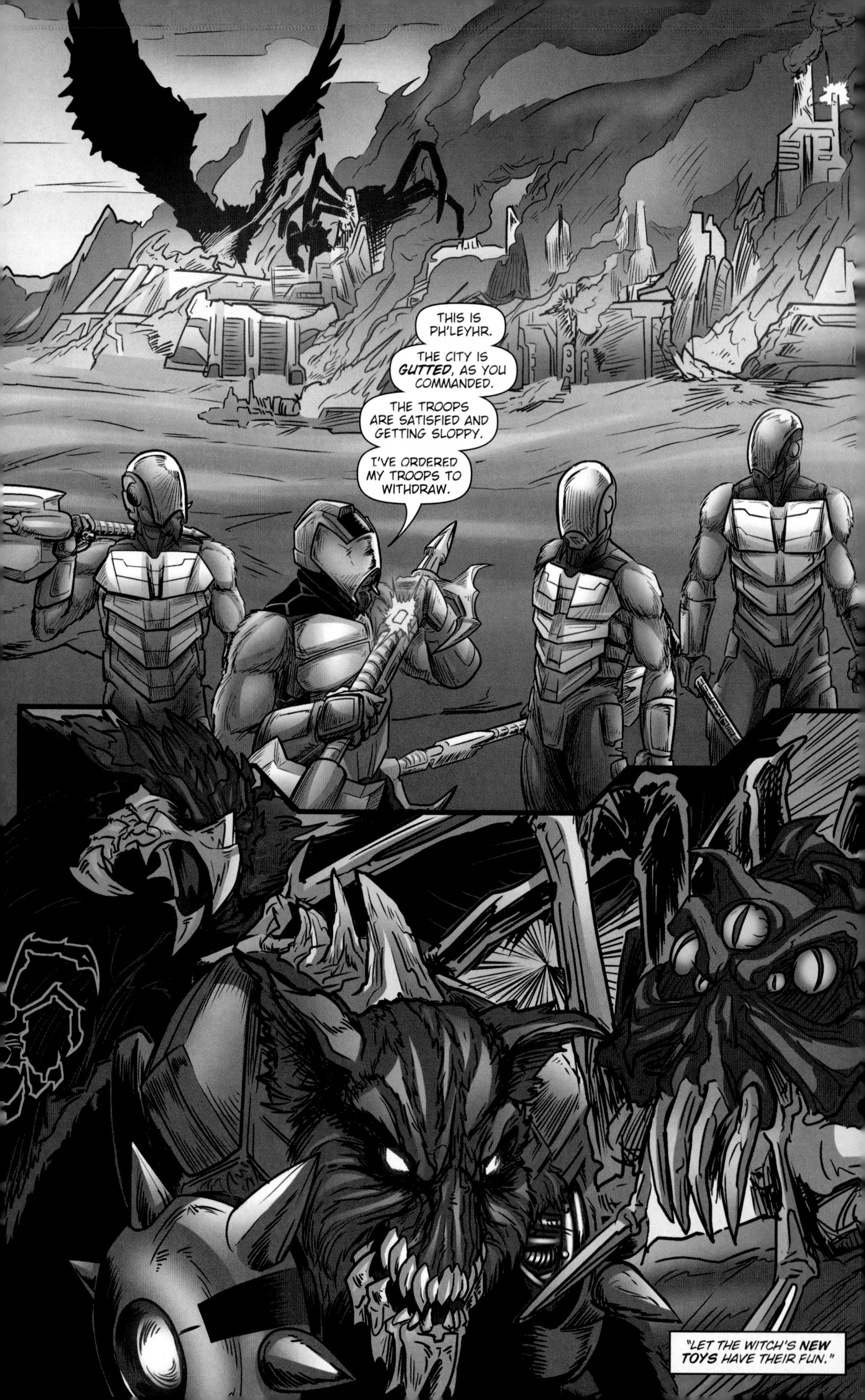
THIS IS PH'LEYHR.
THE CITY IS GUTTED, AS YOU COMMANDED.
THE TROOPS ARE SATISFIED AND GETTING SLOPPY.
I'VE ORDERED MY TROOPS TO WITHDRAW.
"LET THE WITCH'S NEW TOYS HAVE THEIR FUN."

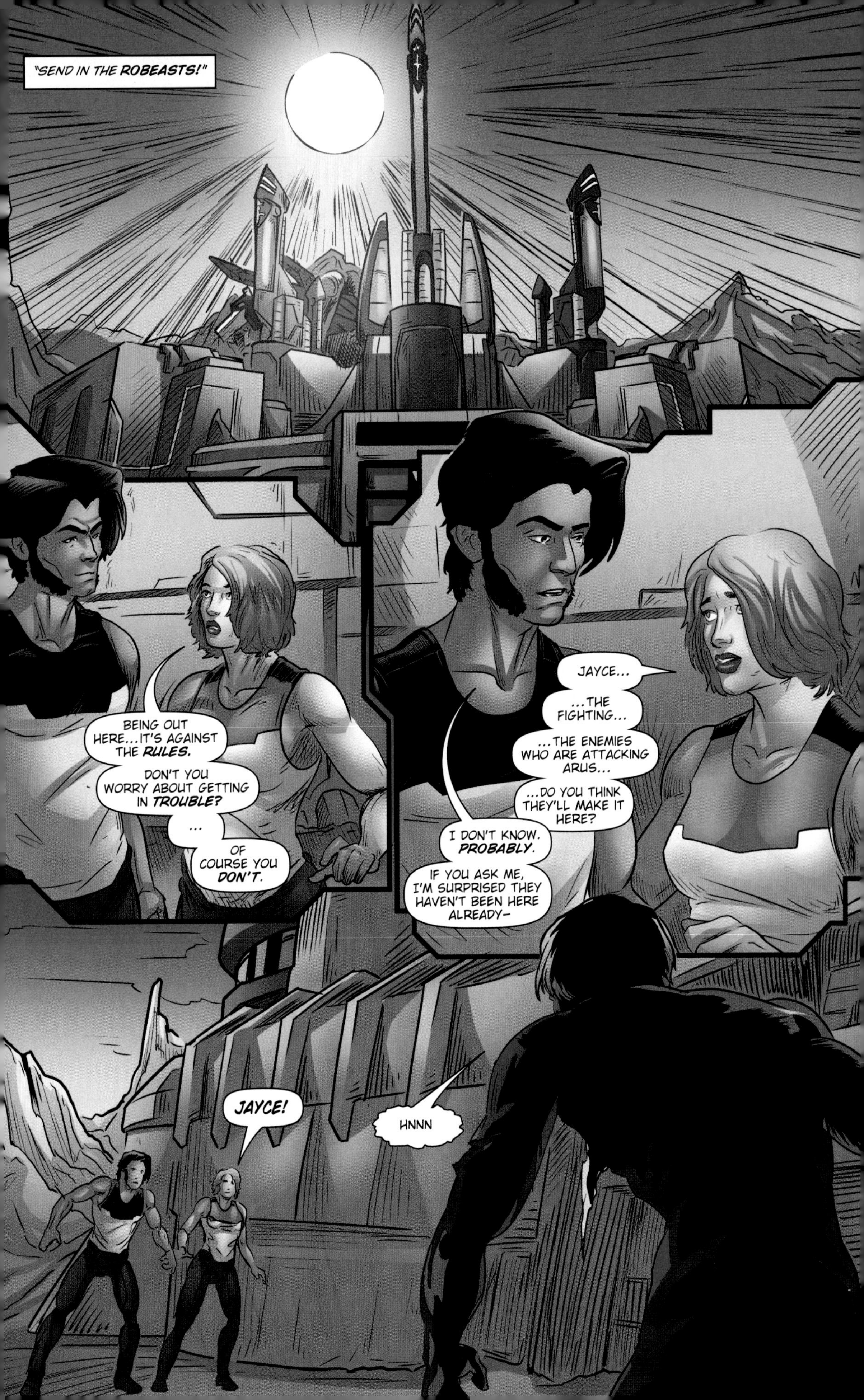
"SEND IN THE ROBEASTS!"
BEING OUT HERE...IT'S AGAINST THE RULES.
DON'T YOU WORRY ABOUT GETTING IN TROUBLE?
...
OF COURSE YOU DON'T.
JAYCE...
...THE FIGHTING...
...THE ENEMIES WHO ARE ATTACKING ARUS...
...DO YOU THINK THEY'LL MAKE IT HERE?
I DON'T KNOW. PROBABLY.
IF YOU ASK ME, I'M SURPRISED THEY HAVEN'T BEEN HERE ALREADY–
JAYCE!
HNNN

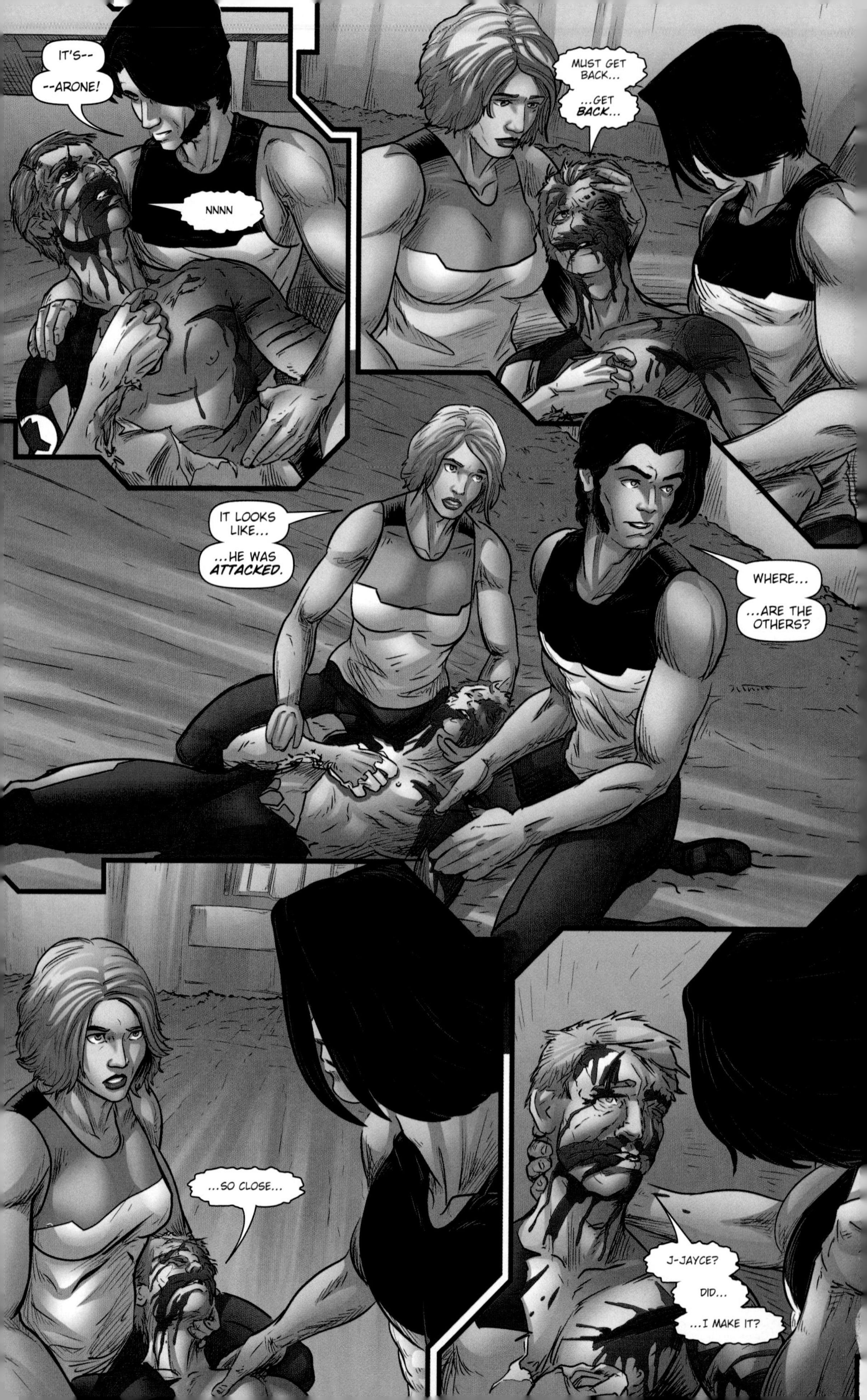
IT'S--
--ARONE!
NNNN
MUST GET BACK...
...GET BACK...
IT LOOKS LIKE...
...HE WAS ATTACKED.
WHERE...
...ARE THE OTHERS?
...SO CLOSE...
J-JAYCE?
DID...
...I MAKE IT?

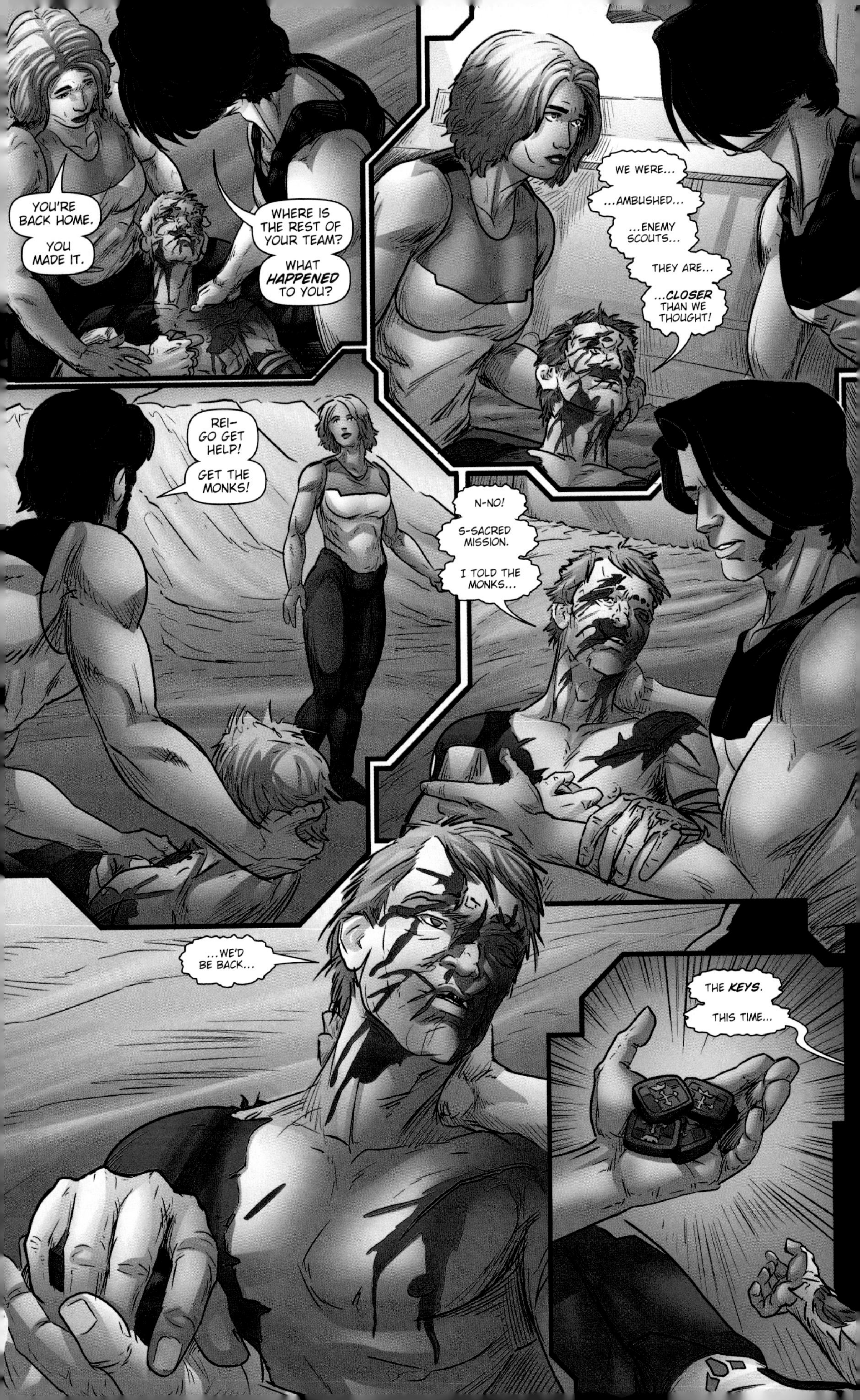
YOU'RE BACK HOME.
YOU MADE IT.
WHERE IS THE REST OF YOUR TEAM?
WHAT HAPPENED TO YOU?
WE WERE...
...AMBUSHED...
...ENEMY SCOUTS...
THEY ARE...
...CLOSER THAN WE THOUGHT!
REI-GO GET HELP!
GET THE MONKS!
N-NO!
S-SACRED MISSION.
I TOLD THE MONKS...
...WE'D BE BACK...
THE KEYS.
THIS TIME...

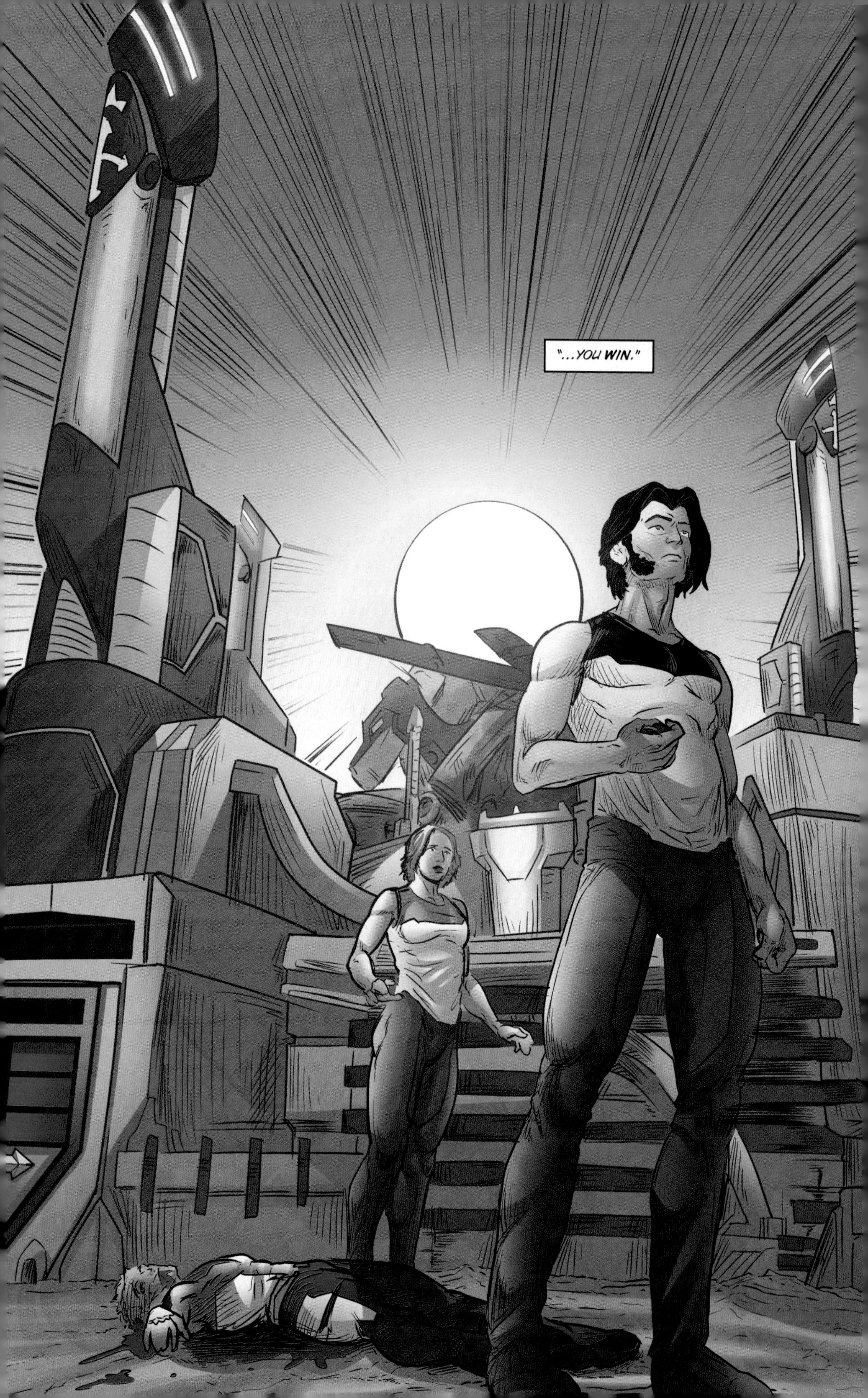
"...YOU WIN."

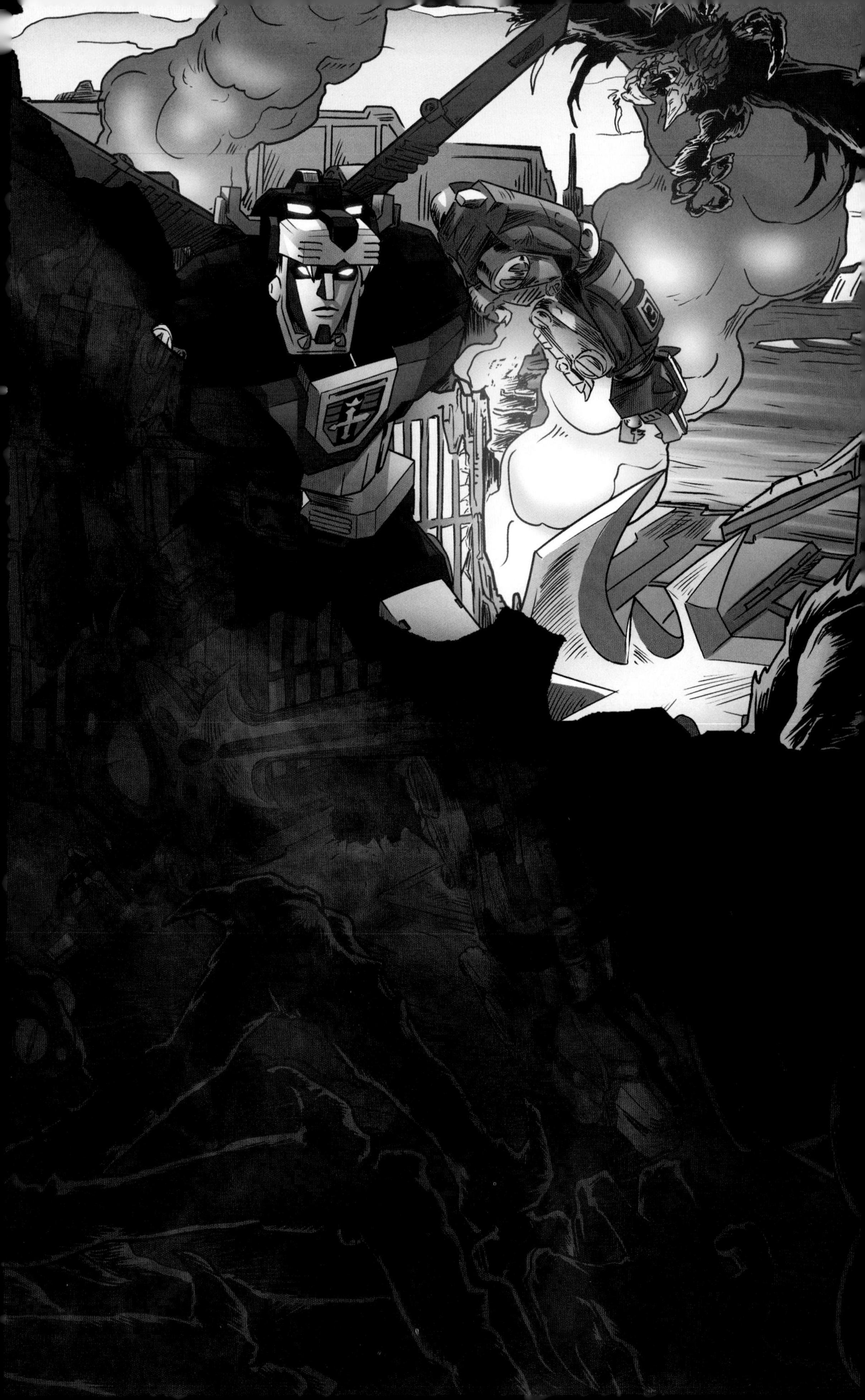

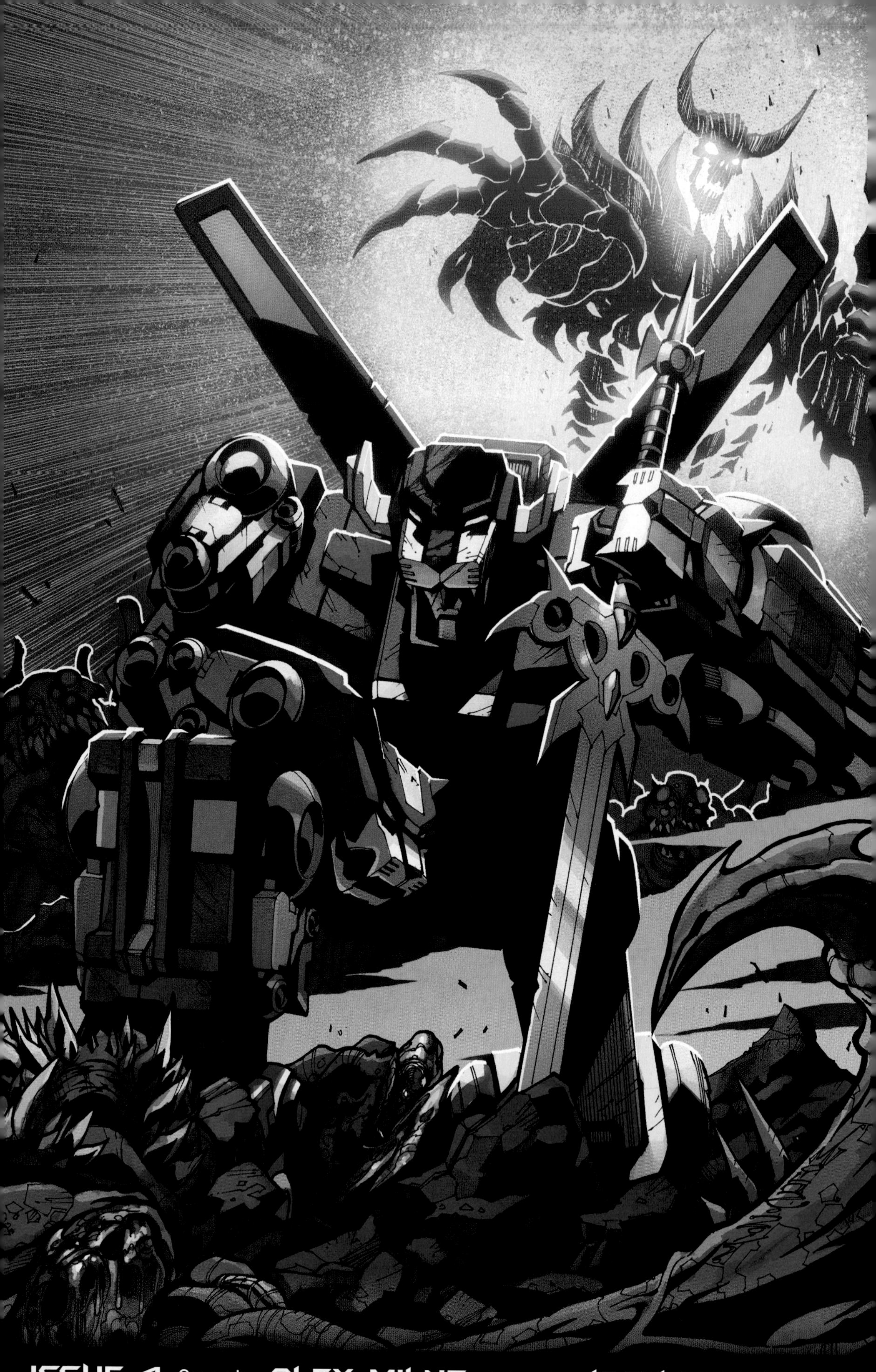

ISSUE 4 Cover by ALEX MILNE Colors by JOSH PEREZ

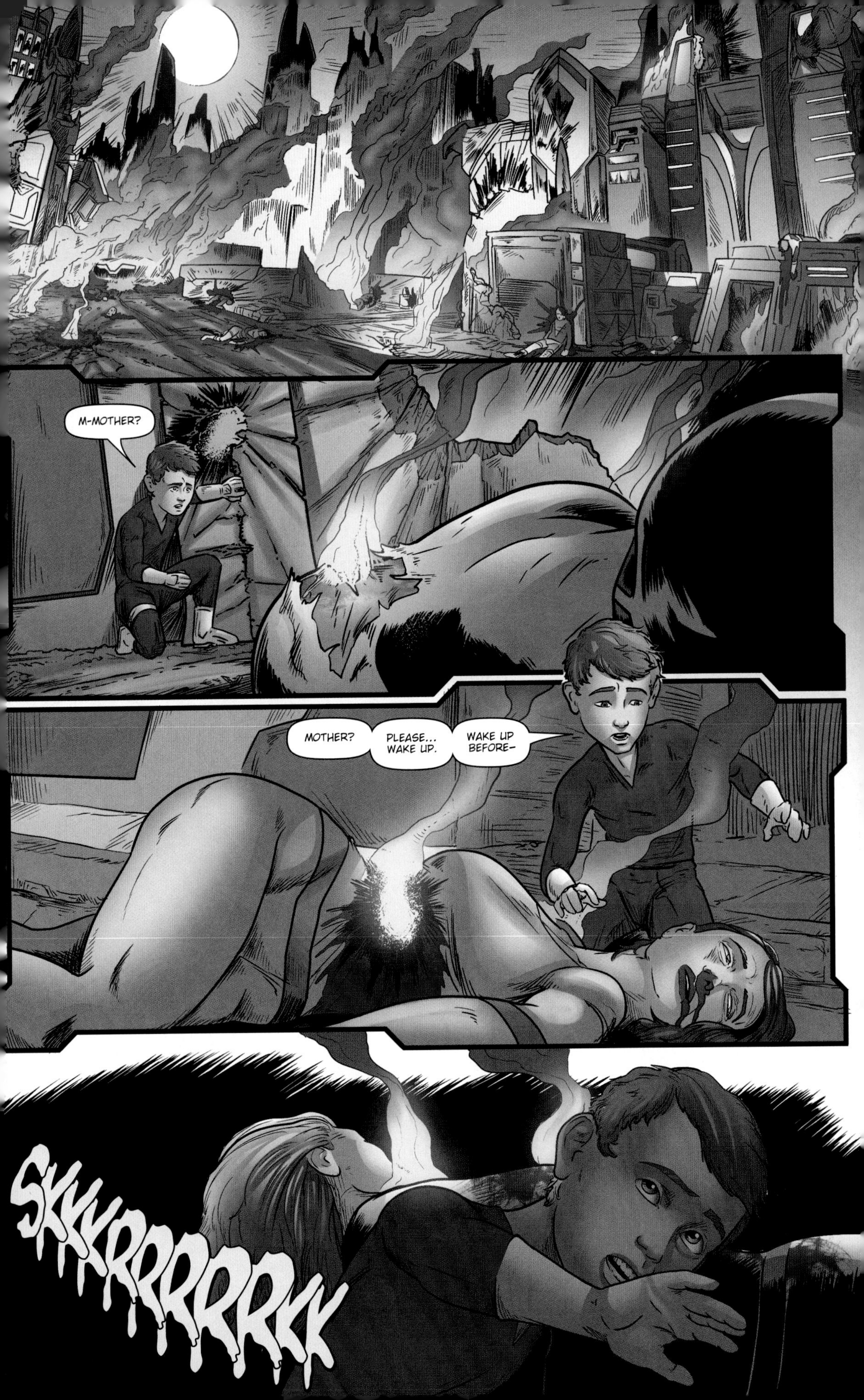
M-MOTHER?
MOTHER?
PLEASE... WAKE UP.
WAKE UP BEFORE-
SKKRRRRRKK

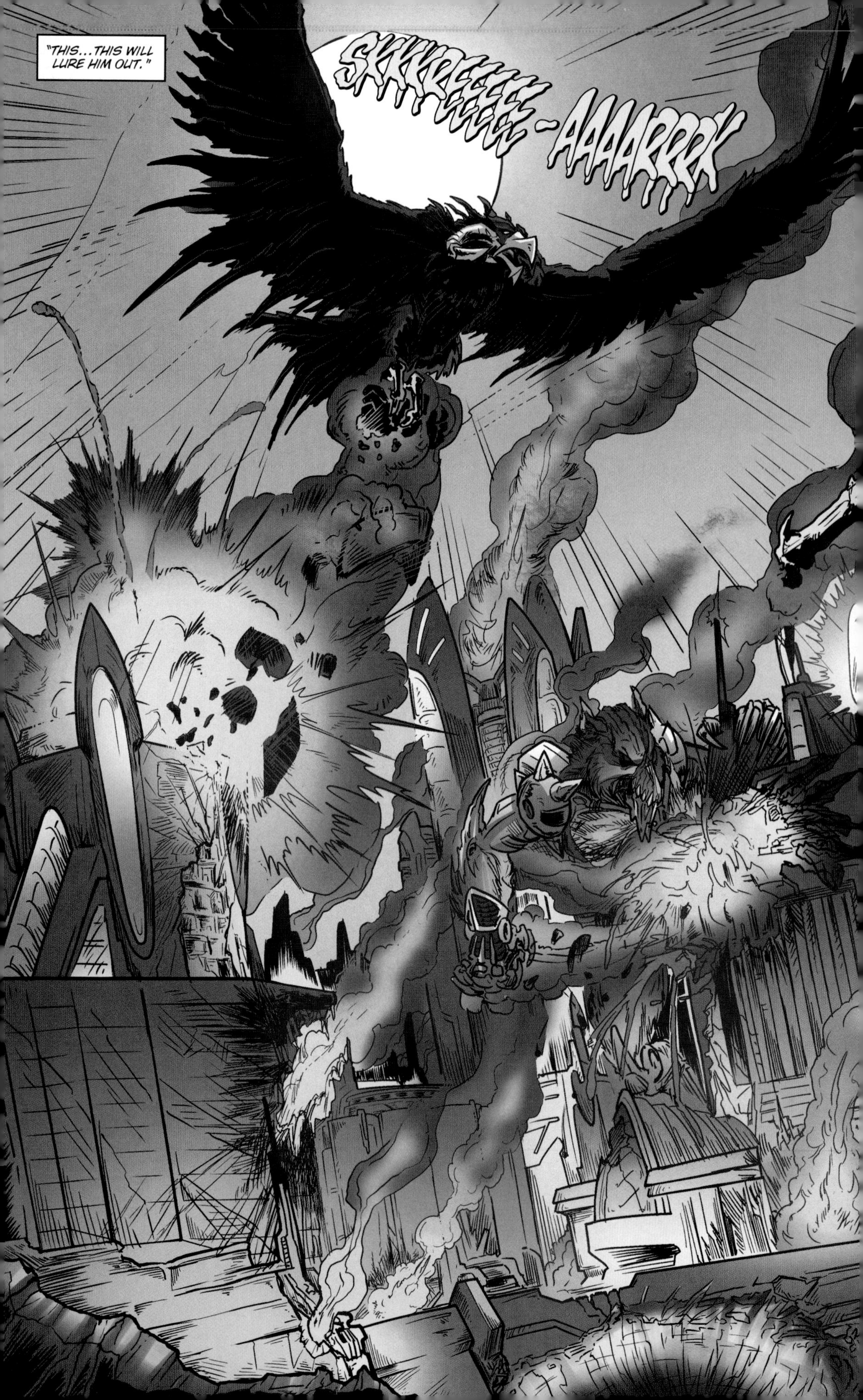
"THIS...THIS WILL LURE HIM OUT."
SKKKREEEEEE-AAAARRRK

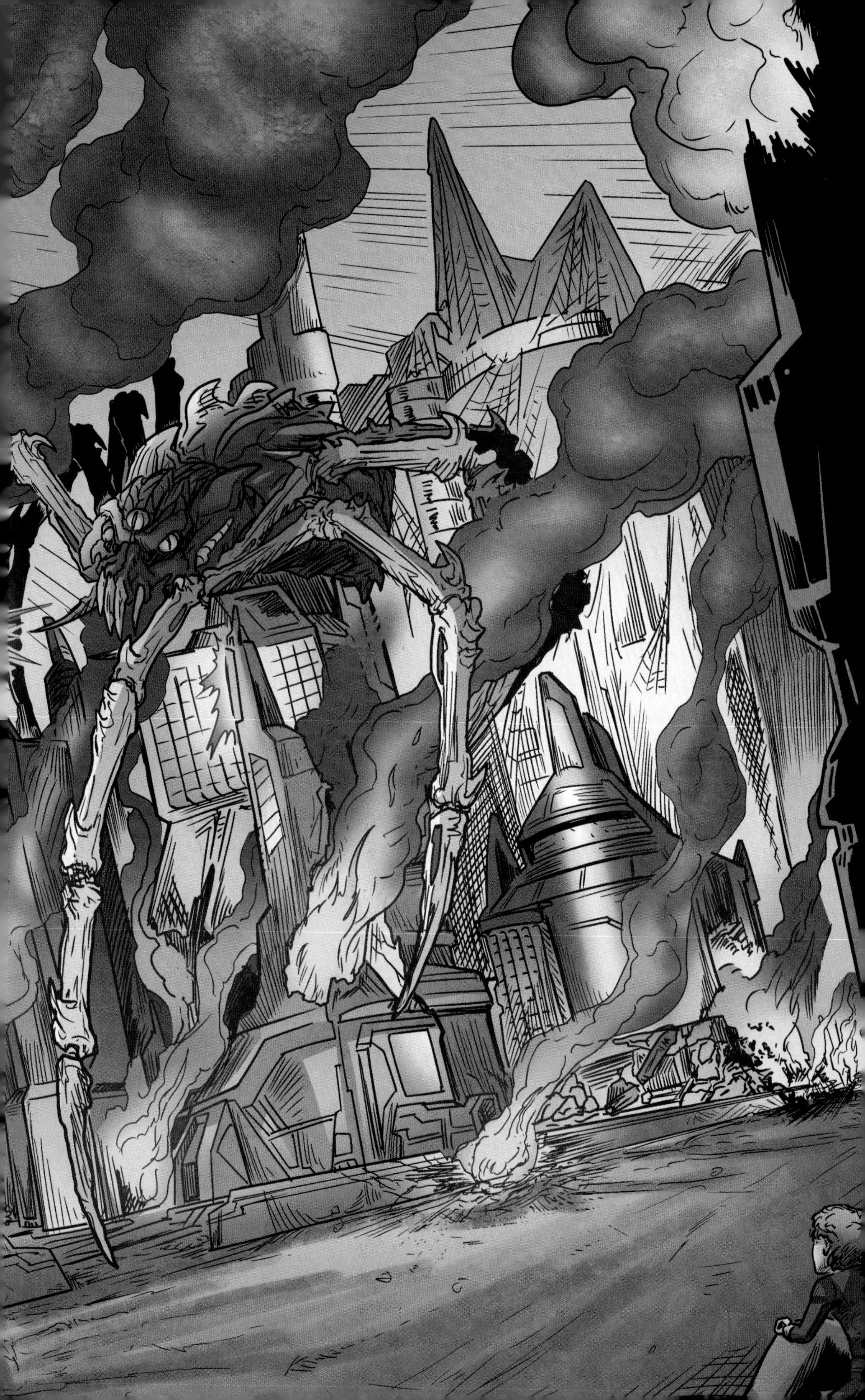

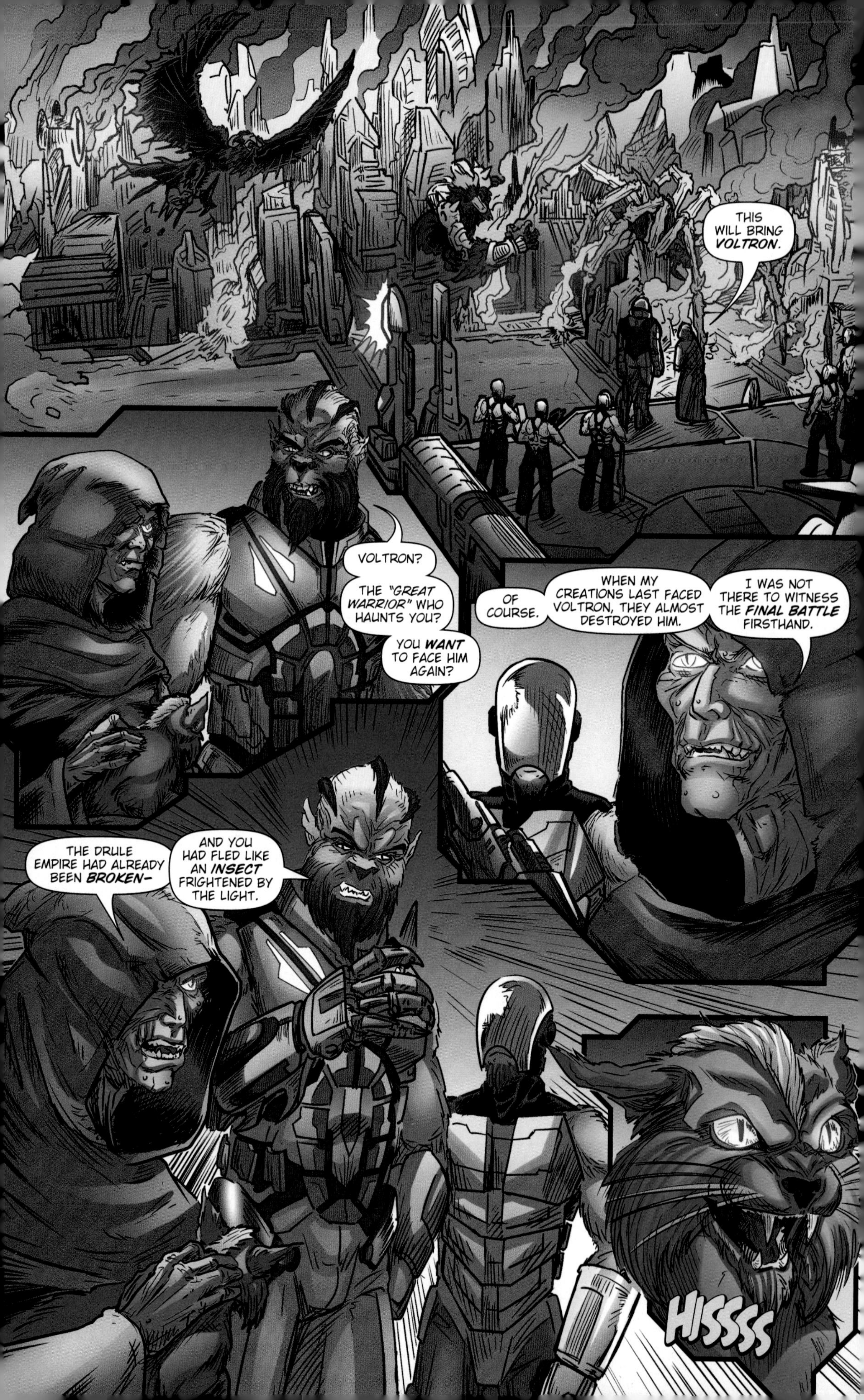

THIS WILL BRING **VOLTRON**.
VOLTRON?
THE "*GREAT WARRIOR*" WHO HAUNTS YOU?
YOU ***WANT*** TO FACE HIM AGAIN?
OF COURSE.
WHEN MY CREATIONS LAST FACED VOLTRON, THEY ALMOST DESTROYED HIM.
I WAS NOT THERE TO WITNESS THE ***FINAL BATTLE*** FIRSTHAND.
THE DRULE EMPIRE HAD ALREADY BEEN **BROKEN**–
AND YOU HAD FLED LIKE AN ***INSECT*** FRIGHTENED BY THE LIGHT.
HISSSS

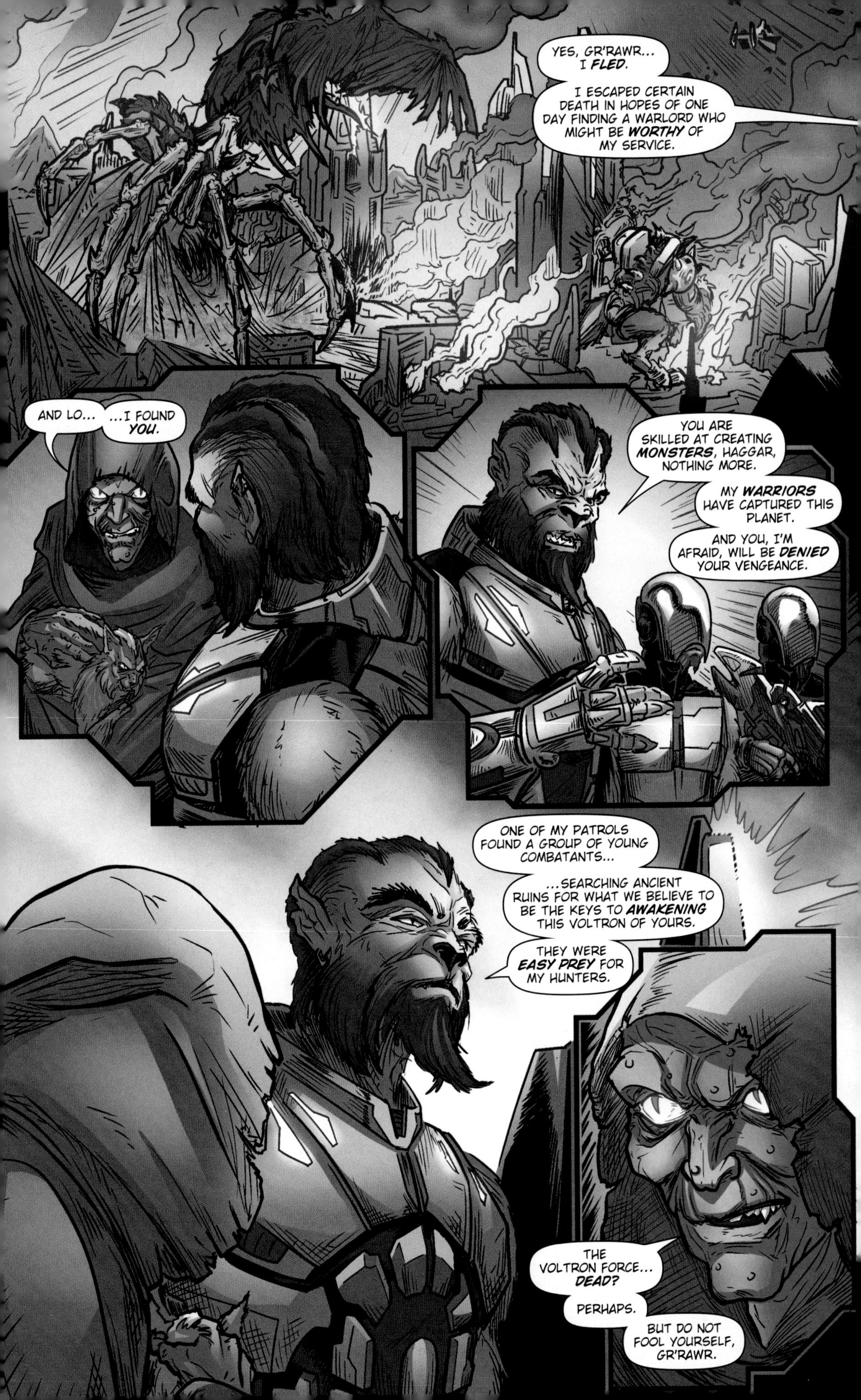
YES, GR'RAWR... I **FLED**.
I ESCAPED CERTAIN DEATH IN HOPES OF ONE DAY FINDING A WARLORD WHO MIGHT BE **WORTHY** OF MY SERVICE.
AND LO...
...I FOUND **YOU**.
YOU ARE SKILLED AT CREATING **MONSTERS**, HAGGAR, NOTHING MORE.
MY **WARRIORS** HAVE CAPTURED THIS PLANET.
AND YOU, I'M AFRAID, WILL BE **DENIED** YOUR VENGEANCE.
ONE OF MY PATROLS FOUND A GROUP OF YOUNG COMBATANTS...
...SEARCHING ANCIENT RUINS FOR WHAT WE BELIEVE TO BE THE KEYS TO **AWAKENING** THIS VOLTRON OF YOURS.
THEY WERE **EASY PREY** FOR MY HUNTERS.
THE VOLTRON FORCE... **DEAD?**
PERHAPS.
BUT DO NOT FOOL YOURSELF, GR'RAWR.

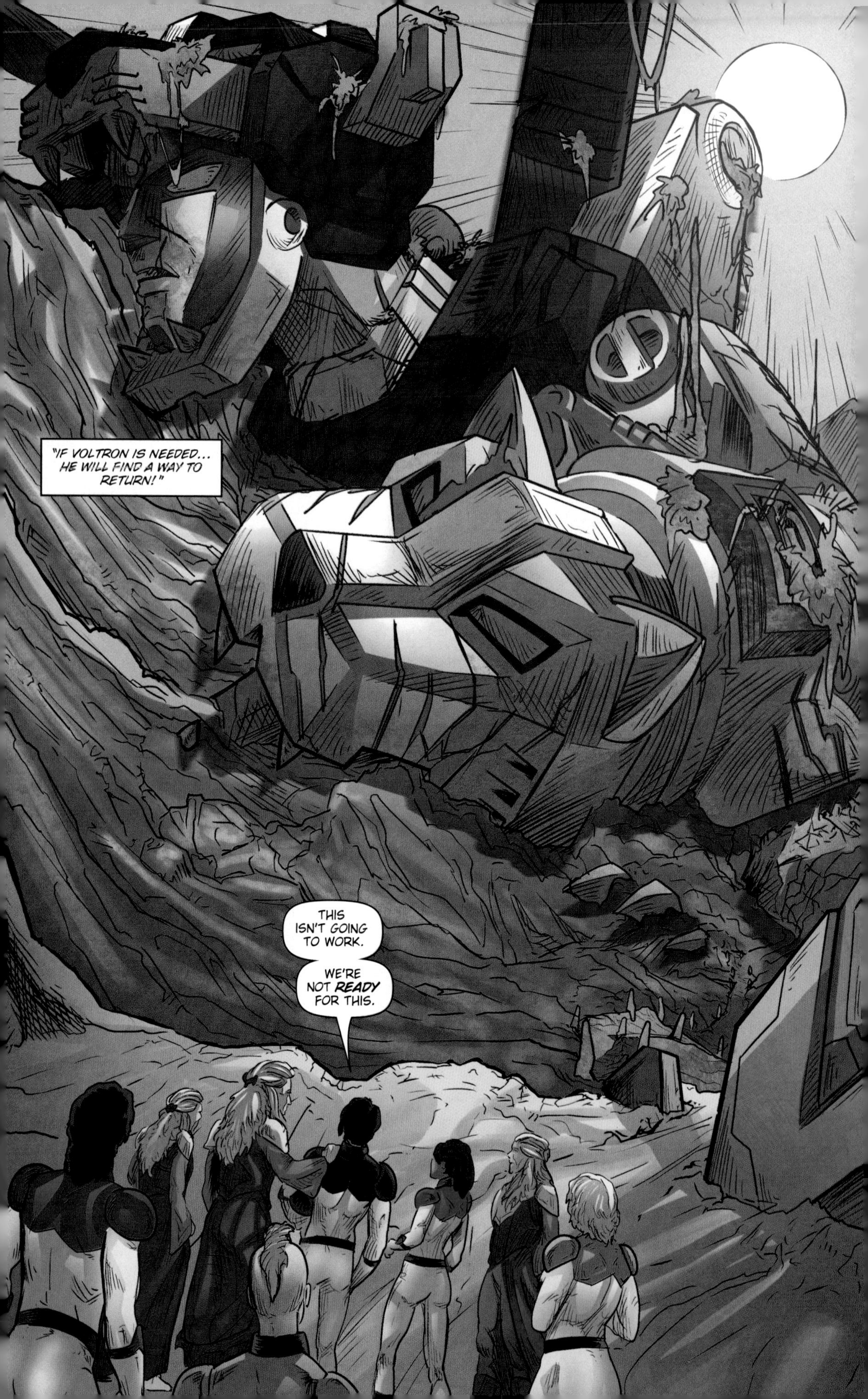
"IF VOLTRON IS NEEDED... HE WILL FIND A WAY TO RETURN!"
THIS ISN'T GOING TO WORK.
WE'RE NOT *READY* FOR THIS.

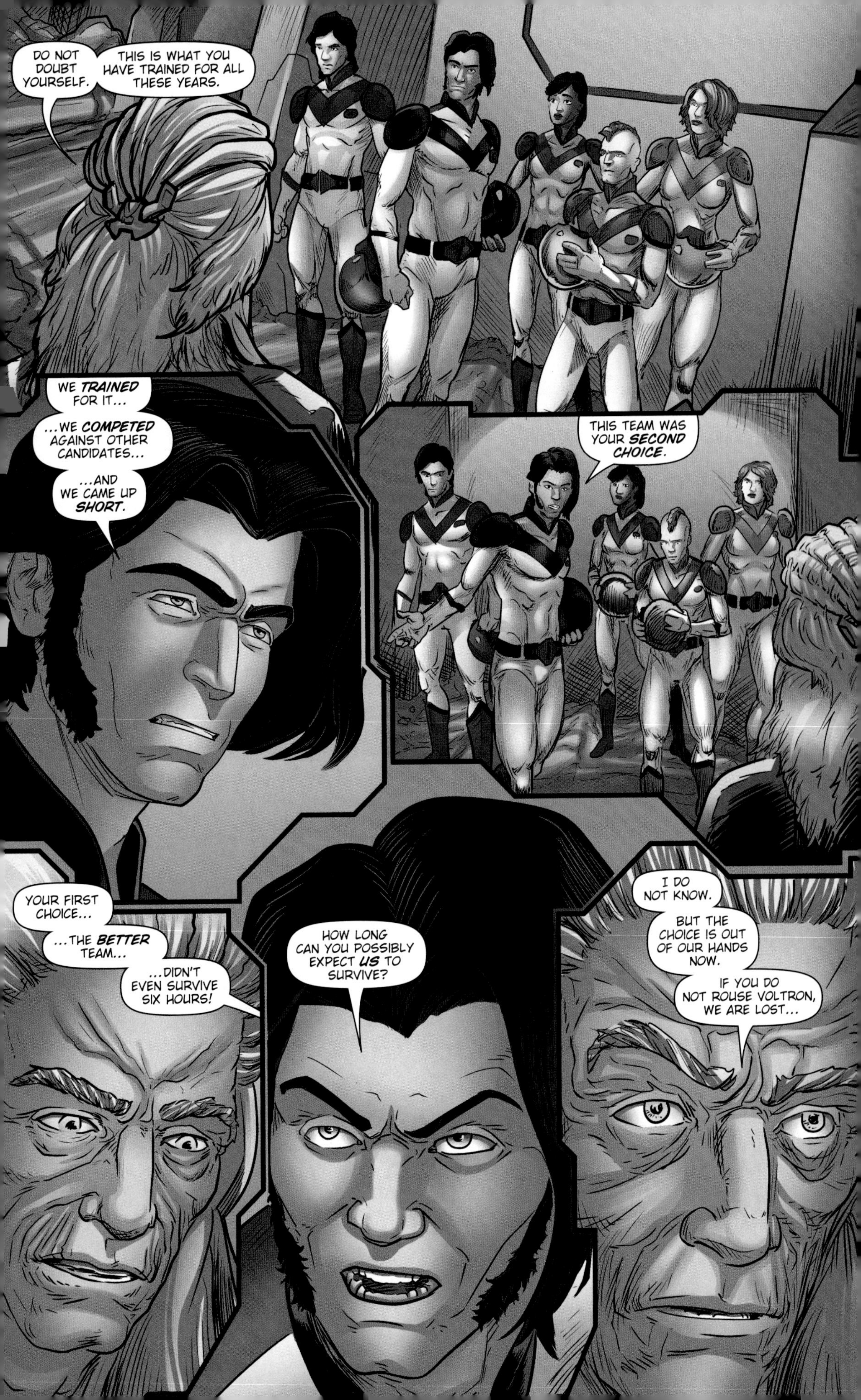
DO NOT DOUBT YOURSELF.
THIS IS WHAT YOU HAVE TRAINED FOR ALL THESE YEARS.
WE *TRAINED* FOR IT...
...WE *COMPETED* AGAINST OTHER CANDIDATES...
...AND WE CAME UP *SHORT*.
THIS TEAM WAS YOUR *SECOND CHOICE*.
YOUR FIRST CHOICE...
...THE *BETTER* TEAM...
...DIDN'T EVEN SURVIVE SIX HOURS!
HOW LONG CAN YOU POSSIBLY EXPECT *US* TO SURVIVE?
I DO NOT KNOW.
BUT THE CHOICE IS OUT OF OUR HANDS NOW.
IF YOU DO NOT ROUSE VOLTRON, WE ARE LOST...

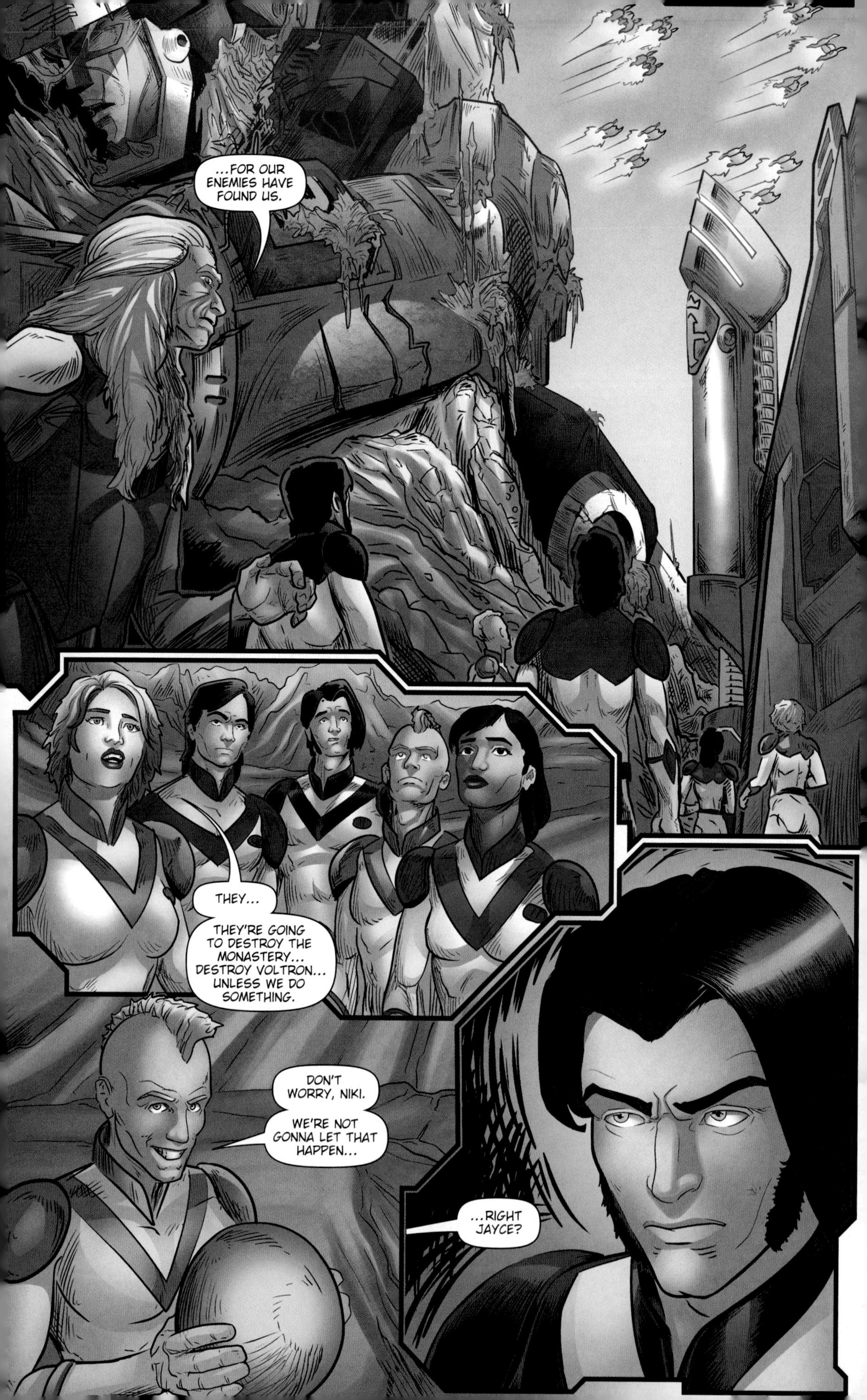
...FOR OUR ENEMIES HAVE FOUND US.
THEY...
THEY'RE GOING TO DESTROY THE MONASTERY... DESTROY VOLTRON... UNLESS WE DO SOMETHING.
DON'T WORRY, NIKI.
WE'RE NOT GONNA LET THAT HAPPEN...
...RIGHT JAYCE?

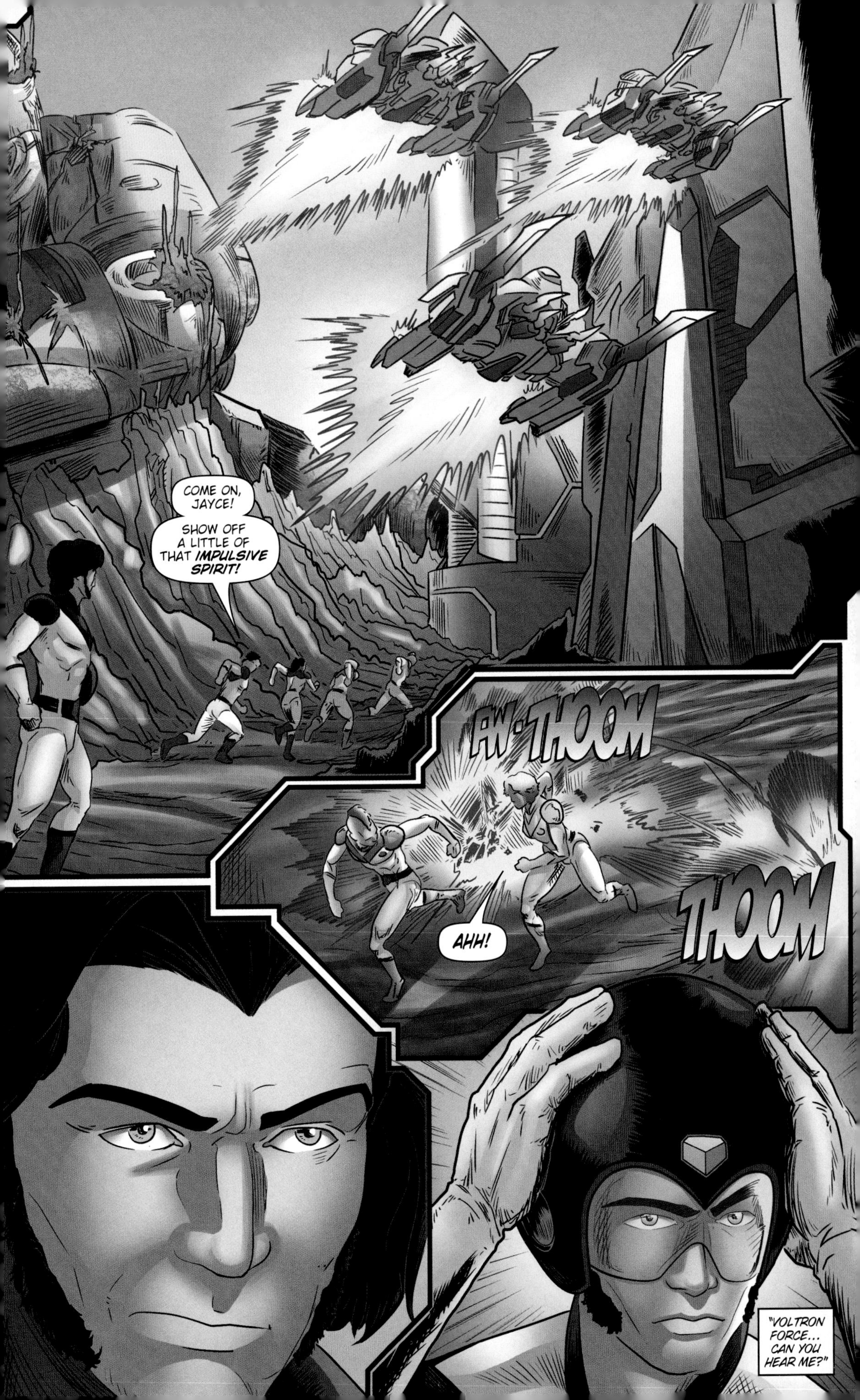
COME ON, JAYCE!
SHOW OFF A LITTLE OF THAT *IMPULSIVE SPIRIT!*
FW-THOOM
THOOM
AHH!
"VOLTRON FORCE... CAN YOU HEAR ME?"

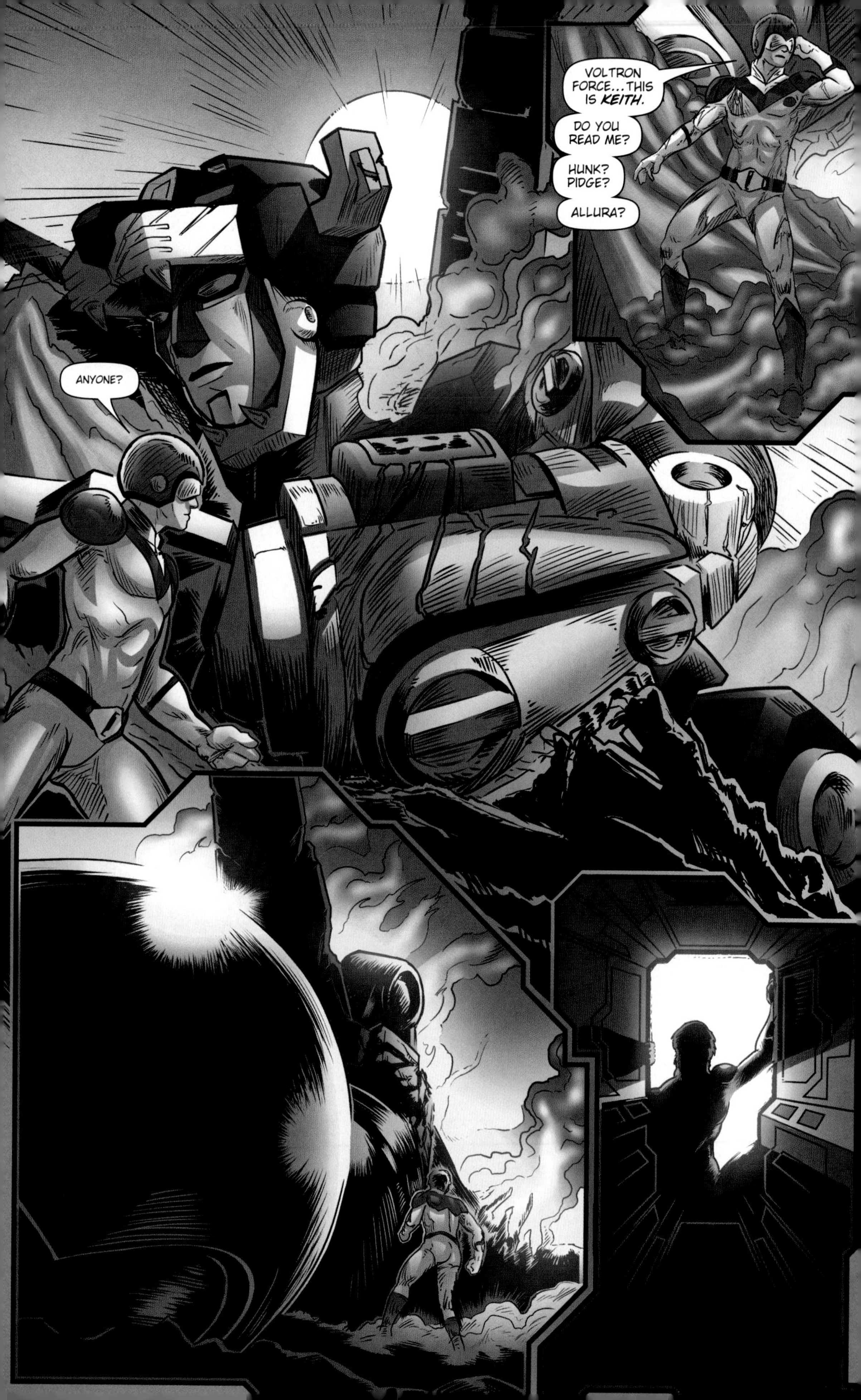
VOLTRON FORCE... THIS IS *KEITH*.
DO YOU READ ME?
HUNK? PIDGE?
ALLURA?
ANYONE?

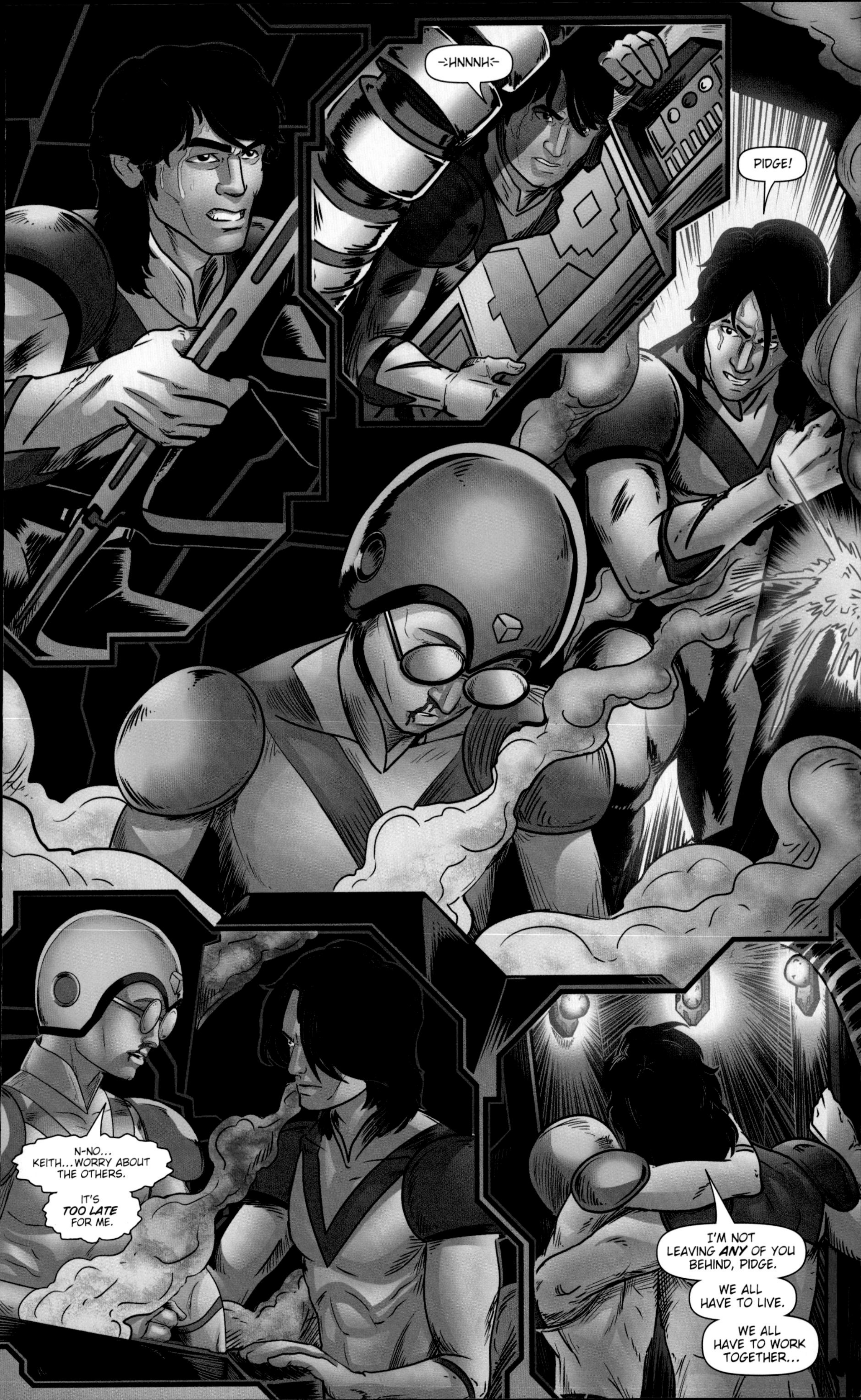
-HNNNH-
PIDGE!
N-NO... KEITH...WORRY ABOUT THE OTHERS.
IT'S *TOO LATE* FOR ME.
I'M NOT LEAVING *ANY* OF YOU BEHIND, PIDGE.
WE ALL HAVE TO LIVE.
WE ALL HAVE TO WORK TOGETHER...

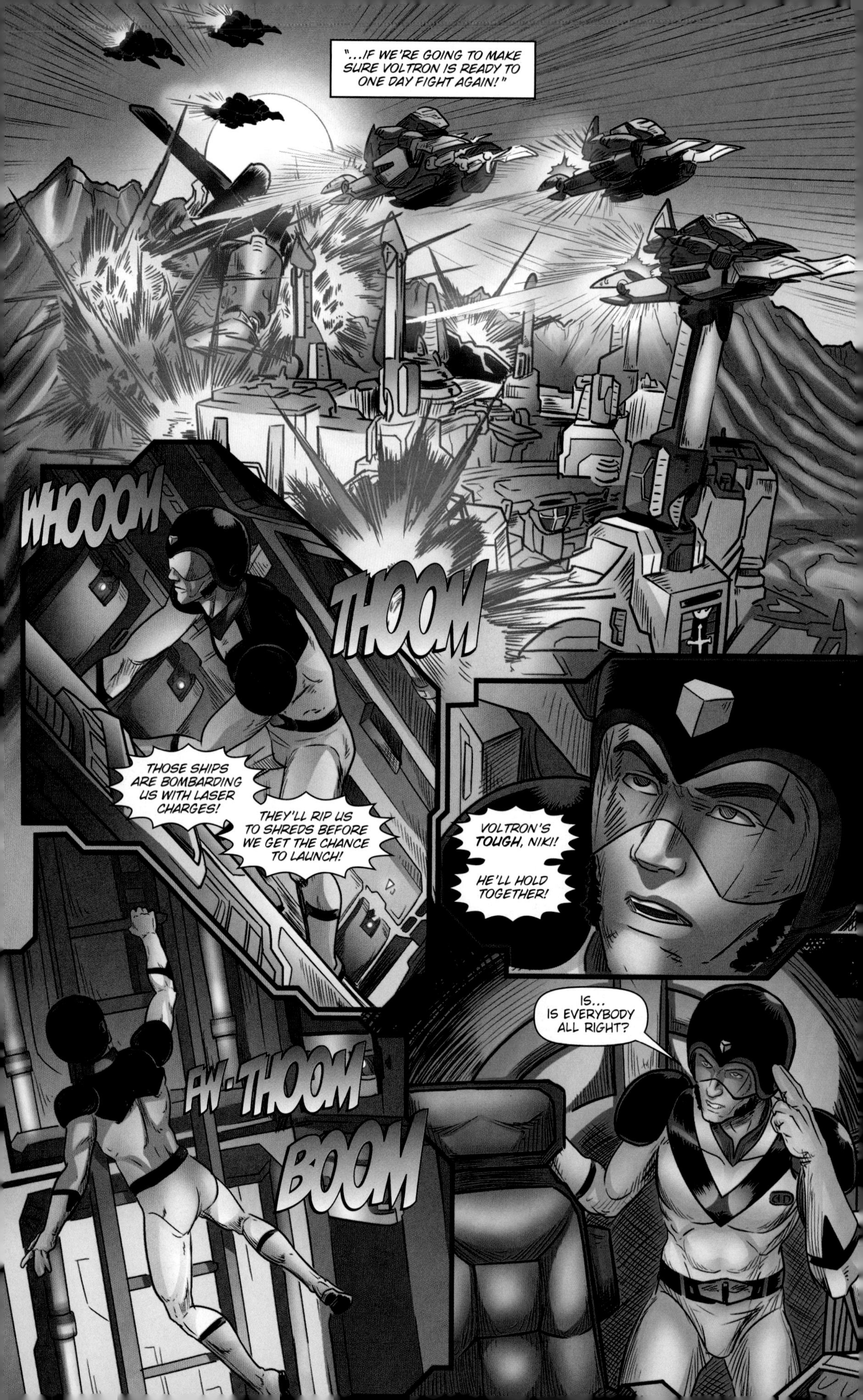
"...IF WE'RE GOING TO MAKE SURE VOLTRON IS READY TO ONE DAY FIGHT AGAIN!"
WHOOOM
THOOM
THOSE SHIPS ARE BOMBARDING US WITH LASER CHARGES!
THEY'LL RIP US TO SHREDS BEFORE WE GET THE CHANCE TO LAUNCH!
VOLTRON'S TOUGH, NIKI!
HE'LL HOLD TOGETHER!
FW-THOOM
BOOM
IS... IS EVERYBODY ALL RIGHT?

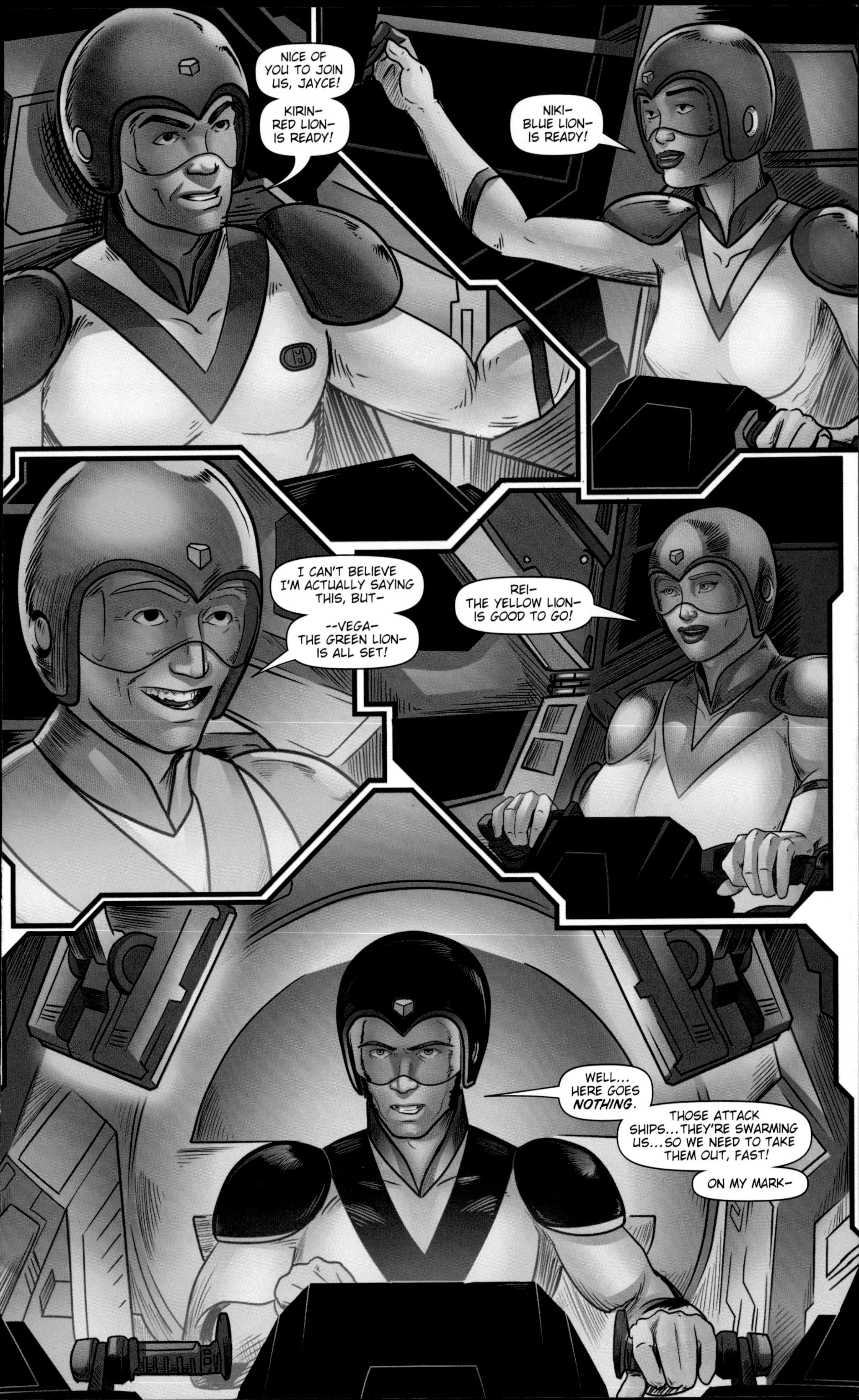
NICE OF YOU TO JOIN US, JAYCE!
KIRIN- RED LION- IS READY!
NIKI- BLUE LION- IS READY!
I CAN'T BELIEVE I'M ACTUALLY SAYING THIS, BUT-
--VEGA- THE GREEN LION- IS ALL SET!
REI- THE YELLOW LION- IS GOOD TO GO!
WELL... HERE GOES *NOTHING*.
THOSE ATTACK SHIPS...THEY'RE SWARMING US...SO WE NEED TO TAKE THEM OUT, FAST!
ON MY MARK-

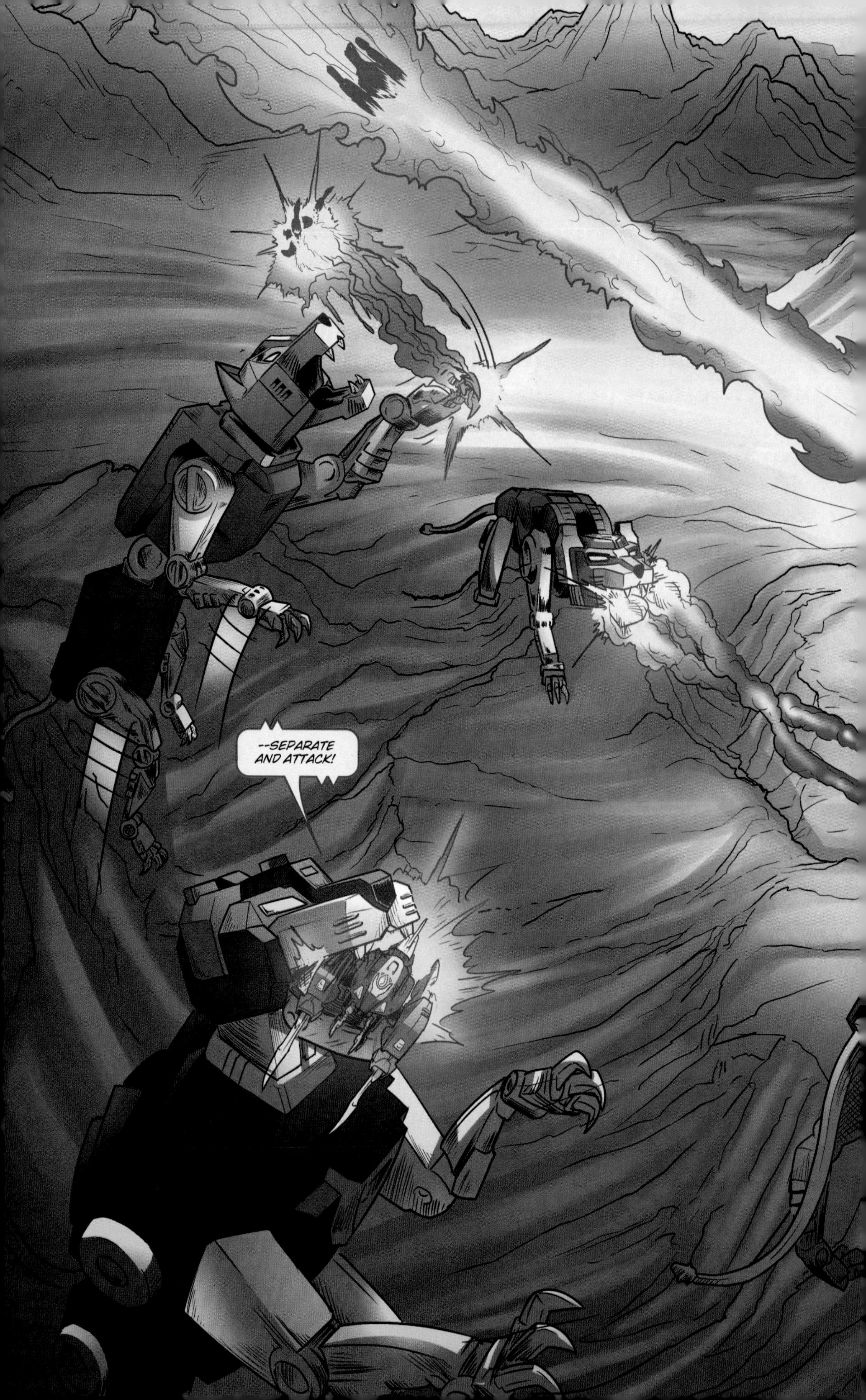
--SEPARATE AND ATTACK!

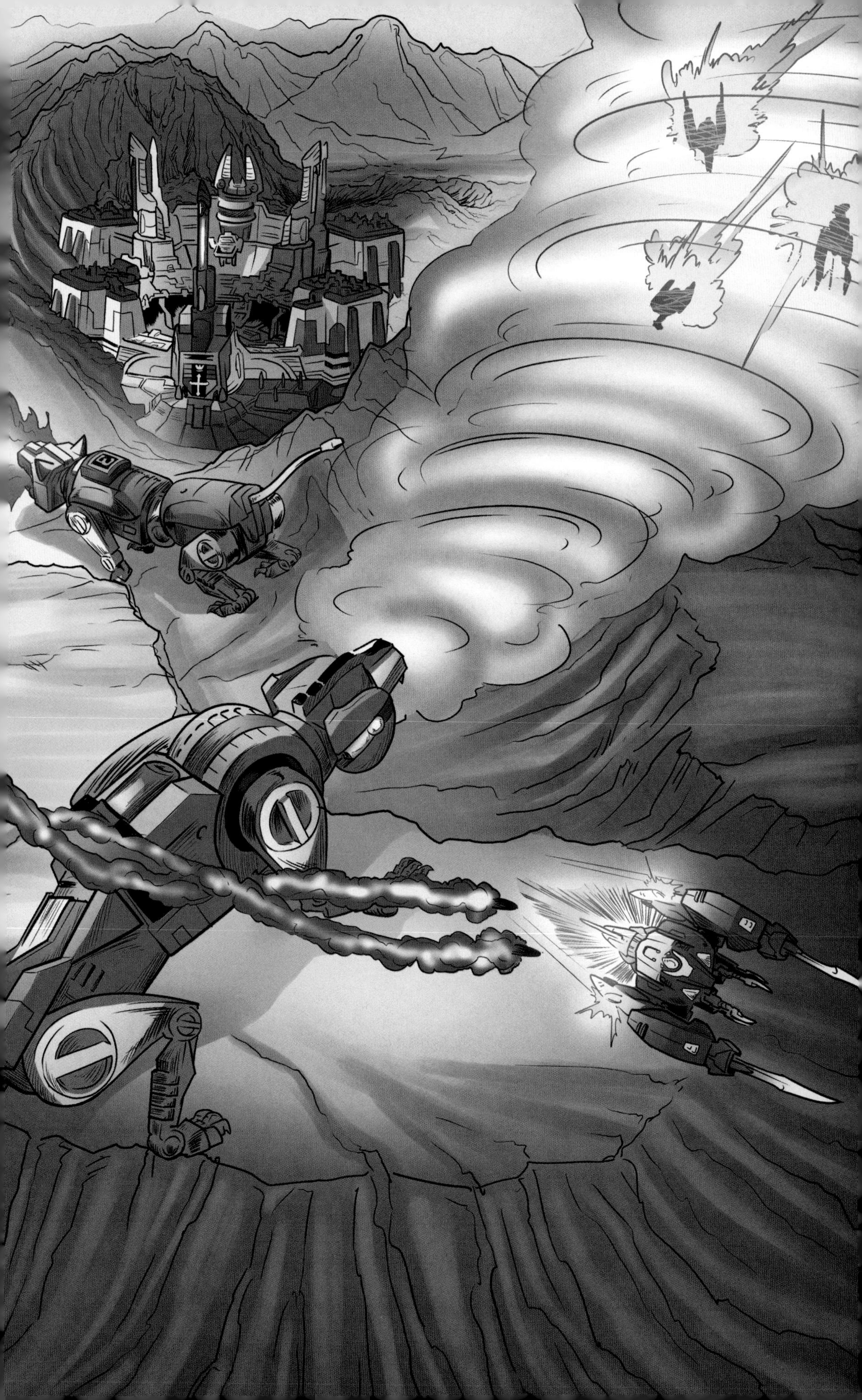

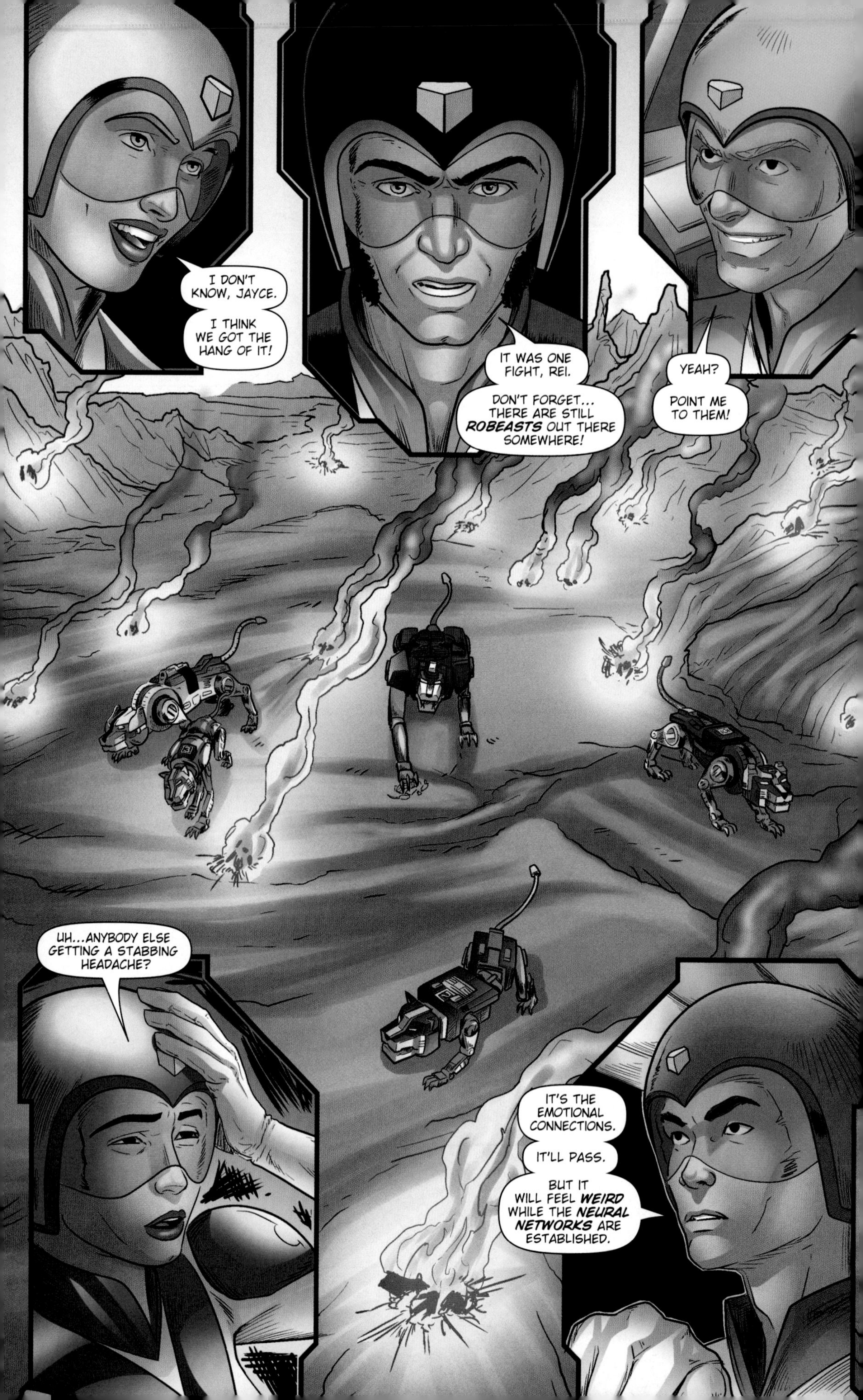
I DON'T KNOW, JAYCE.
I THINK WE GOT THE HANG OF IT!
IT WAS ONE FIGHT, REI.
DON'T FORGET... THERE ARE STILL ROBEASTS OUT THERE SOMEWHERE!
YEAH?
POINT ME TO THEM!
UH...ANYBODY ELSE GETTING A STABBING HEADACHE?
IT'S THE EMOTIONAL CONNECTIONS.
IT'LL PASS.
BUT IT WILL FEEL WEIRD WHILE THE NEURAL NETWORKS ARE ESTABLISHED.

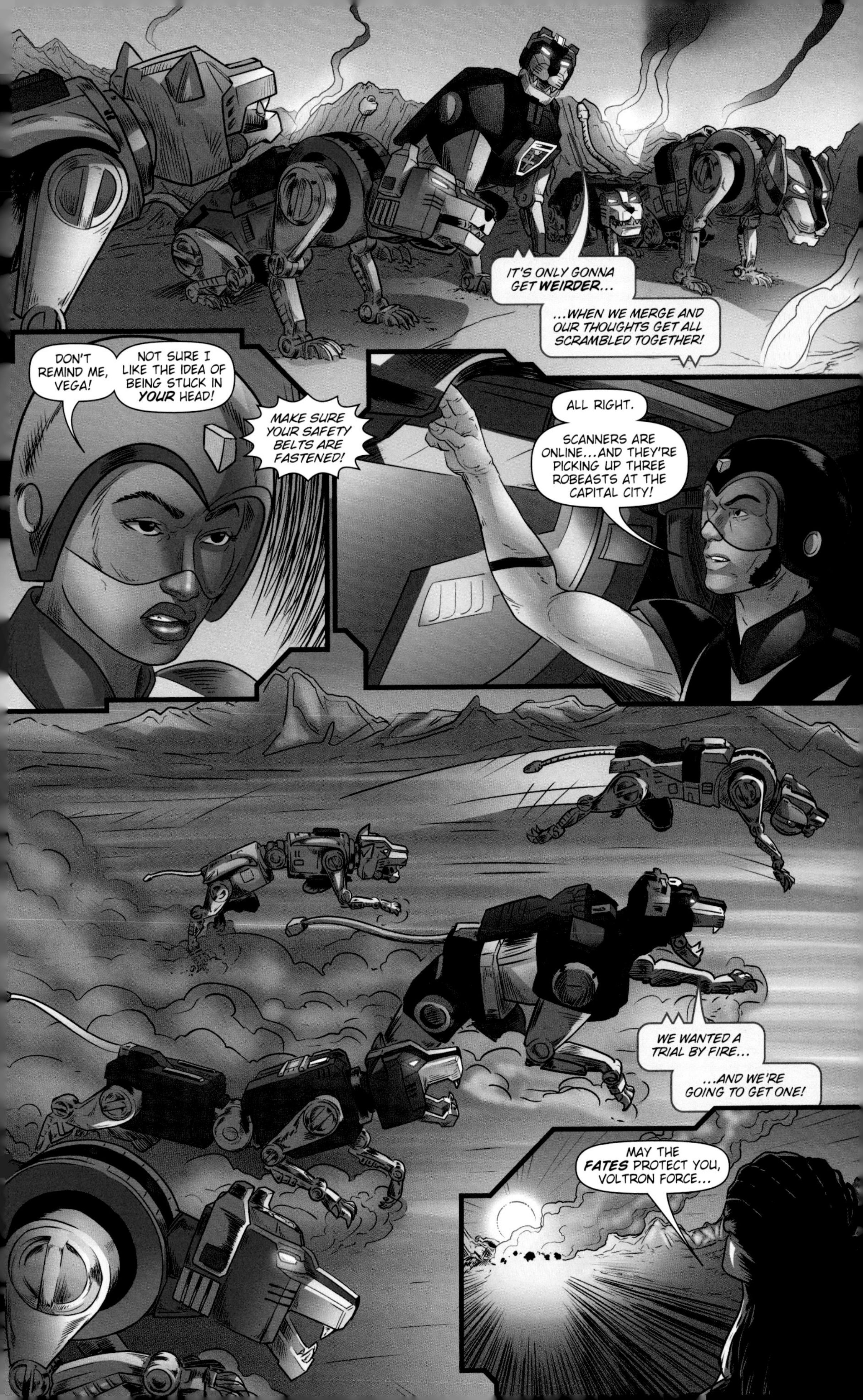
IT'S ONLY GONNA GET WEIRDER...
...WHEN WE MERGE AND OUR THOUGHTS GET ALL SCRAMBLED TOGETHER!
DON'T REMIND ME, VEGA!
NOT SURE I LIKE THE IDEA OF BEING STUCK IN YOUR HEAD!
MAKE SURE YOUR SAFETY BELTS ARE FASTENED!
ALL RIGHT.
SCANNERS ARE ONLINE...AND THEY'RE PICKING UP THREE ROBEASTS AT THE CAPITAL CITY!
WE WANTED A TRIAL BY FIRE...
...AND WE'RE GOING TO GET ONE!
MAY THE FATES PROTECT YOU, VOLTRON FORCE...

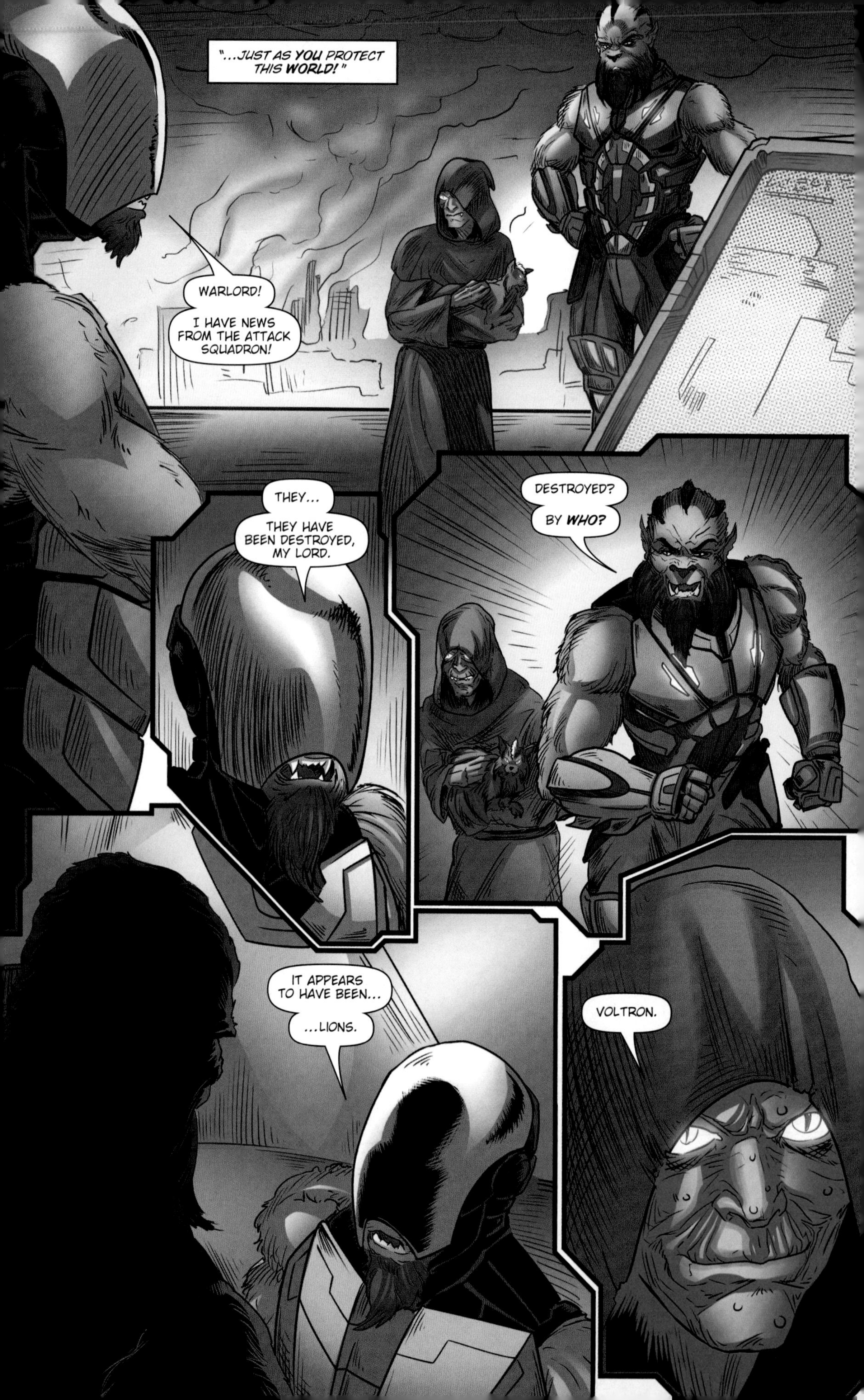
"...JUST AS YOU PROTECT THIS WORLD!"
WARLORD!
I HAVE NEWS FROM THE ATTACK SQUADRON!
THEY...
THEY HAVE BEEN DESTROYED, MY LORD.
DESTROYED?
BY WHO?
IT APPEARS TO HAVE BEEN...
...LIONS.
VOLTRON.

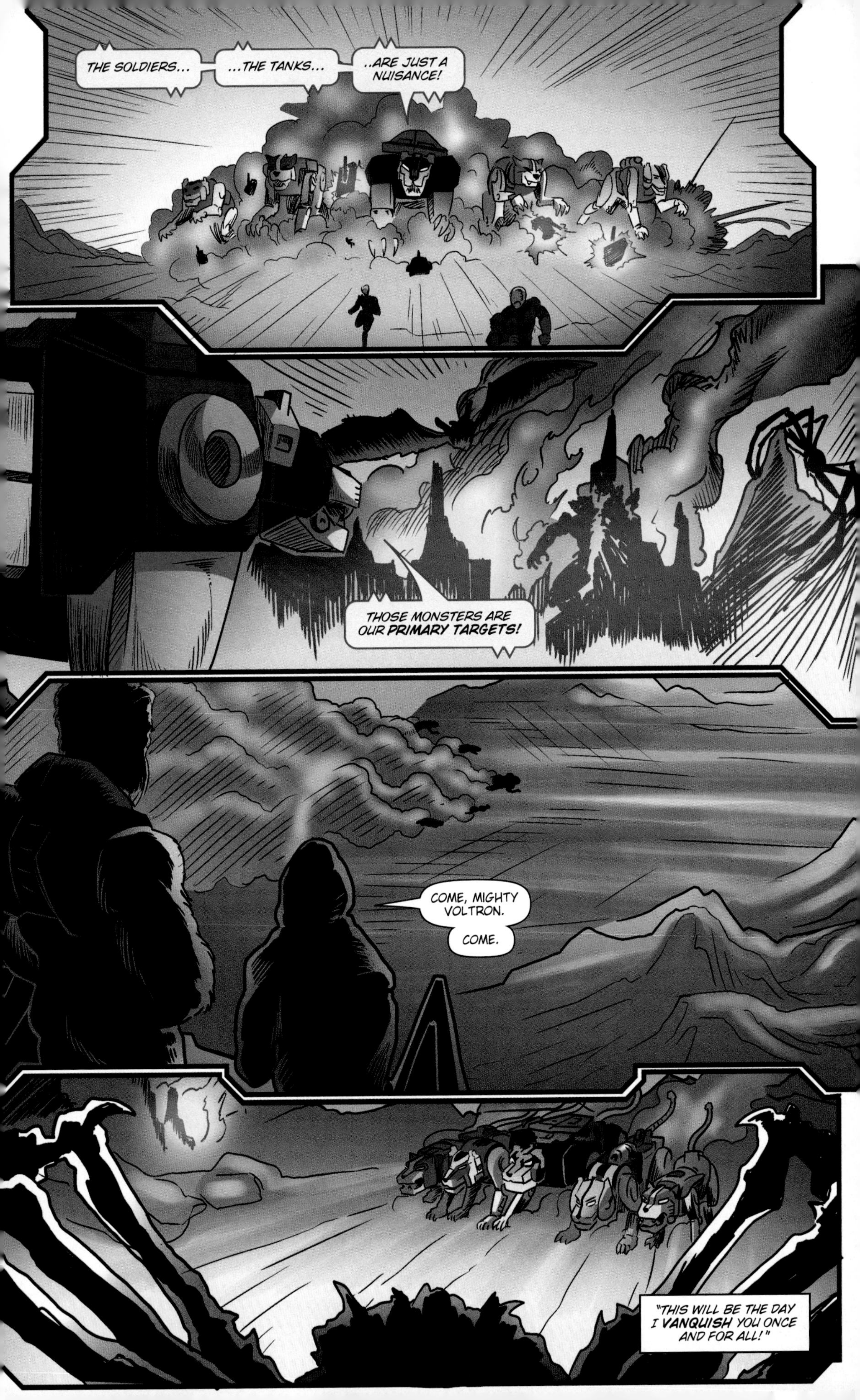
THE SOLDIERS...
...THE TANKS...
..ARE JUST A NUISANCE!
THOSE MONSTERS ARE OUR **PRIMARY TARGETS!**
COME, MIGHTY VOLTRON.
COME.
"THIS WILL BE THE DAY I **VANQUISH** YOU ONCE AND FOR ALL!"

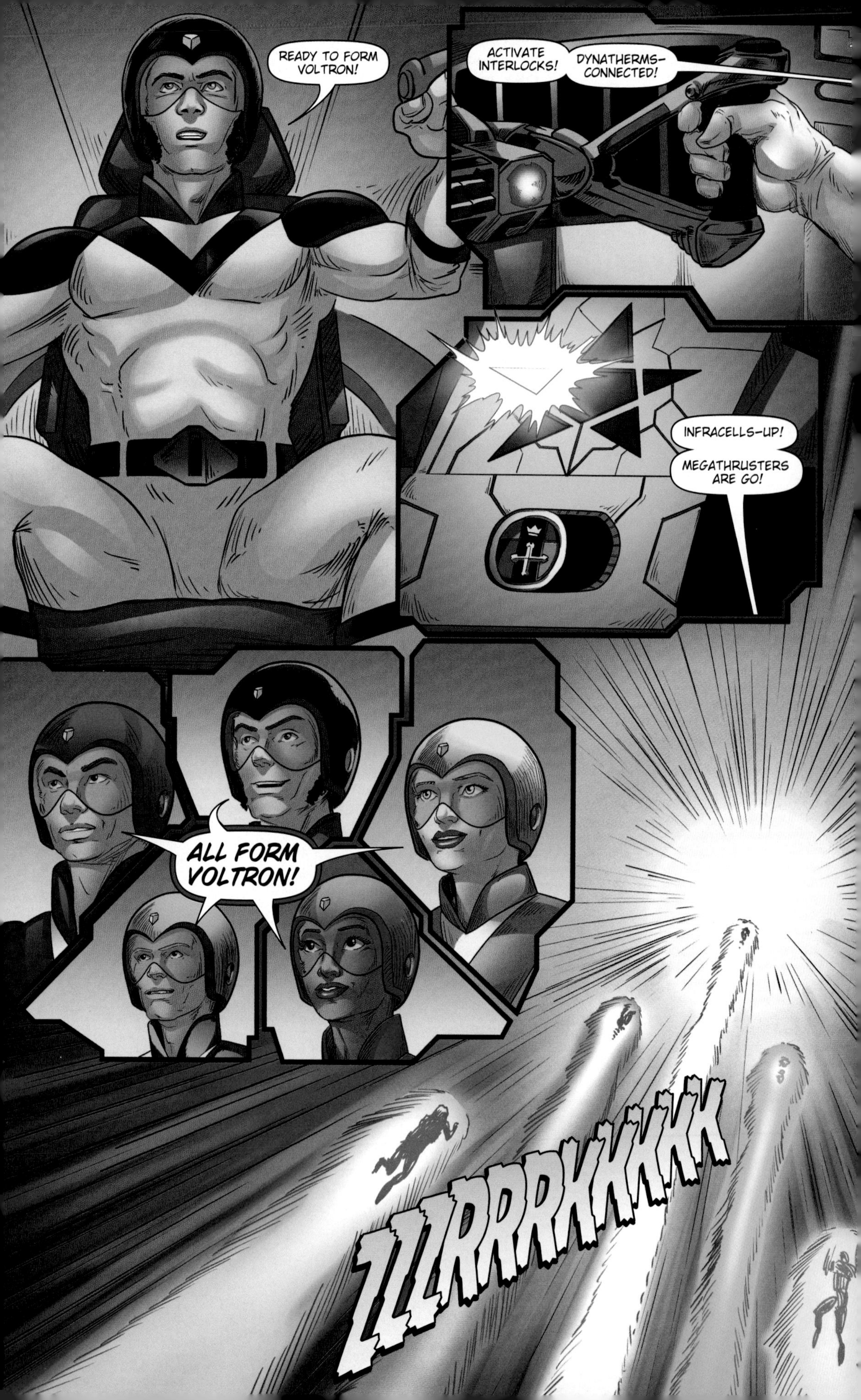
READY TO FORM VOLTRON!
ACTIVATE INTERLOCKS!
DYNATHERMS-CONNECTED!
INFRACELLS-UP!
MEGATHRUSTERS ARE GO!
ALL FORM VOLTRON!
ZZRRRKKKKK

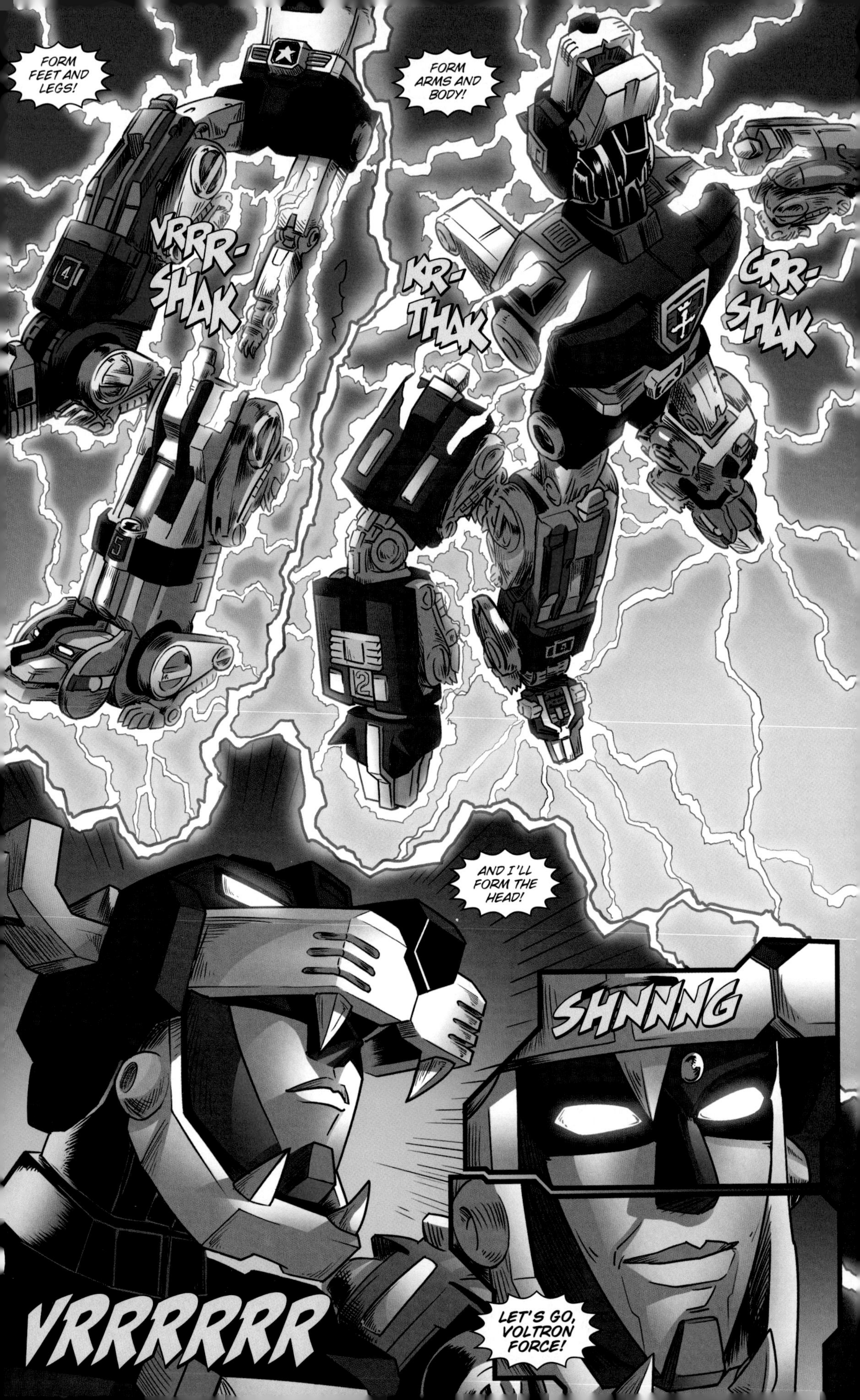
FORM FEET AND LEGS!
FORM ARMS AND BODY!
VRRR-SHAK
KR-THAK
GRR-SHAK
AND I'LL FORM THE HEAD!
SHNNNG
VRRRRRR
LET'S GO, VOLTRON FORCE!

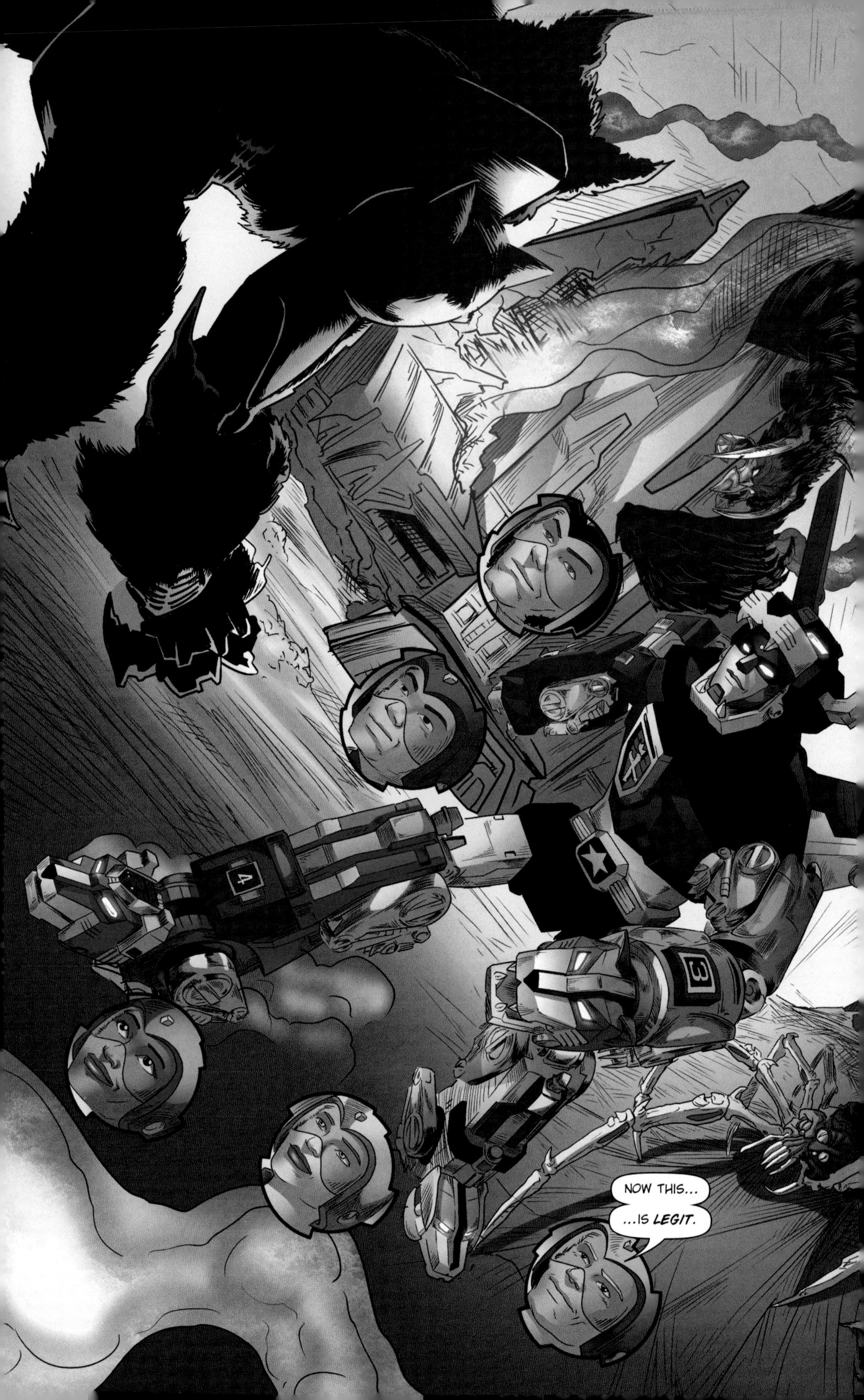
NOW THIS...
...IS *LEGIT*.

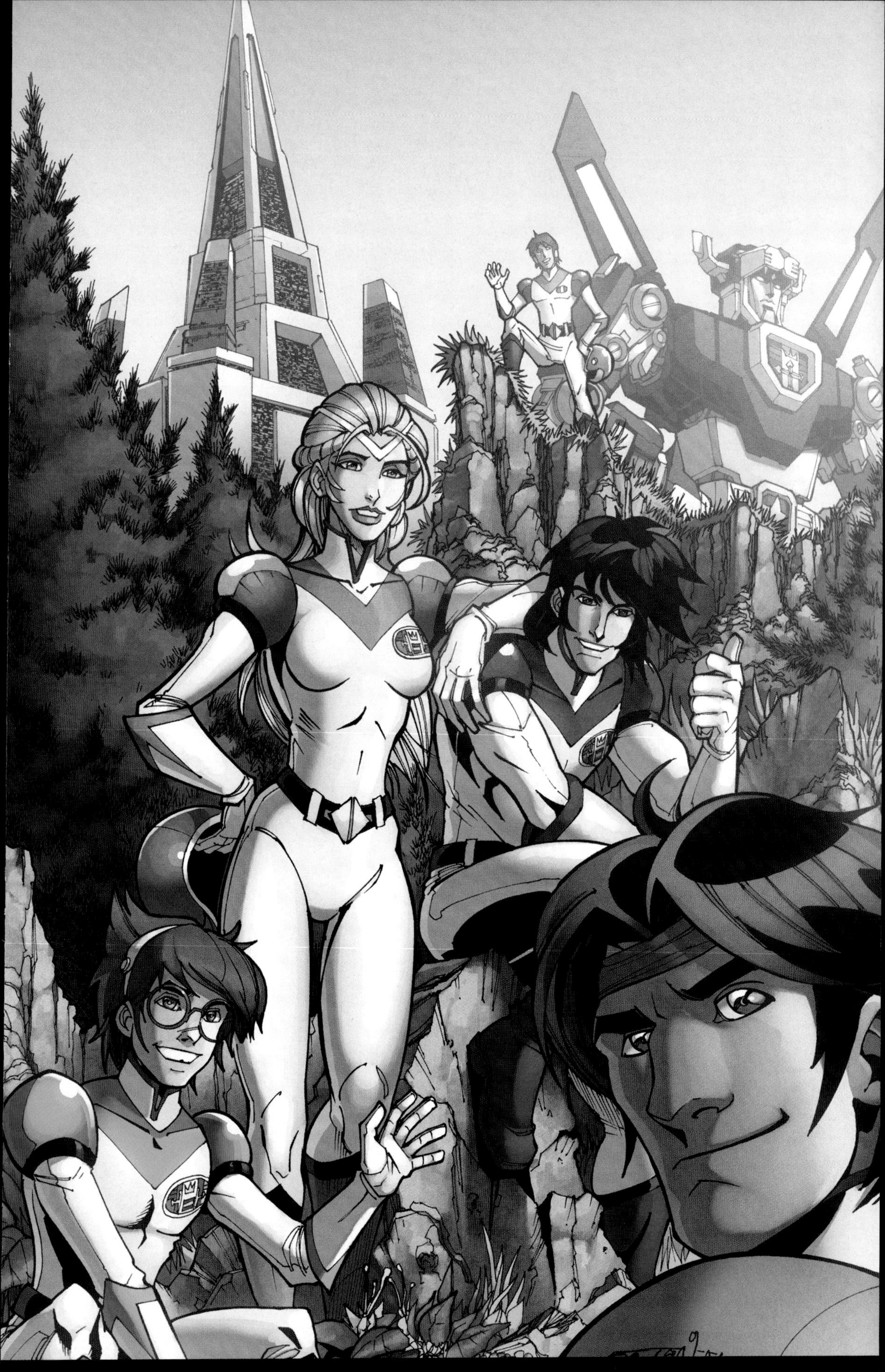

ISSUE 5 Cover by ALEX MILNE Colors by JOSH PEREZ

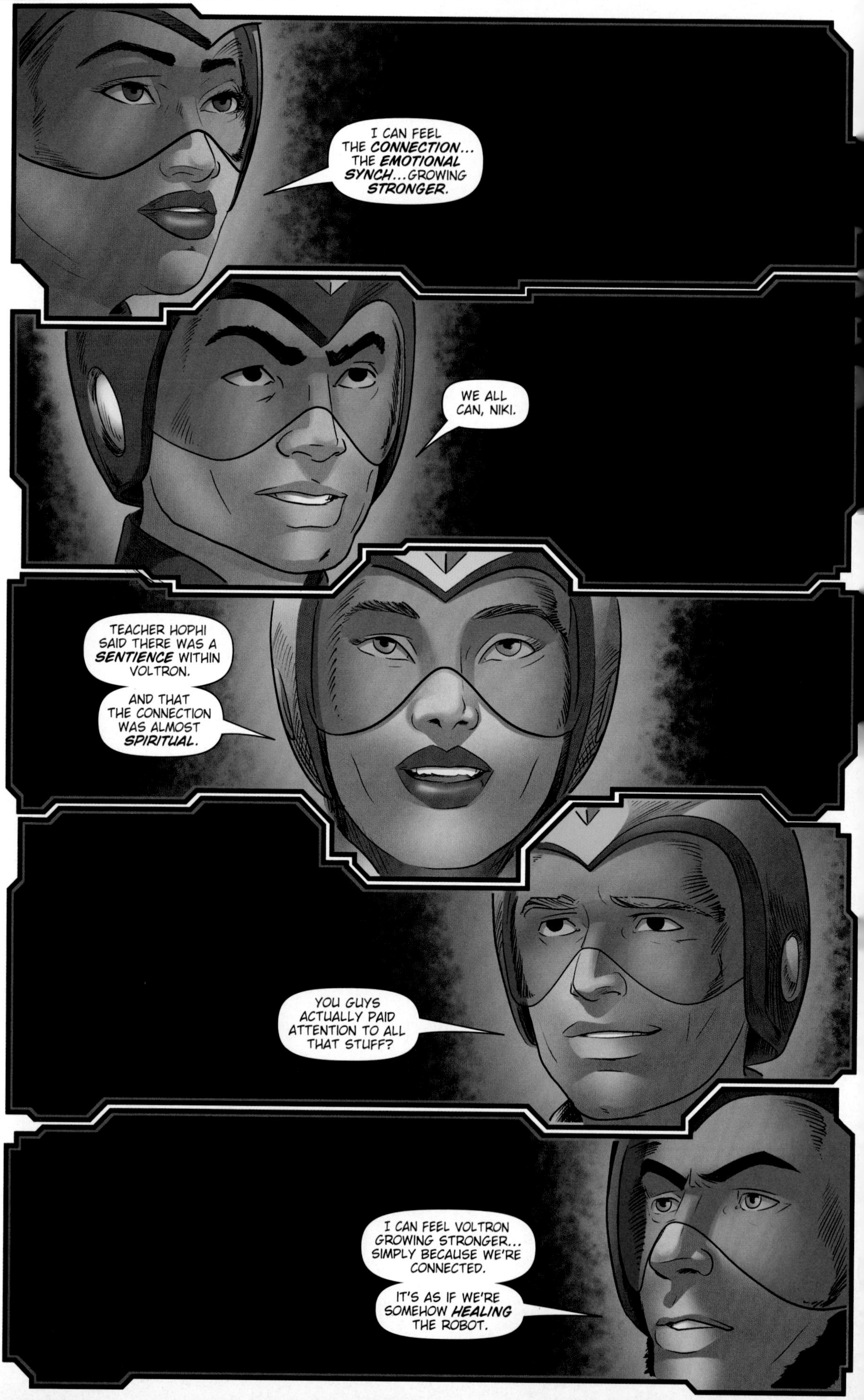
I CAN FEEL THE CONNECTION... THE EMOTIONAL SYNCH...GROWING STRONGER.
WE ALL CAN, NIKI.
TEACHER HOPHI SAID THERE WAS A SENTIENCE WITHIN VOLTRON.
AND THAT THE CONNECTION WAS ALMOST SPIRITUAL.
YOU GUYS ACTUALLY PAID ATTENTION TO ALL THAT STUFF?
I CAN FEEL VOLTRON GROWING STRONGER... SIMPLY BECAUSE WE'RE CONNECTED.
IT'S AS IF WE'RE SOMEHOW HEALING THE ROBOT.

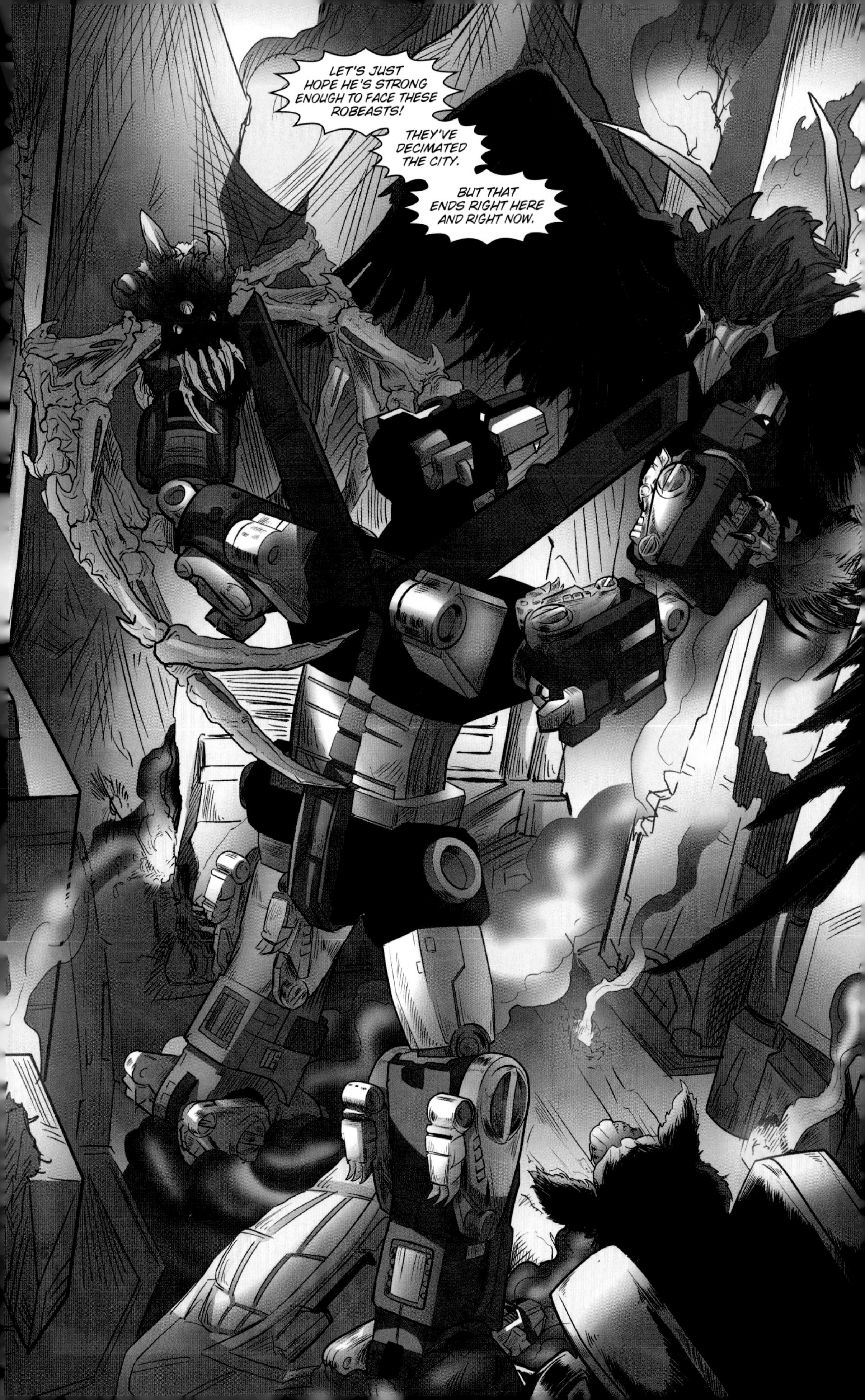
LET'S JUST HOPE HE'S STRONG ENOUGH TO FACE THESE ROBEASTS!
THEY'VE DECIMATED THE CITY.
BUT THAT ENDS RIGHT HERE AND RIGHT NOW.

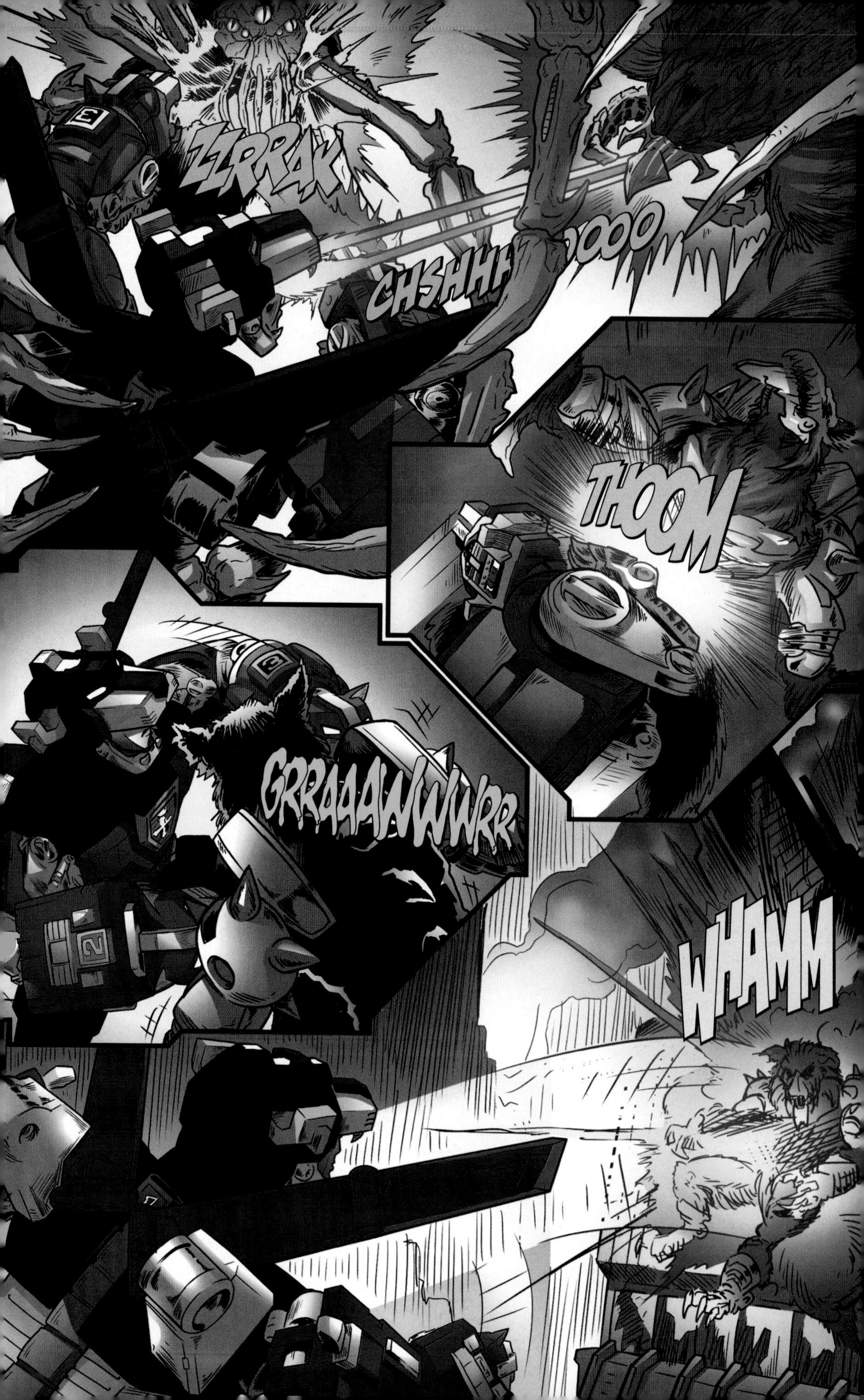
ZZRRAK
CHSHHH
OOOO
THOOM
GRRAAAWWWRR
WHAMM

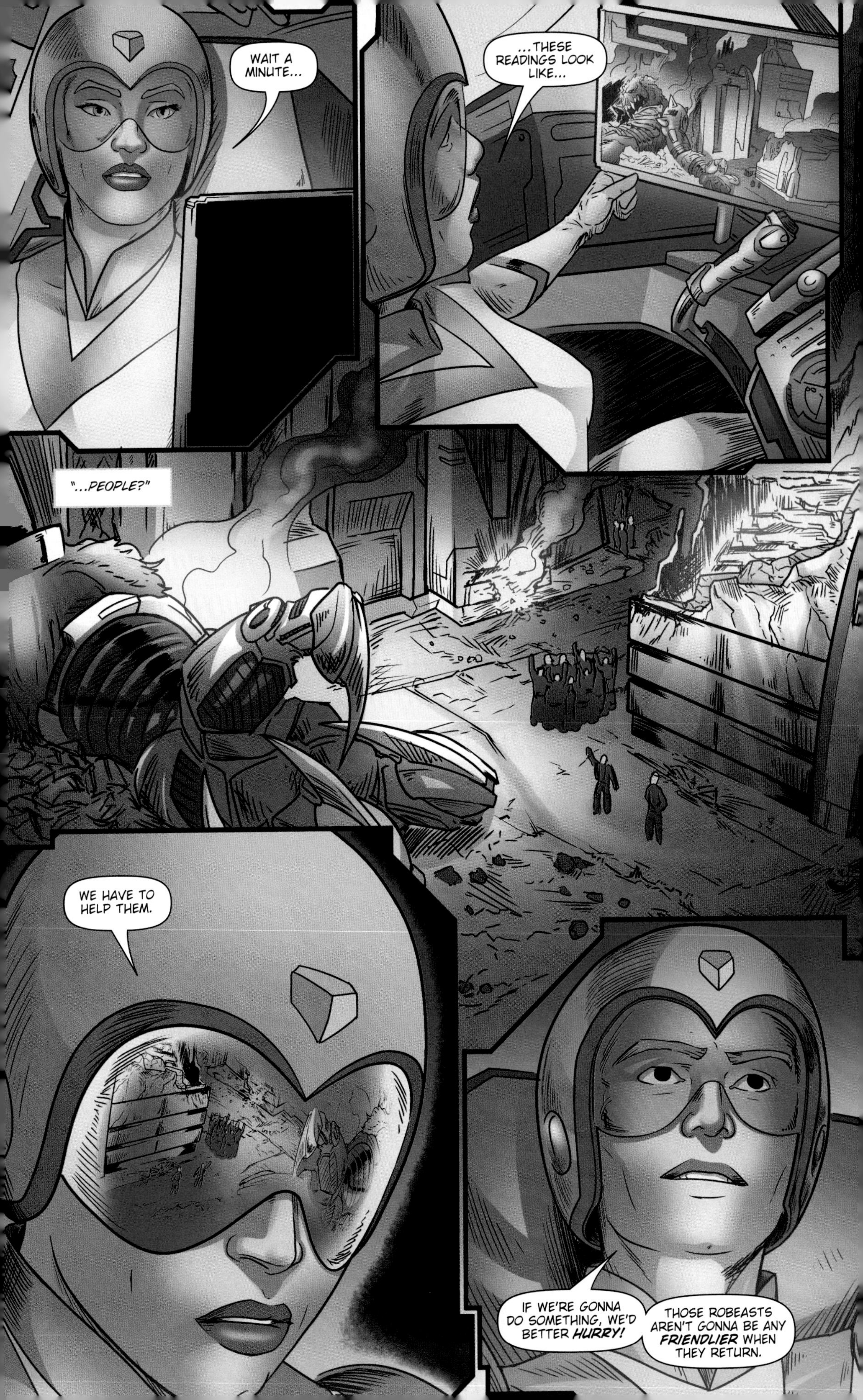
WAIT A MINUTE...
...THESE READINGS LOOK LIKE...
"...PEOPLE?"
WE HAVE TO HELP THEM.
IF WE'RE GONNA DO SOMETHING, WE'D BETTER HURRY!
THOSE ROBEASTS AREN'T GONNA BE ANY FRIENDLIER WHEN THEY RETURN.

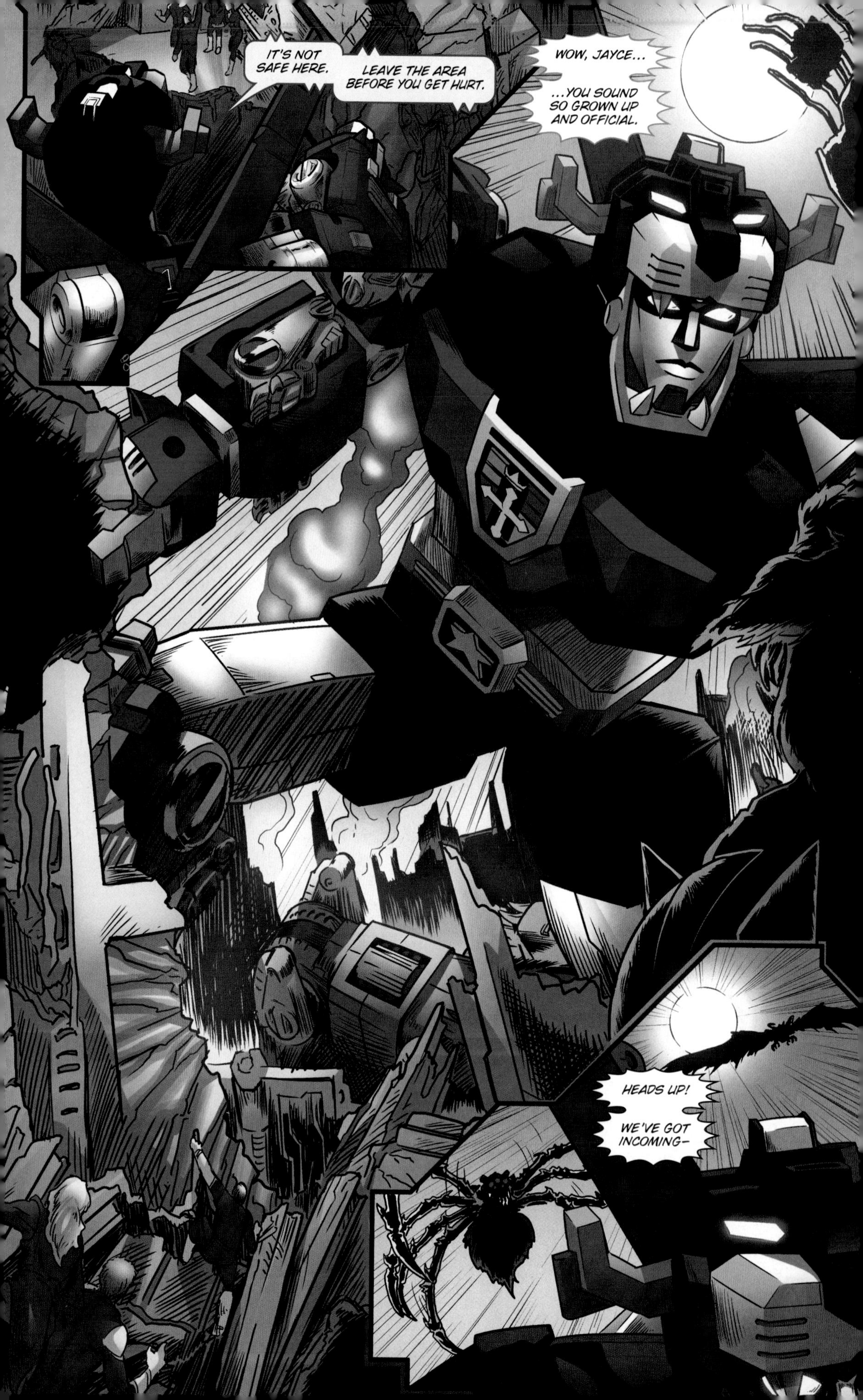
IT'S NOT SAFE HERE.
LEAVE THE AREA BEFORE YOU GET HURT.
WOW, JAYCE...
...YOU SOUND SO GROWN UP AND OFFICIAL.
HEADS UP!
WE'VE GOT INCOMING-

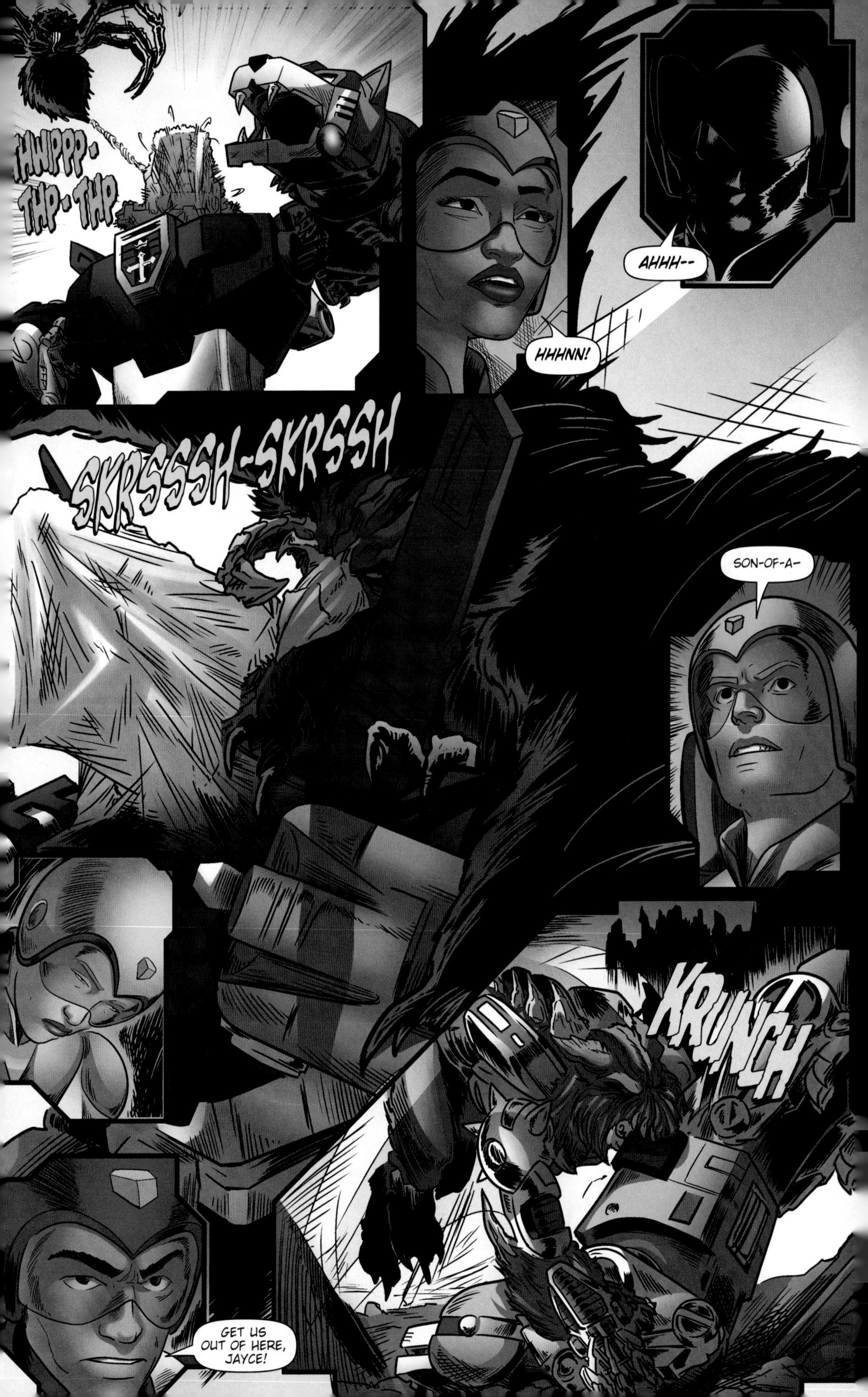
THWIPPP-
THP-THP
AHHH--
HHHNN!
SKRSSSSH-SKRSSH
SON-OF-A-
KRUNCH
GET US
OUT OF HERE,
JAYCE!

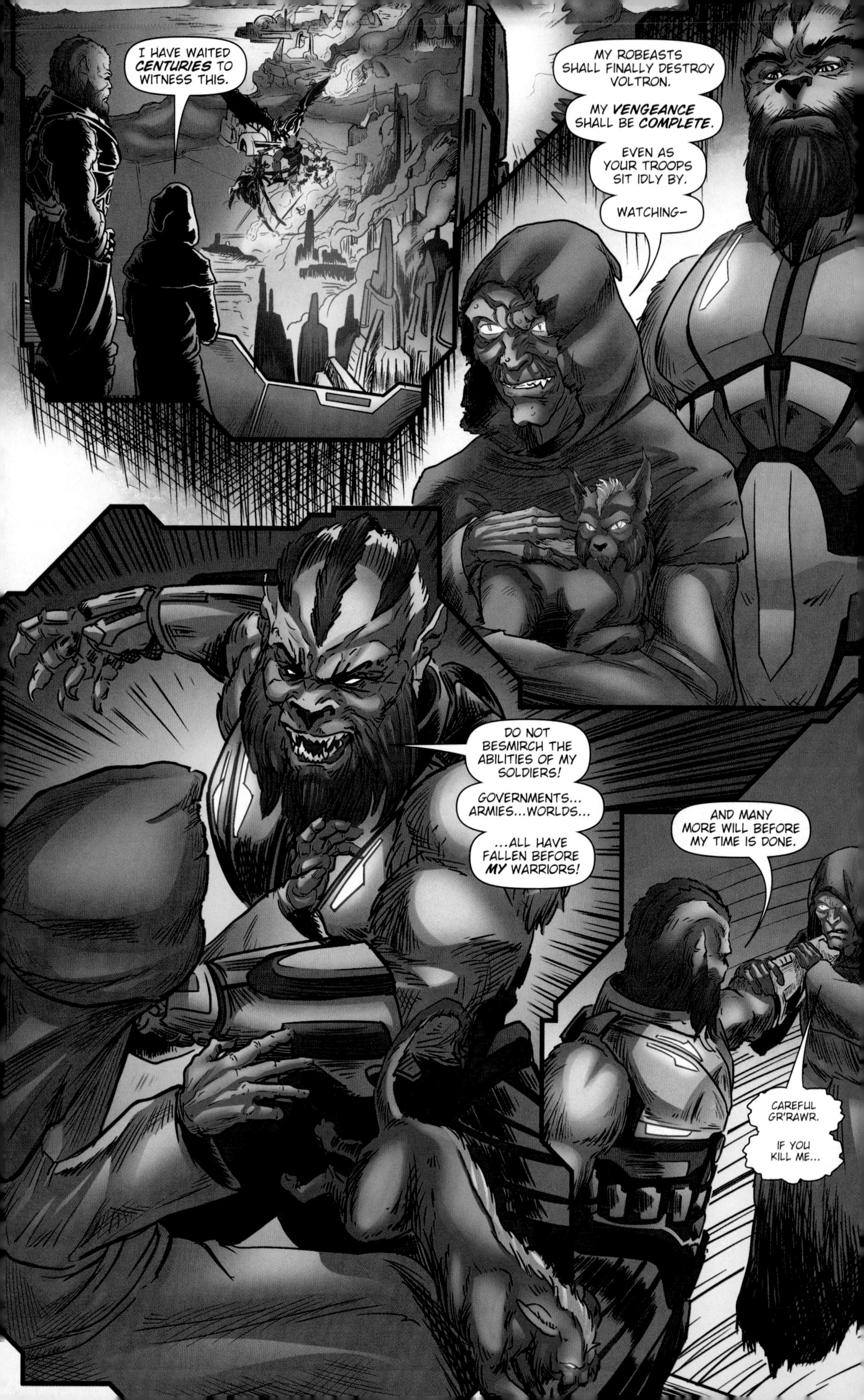
I HAVE WAITED *CENTURIES* TO WITNESS THIS.
MY ROBEASTS SHALL FINALLY DESTROY VOLTRON.
MY *VENGEANCE* SHALL BE *COMPLETE*.
EVEN AS YOUR TROOPS SIT IDLY BY.
WATCHING-
DO NOT BESMIRCH THE ABILITIES OF MY SOLDIERS!
GOVERNMENTS... ARMIES...WORLDS...
...ALL HAVE FALLEN BEFORE *MY* WARRIORS!
AND MANY MORE WILL BEFORE MY TIME IS DONE.
CAREFUL GR'RAWR.
IF YOU KILL ME...

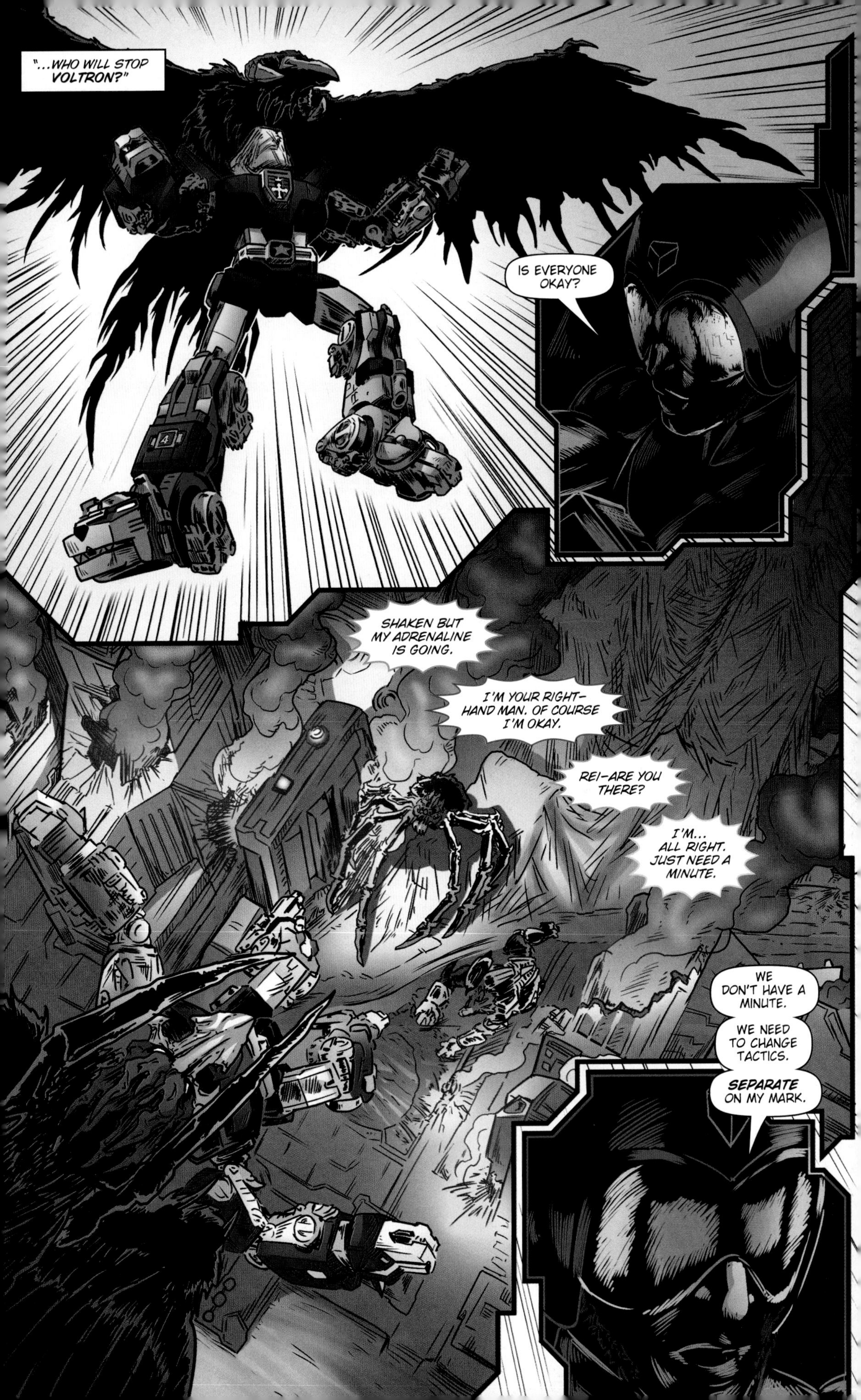
"...WHO WILL STOP VOLTRON?"
IS EVERYONE OKAY?
SHAKEN BUT MY ADRENALINE IS GOING.
I'M YOUR RIGHT-HAND MAN. OF COURSE I'M OKAY.
REI-ARE YOU THERE?
I'M... ALL RIGHT. JUST NEED A MINUTE.
WE DON'T HAVE A MINUTE.
WE NEED TO CHANGE TACTICS.
SEPARATE ON MY MARK.

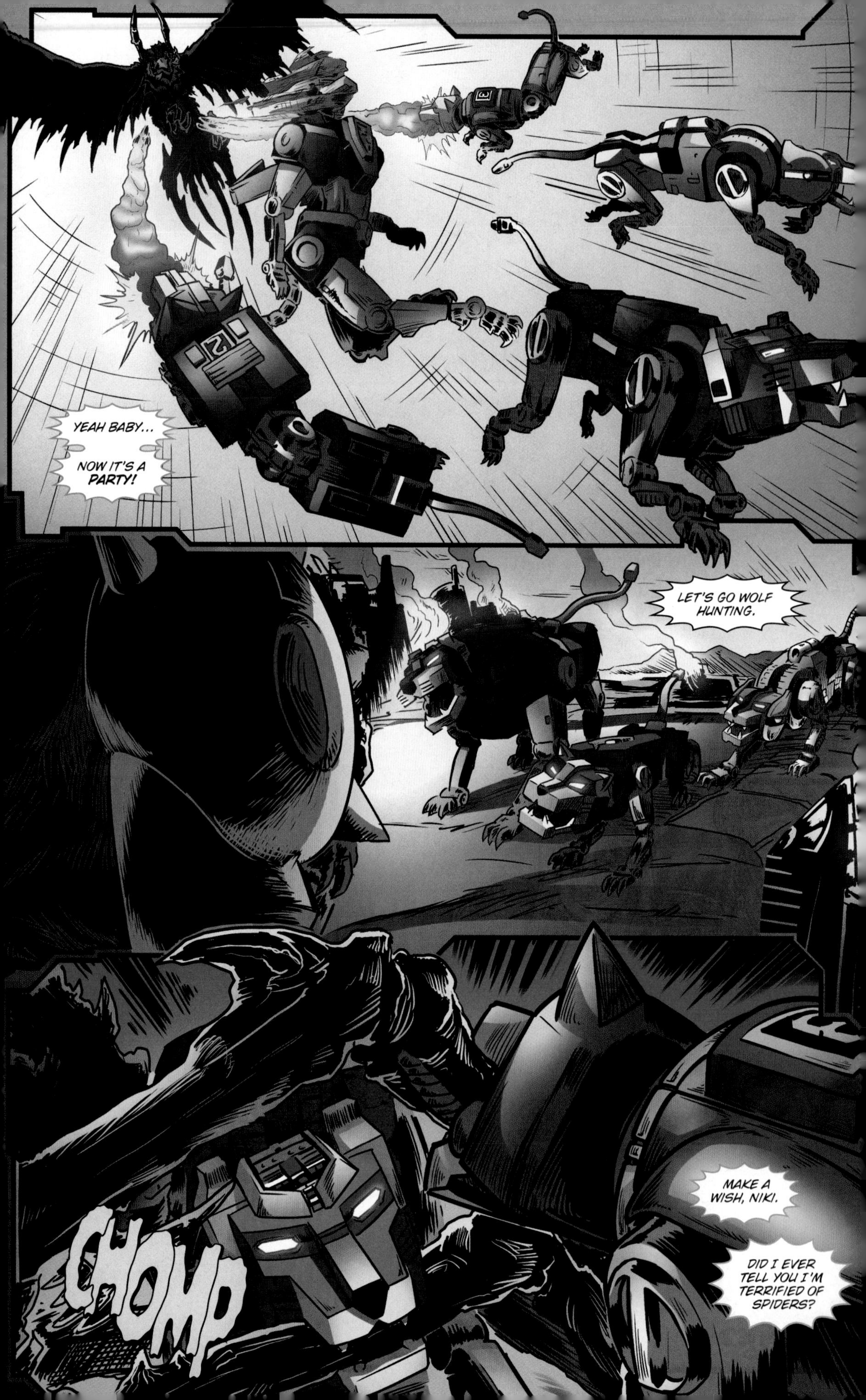
YEAH BABY...
NOW IT'S A PARTY!
LET'S GO WOLF HUNTING.
CHOMP
MAKE A WISH, NIKI.
DID I EVER TELL YOU I'M TERRIFIED OF SPIDERS?

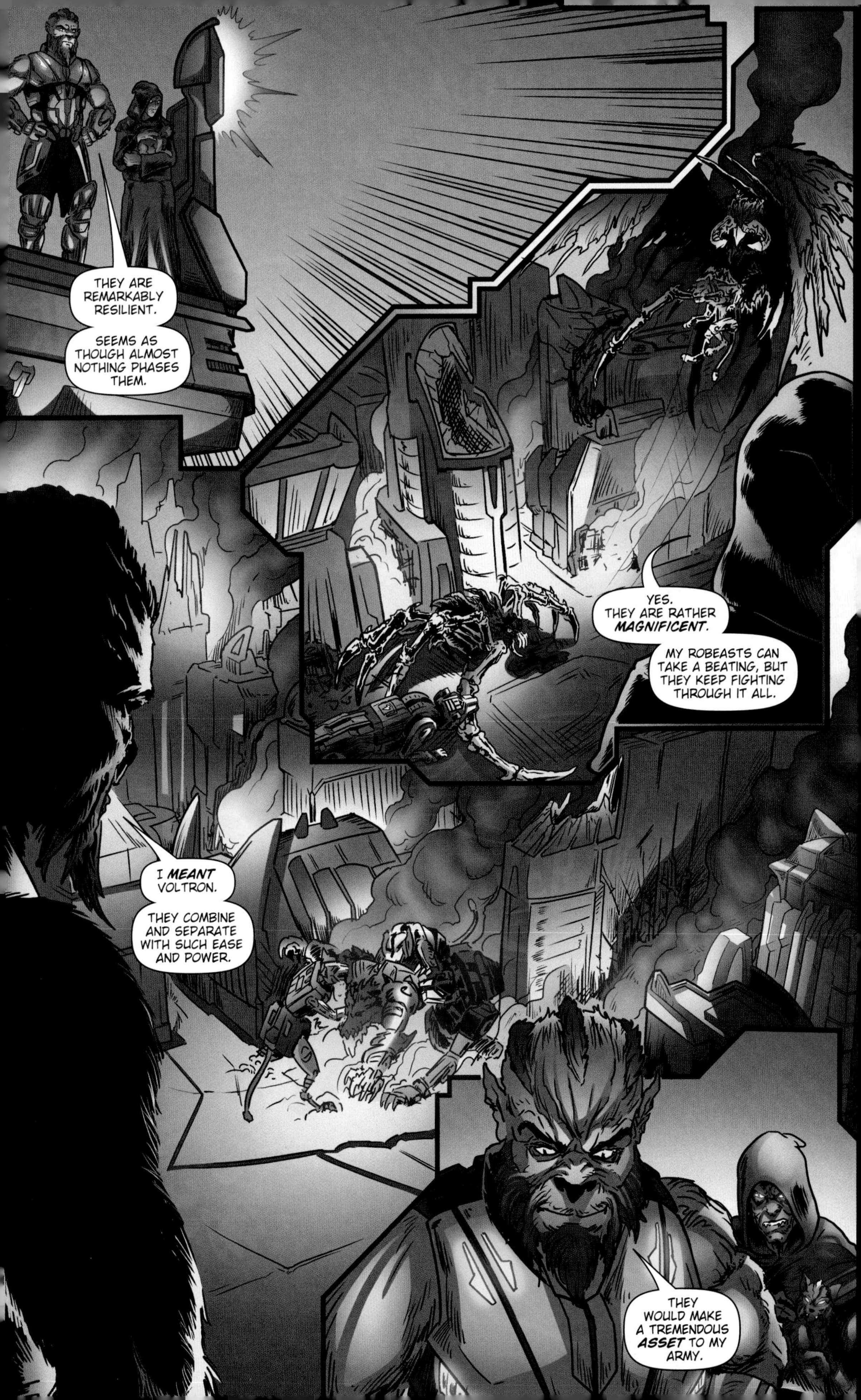

THEY ARE REMARKABLY RESILIENT.
SEEMS AS THOUGH ALMOST NOTHING PHASES THEM.
YES. THEY ARE RATHER MAGNIFICENT.
MY ROBEASTS CAN TAKE A BEATING, BUT THEY KEEP FIGHTING THROUGH IT ALL.
I MEANT VOLTRON.
THEY COMBINE AND SEPARATE WITH SUCH EASE AND POWER.
THEY WOULD MAKE A TREMENDOUS ASSET TO MY ARMY.

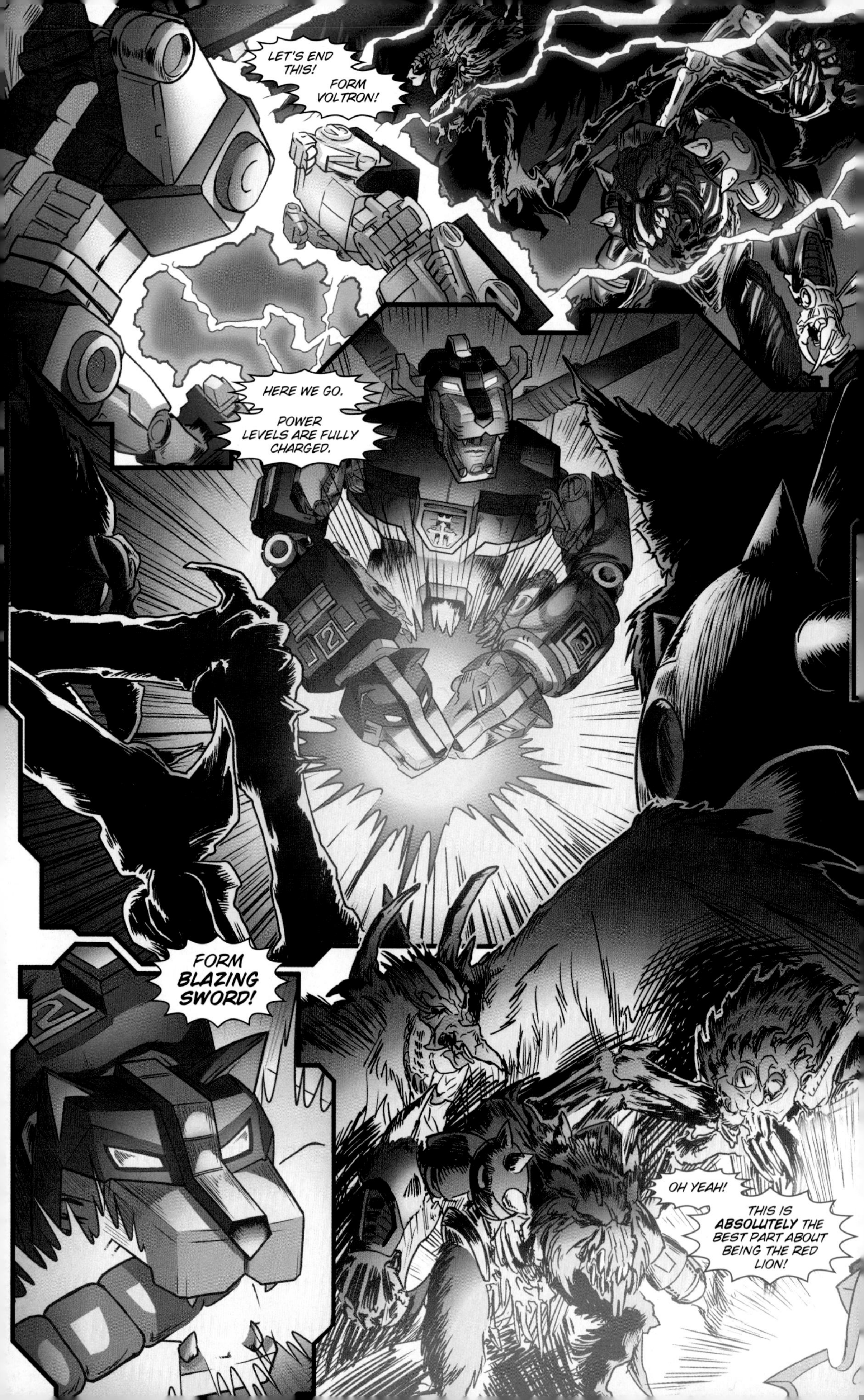
LET'S END THIS!
FORM VOLTRON!
HERE WE GO.
POWER LEVELS ARE FULLY CHARGED.
FORM BLAZING SWORD!
OH YEAH!
THIS IS ABSOLUTELY THE BEST PART ABOUT BEING THE RED LION!

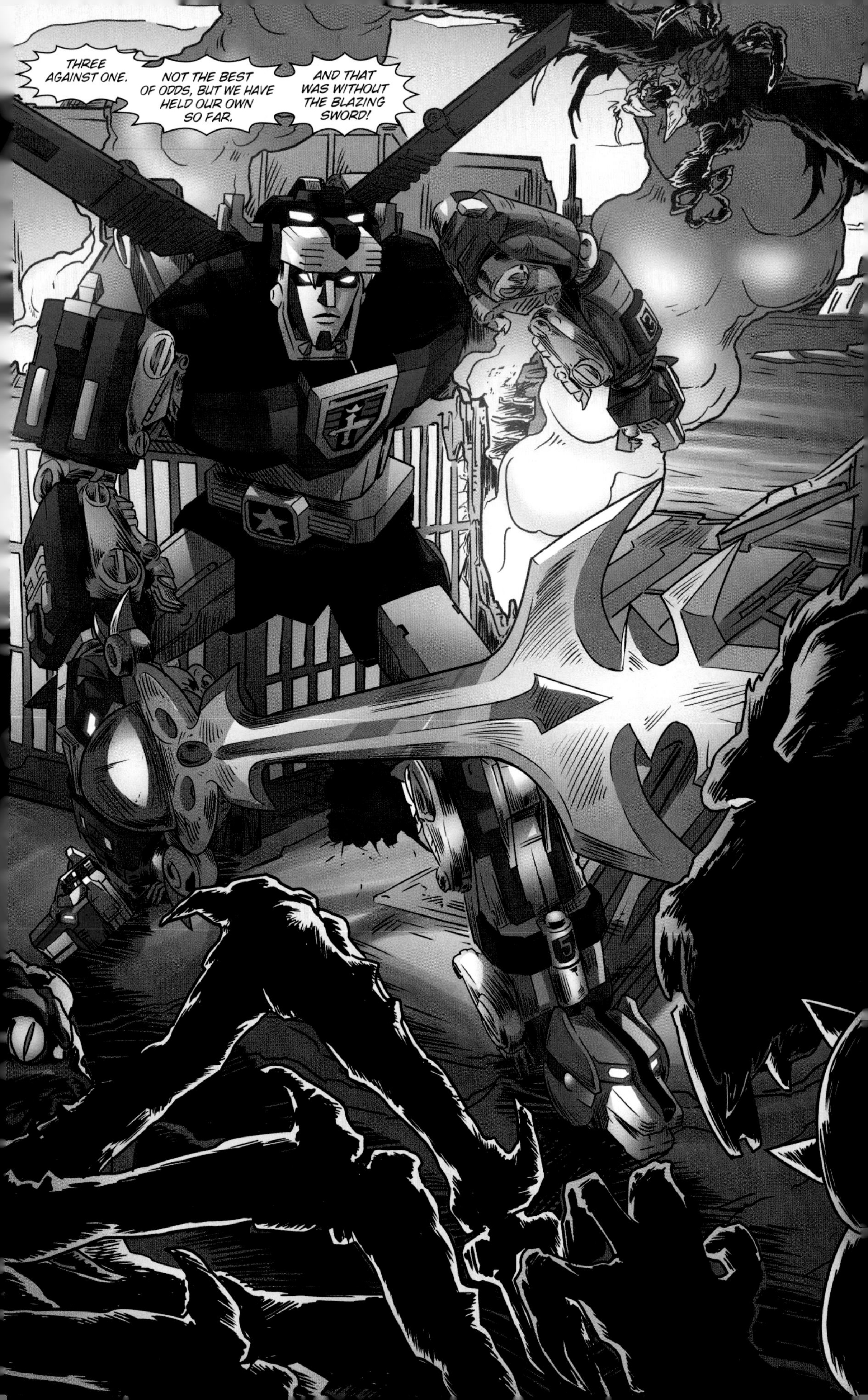
THREE AGAINST ONE.
NOT THE BEST OF ODDS, BUT WE HAVE HELD OUR OWN SO FAR.
AND THAT WAS WITHOUT THE BLAZING SWORD!

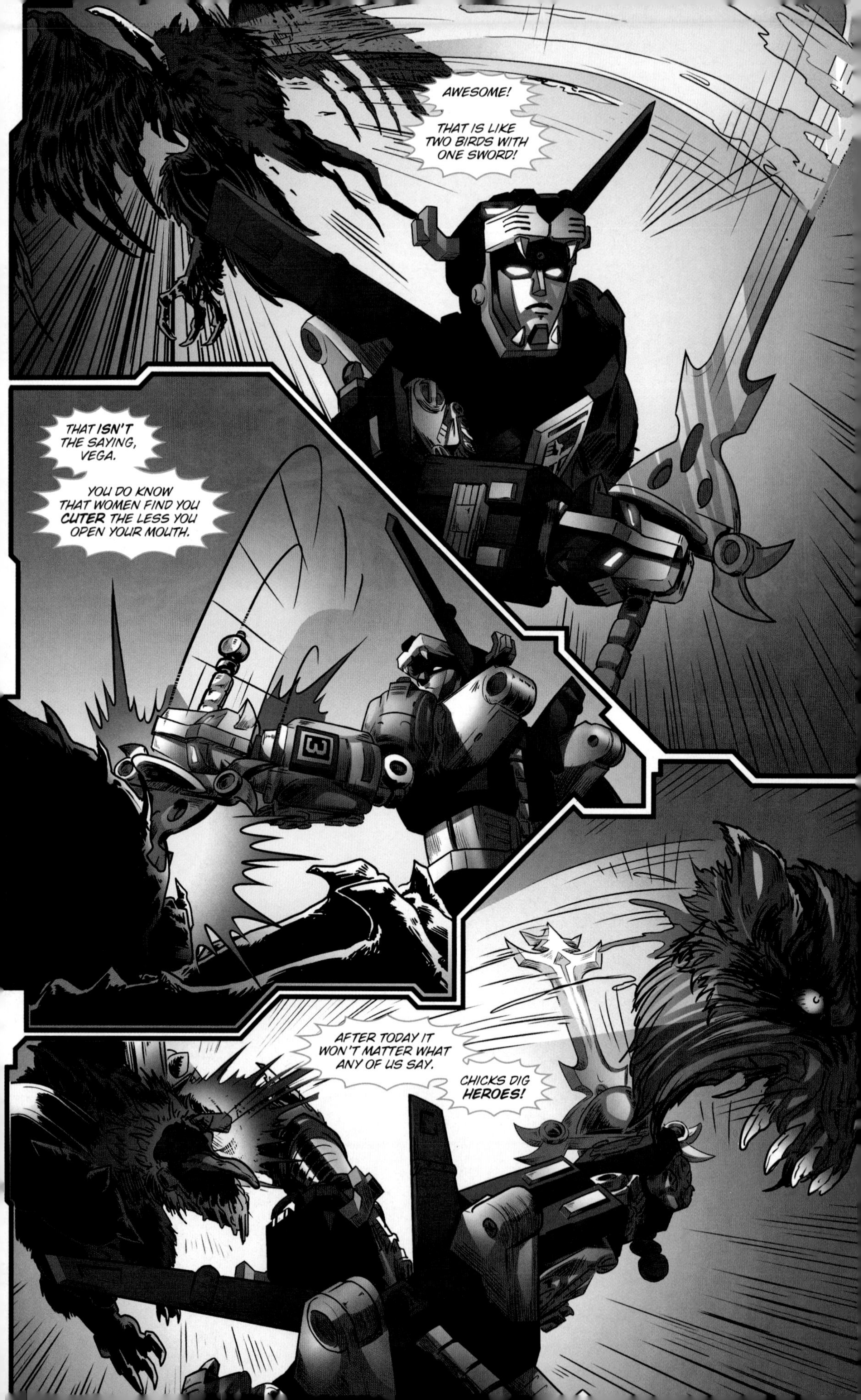
AWESOME!
THAT IS LIKE TWO BIRDS WITH ONE SWORD!
THAT ISN'T THE SAYING, VEGA.
YOU DO KNOW THAT WOMEN FIND YOU CUTER THE LESS YOU OPEN YOUR MOUTH.
AFTER TODAY IT WON'T MATTER WHAT ANY OF US SAY.
CHICKS DIG HEROES!
3

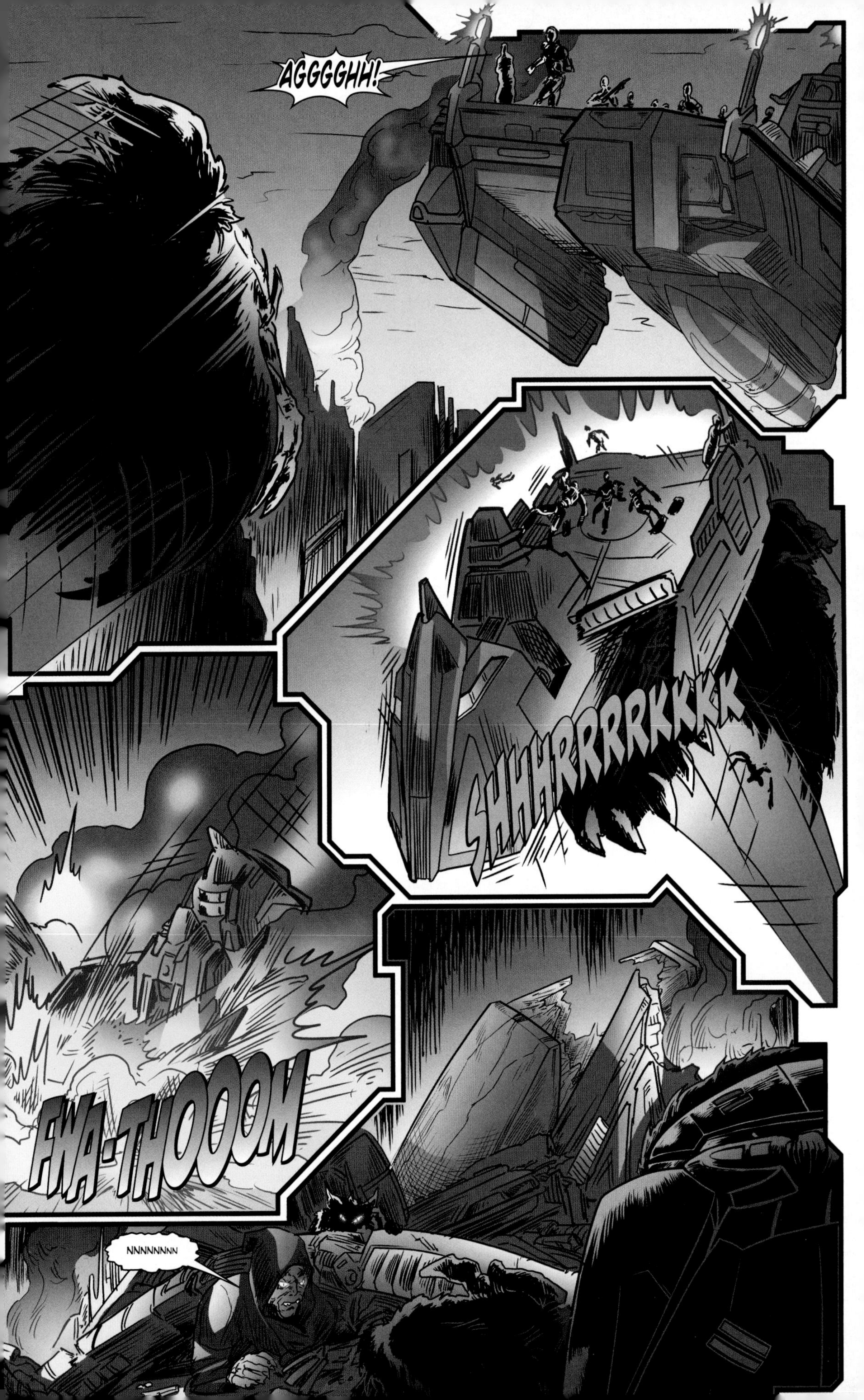
AGGGGHH!
SHHHRRRRKKKK
FWA-THOOOM
NNNNNNNN

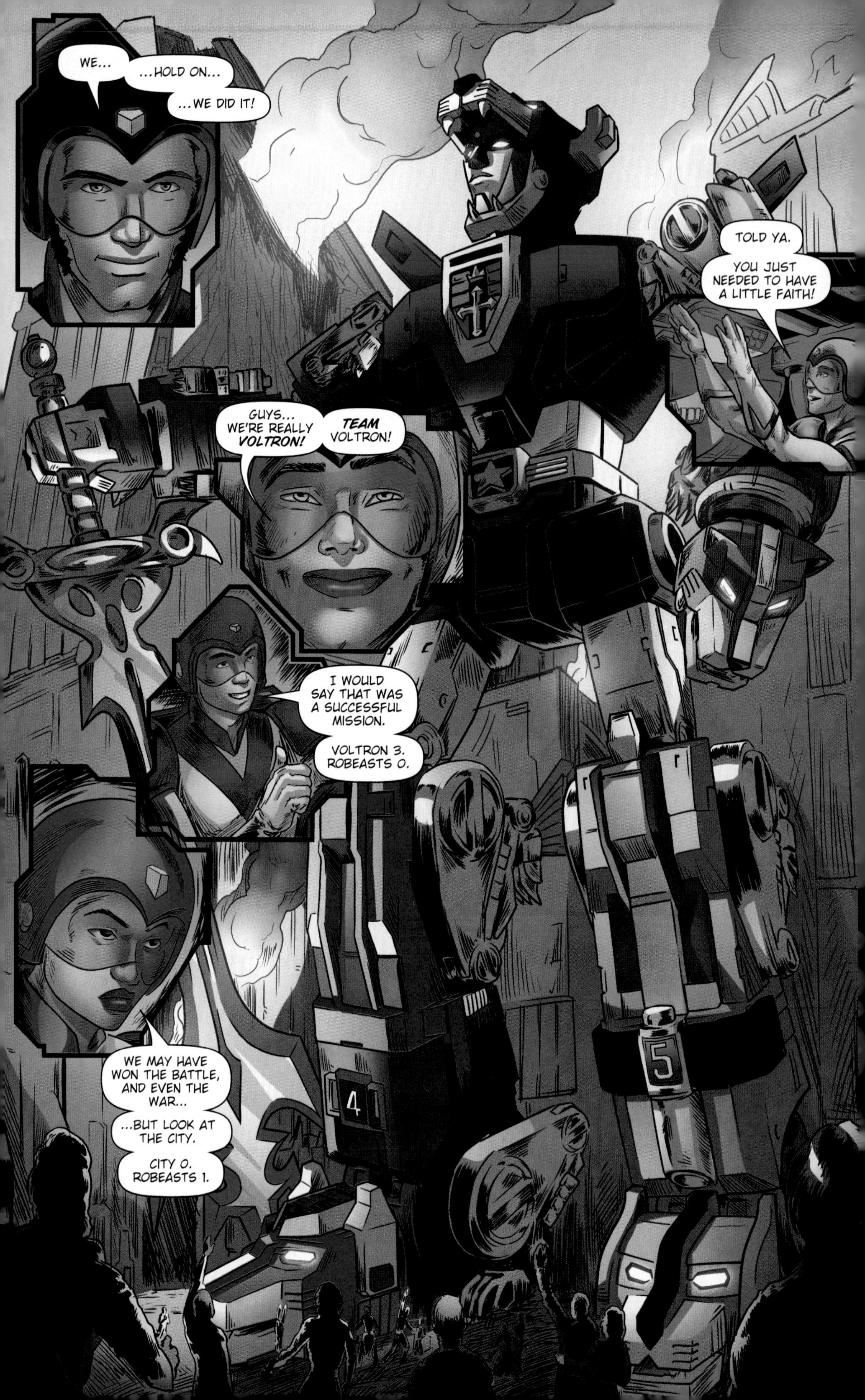

WE...
...HOLD ON...
...WE DID IT!
TOLD YA.
YOU JUST NEEDED TO HAVE A LITTLE FAITH!
GUYS... WE'RE REALLY VOLTRON!
TEAM VOLTRON!
I WOULD SAY THAT WAS A SUCCESSFUL MISSION.
VOLTRON 3. ROBEASTS 0.
WE MAY HAVE WON THE BATTLE, AND EVEN THE WAR...
...BUT LOOK AT THE CITY.
CITY 0. ROBEASTS 1.

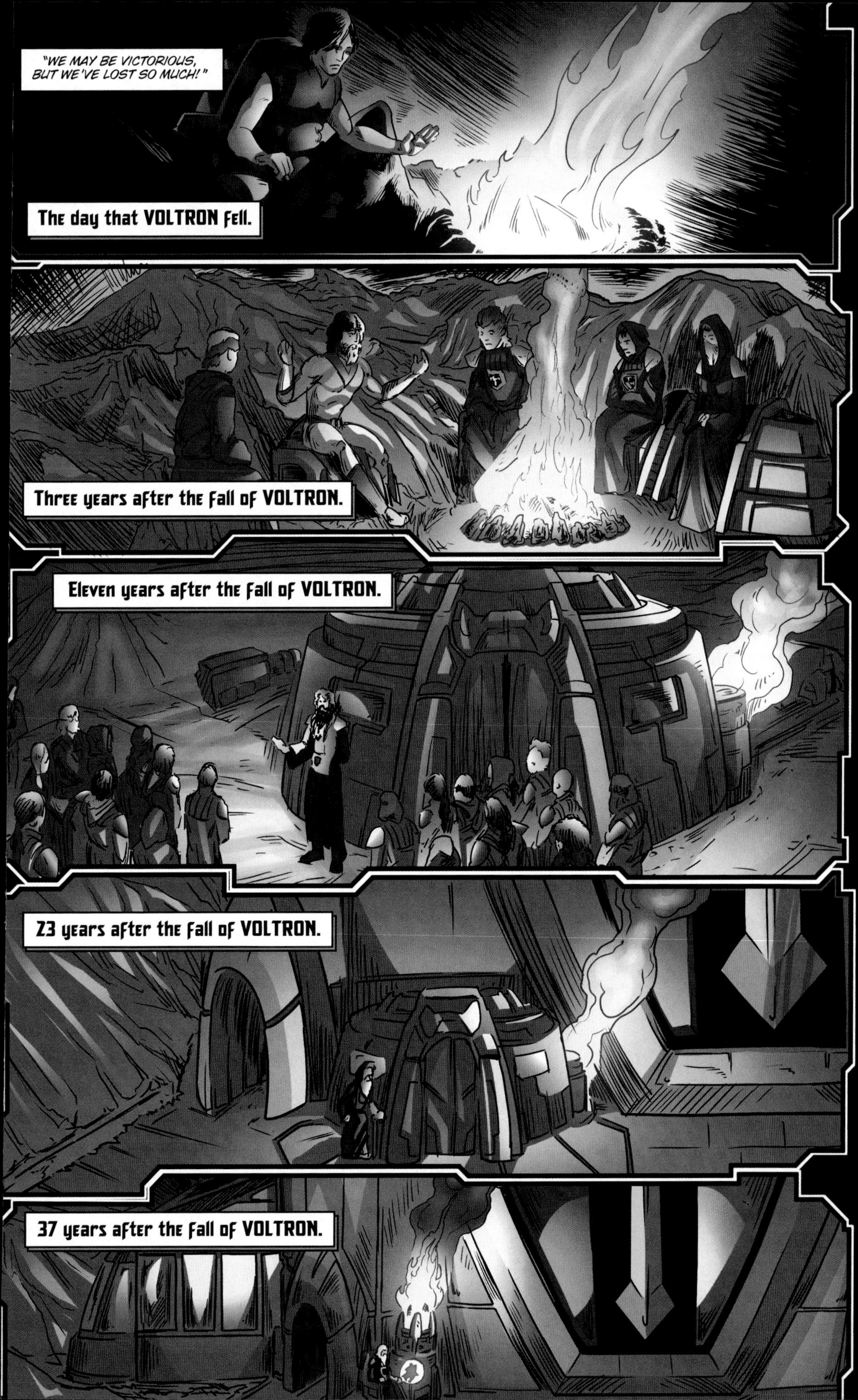
"WE MAY BE VICTORIOUS, BUT WE'VE LOST SO MUCH!"
The day that VOLTRON fell.
Three years after the fall of VOLTRON.
Eleven years after the fall of VOLTRON.
23 years after the fall of VOLTRON.
37 years after the fall of VOLTRON.

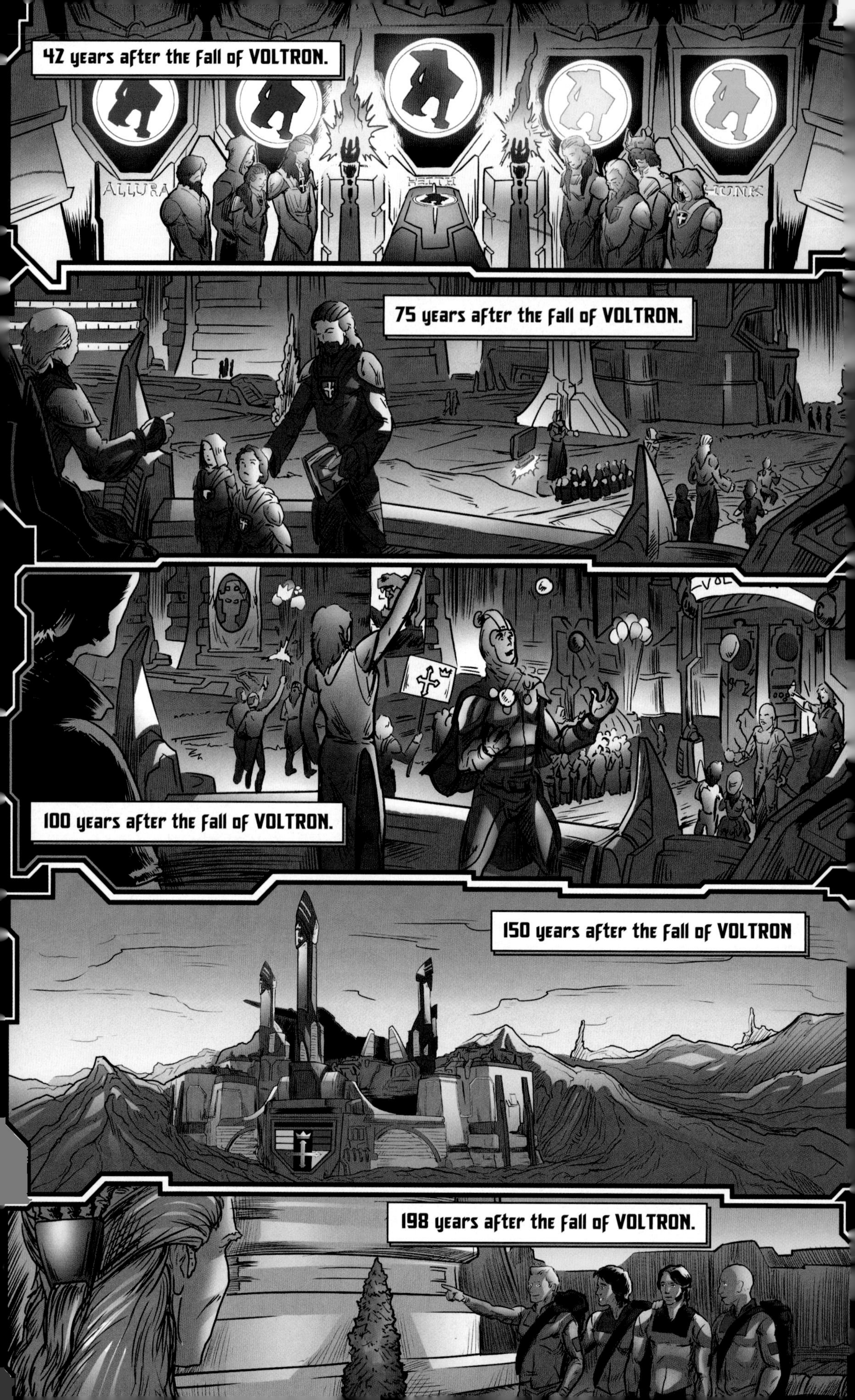
42 years after the fall of VOLTRON.
ALLURA
KEITH
HUNK
75 years after the fall of VOLTRON.
100 years after the fall of VOLTRON.
150 years after the fall of VOLTRON
198 years after the fall of VOLTRON.

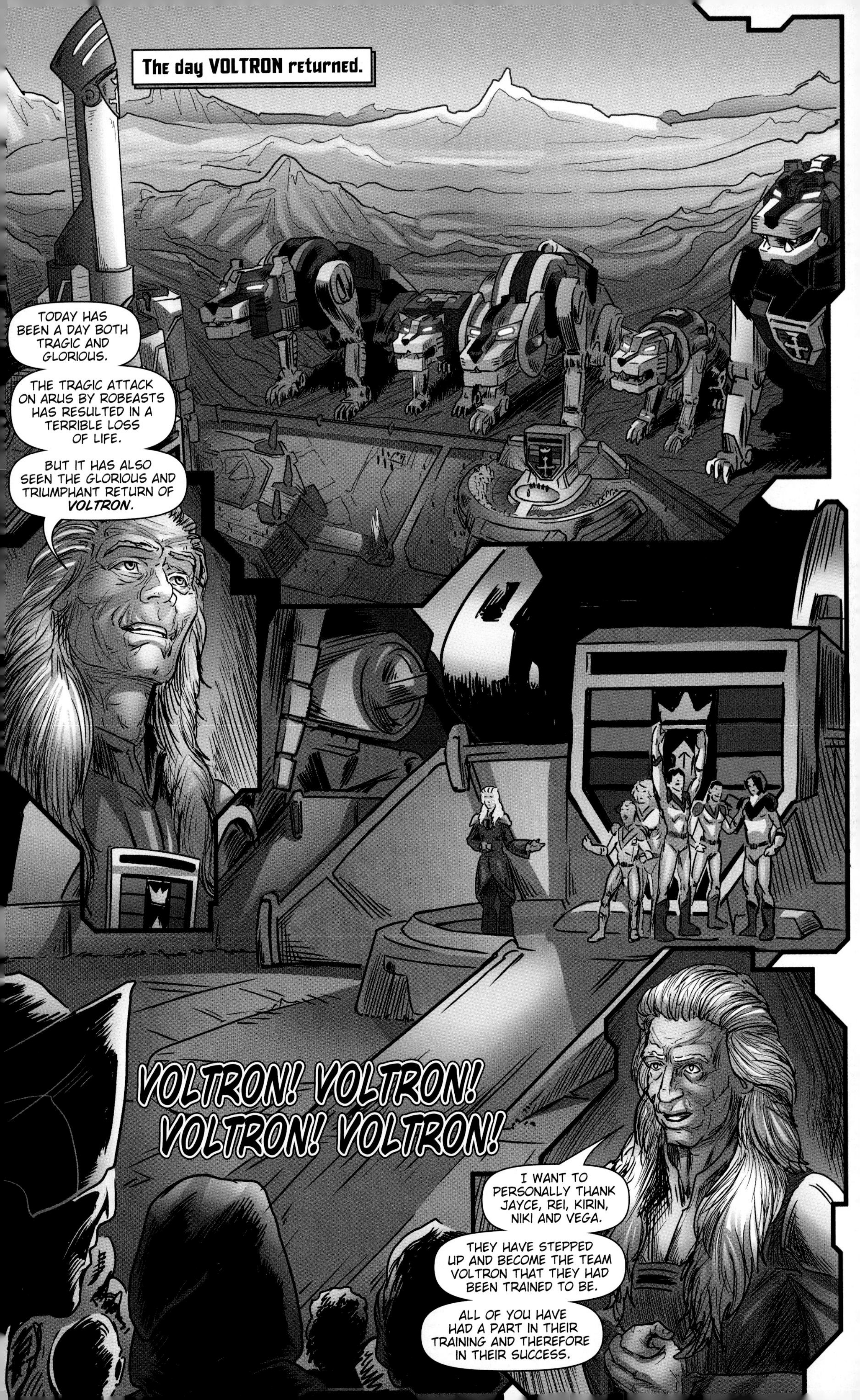

The day VOLTRON returned.
TODAY HAS BEEN A DAY BOTH TRAGIC AND GLORIOUS.
THE TRAGIC ATTACK ON ARUS BY ROBEASTS HAS RESULTED IN A TERRIBLE LOSS OF LIFE.
BUT IT HAS ALSO SEEN THE GLORIOUS AND TRIUMPHANT RETURN OF *VOLTRON*.
VOLTRON! VOLTRON! VOLTRON! VOLTRON!
I WANT TO PERSONALLY THANK JAYCE, REI, KIRIN, NIKI AND VEGA.
THEY HAVE STEPPED UP AND BECOME THE TEAM VOLTRON THAT THEY HAD BEEN TRAINED TO BE.
ALL OF YOU HAVE HAD A PART IN THEIR TRAINING AND THEREFORE IN THEIR SUCCESS.

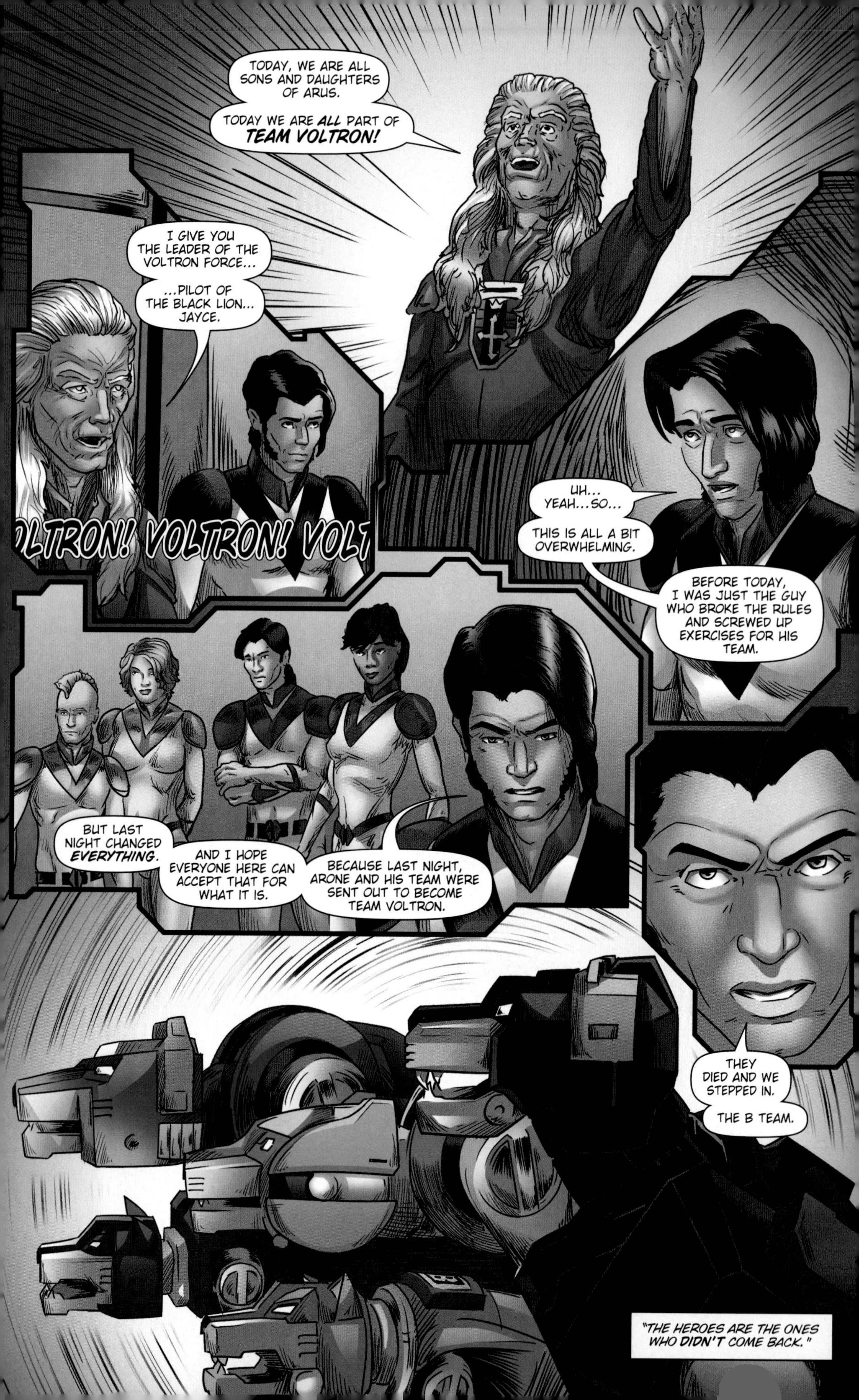
TODAY, WE ARE ALL SONS AND DAUGHTERS OF ARUS.
TODAY WE ARE ALL PART OF TEAM VOLTRON!
I GIVE YOU THE LEADER OF THE VOLTRON FORCE...
...PILOT OF THE BLACK LION... JAYCE.
OLTRON! VOLTRON! VOLT
UH... YEAH... SO...
THIS IS ALL A BIT OVERWHELMING.
BEFORE TODAY, I WAS JUST THE GUY WHO BROKE THE RULES AND SCREWED UP EXERCISES FOR HIS TEAM.
BUT LAST NIGHT CHANGED EVERYTHING.
AND I HOPE EVERYONE HERE CAN ACCEPT THAT FOR WHAT IT IS.
BECAUSE LAST NIGHT, ARONE AND HIS TEAM WERE SENT OUT TO BECOME TEAM VOLTRON.
THEY DIED AND WE STEPPED IN.
THE B TEAM.
"THE HEROES ARE THE ONES WHO DIDN'T COME BACK."

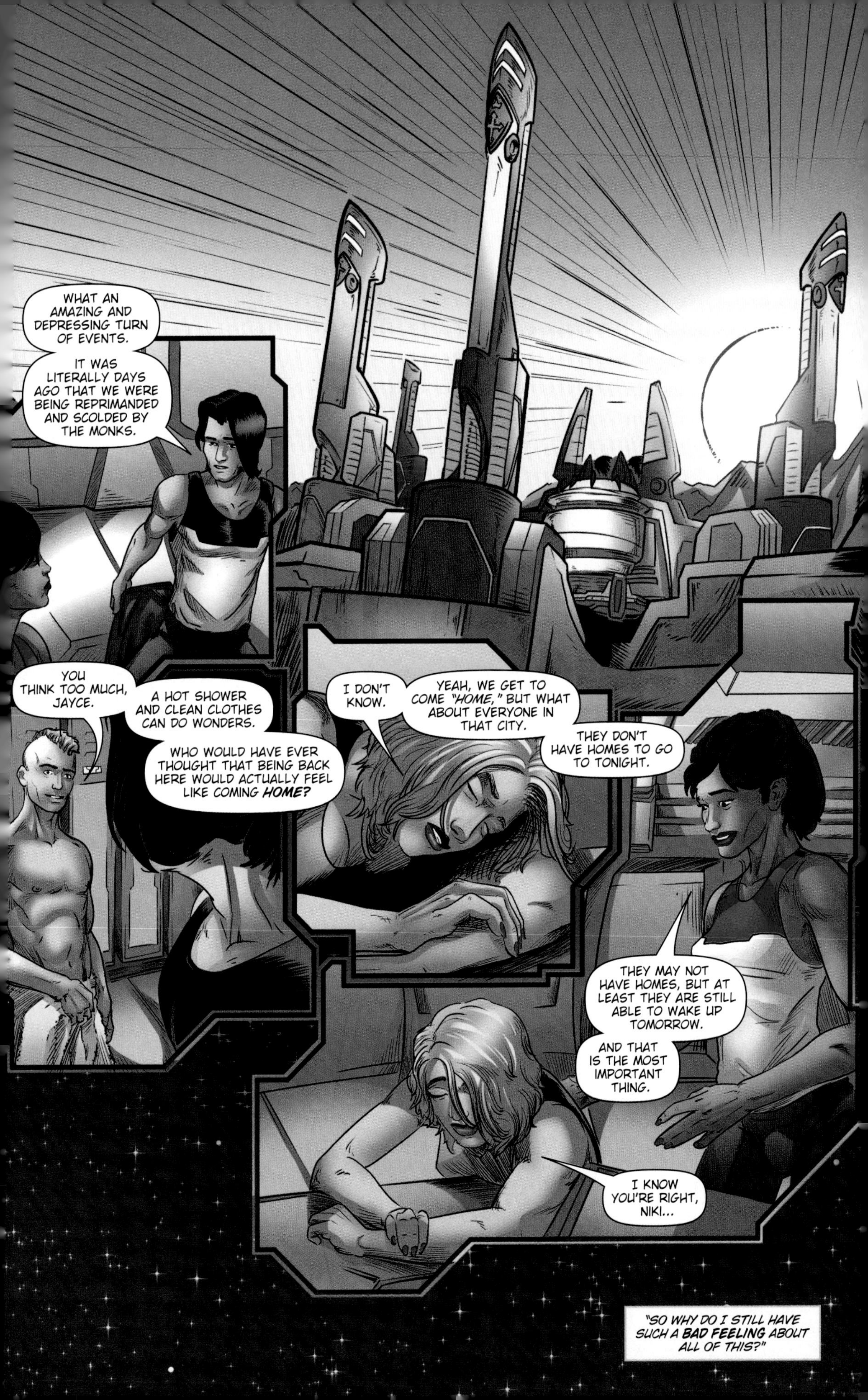
WHAT AN AMAZING AND DEPRESSING TURN OF EVENTS.
IT WAS LITERALLY DAYS AGO THAT WE WERE BEING REPRIMANDED AND SCOLDED BY THE MONKS.
YOU THINK TOO MUCH, JAYCE.
A HOT SHOWER AND CLEAN CLOTHES CAN DO WONDERS.
WHO WOULD HAVE EVER THOUGHT THAT BEING BACK HERE WOULD ACTUALLY FEEL LIKE COMING ***HOME?***
I DON'T KNOW.
YEAH, WE GET TO COME *"HOME,"* BUT WHAT ABOUT EVERYONE IN THAT CITY.
THEY DON'T HAVE HOMES TO GO TO TONIGHT.
THEY MAY NOT HAVE HOMES, BUT AT LEAST THEY ARE STILL ABLE TO WAKE UP TOMORROW.
AND THAT IS THE MOST IMPORTANT THING.
I KNOW YOU'RE RIGHT, NIKI...
*"SO WHY DO I STILL HAVE SUCH A **BAD FEELING** ABOUT ALL OF THIS?"*

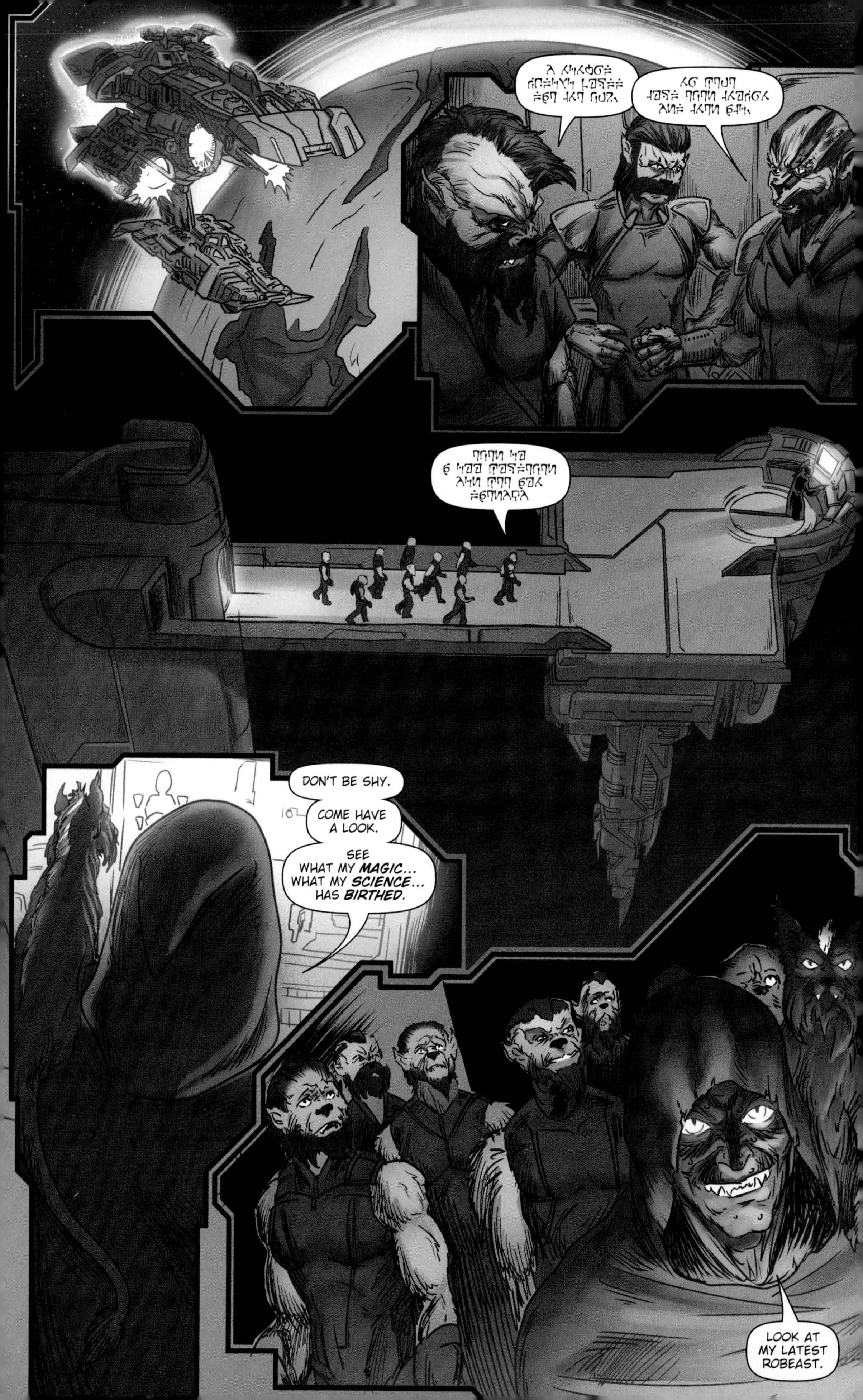
DON'T BE SHY.
COME HAVE A LOOK.
SEE WHAT MY *MAGIC*... WHAT MY *SCIENCE*... HAS *BIRTHED*.
LOOK AT MY LATEST ROBEAST.

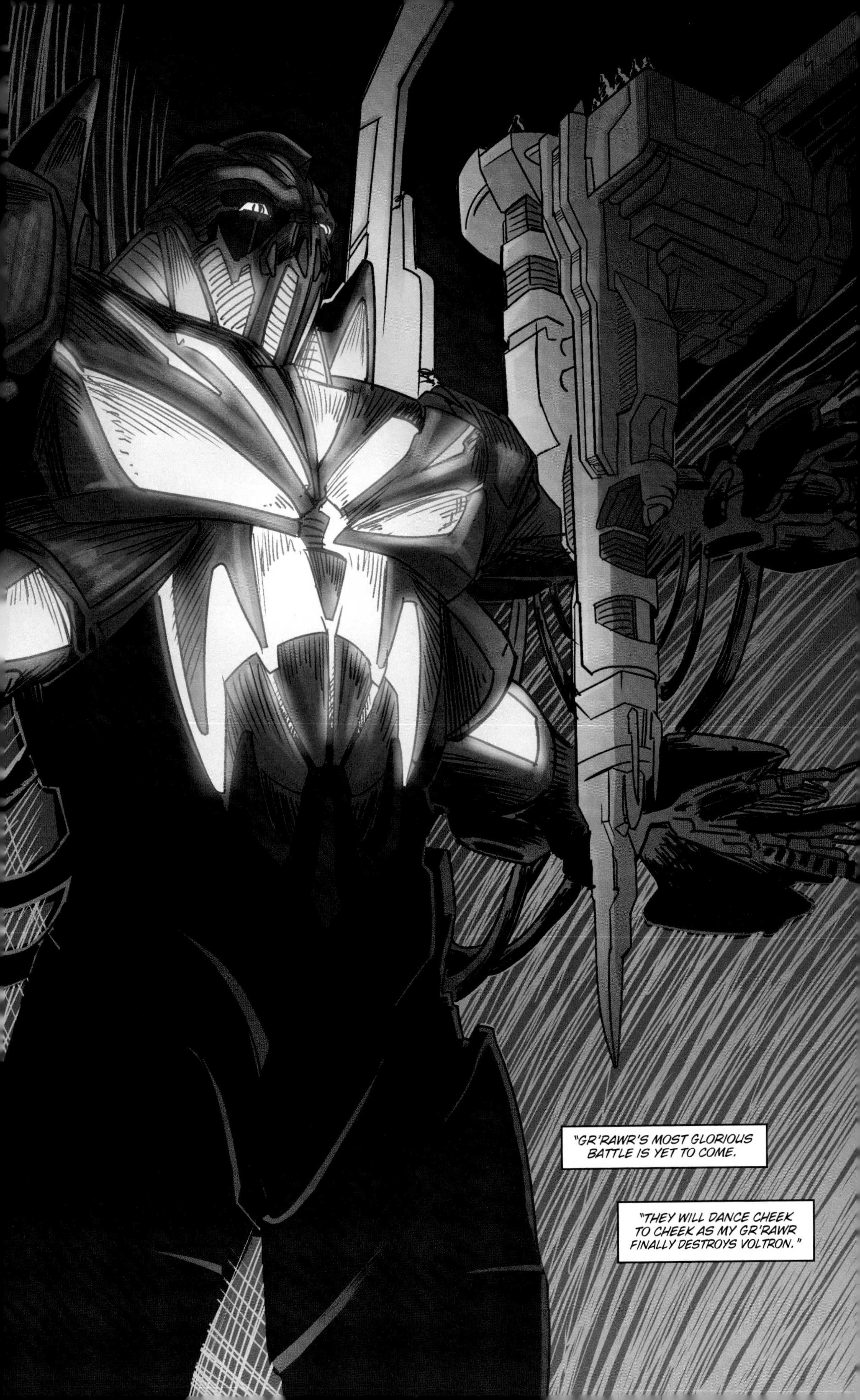
"GR'RAWR'S MOST GLORIOUS BATTLE IS YET TO COME.
"THEY WILL DANCE CHEEK TO CHEEK AS MY GR'RAWR FINALLY DESTROYS VOLTRON."

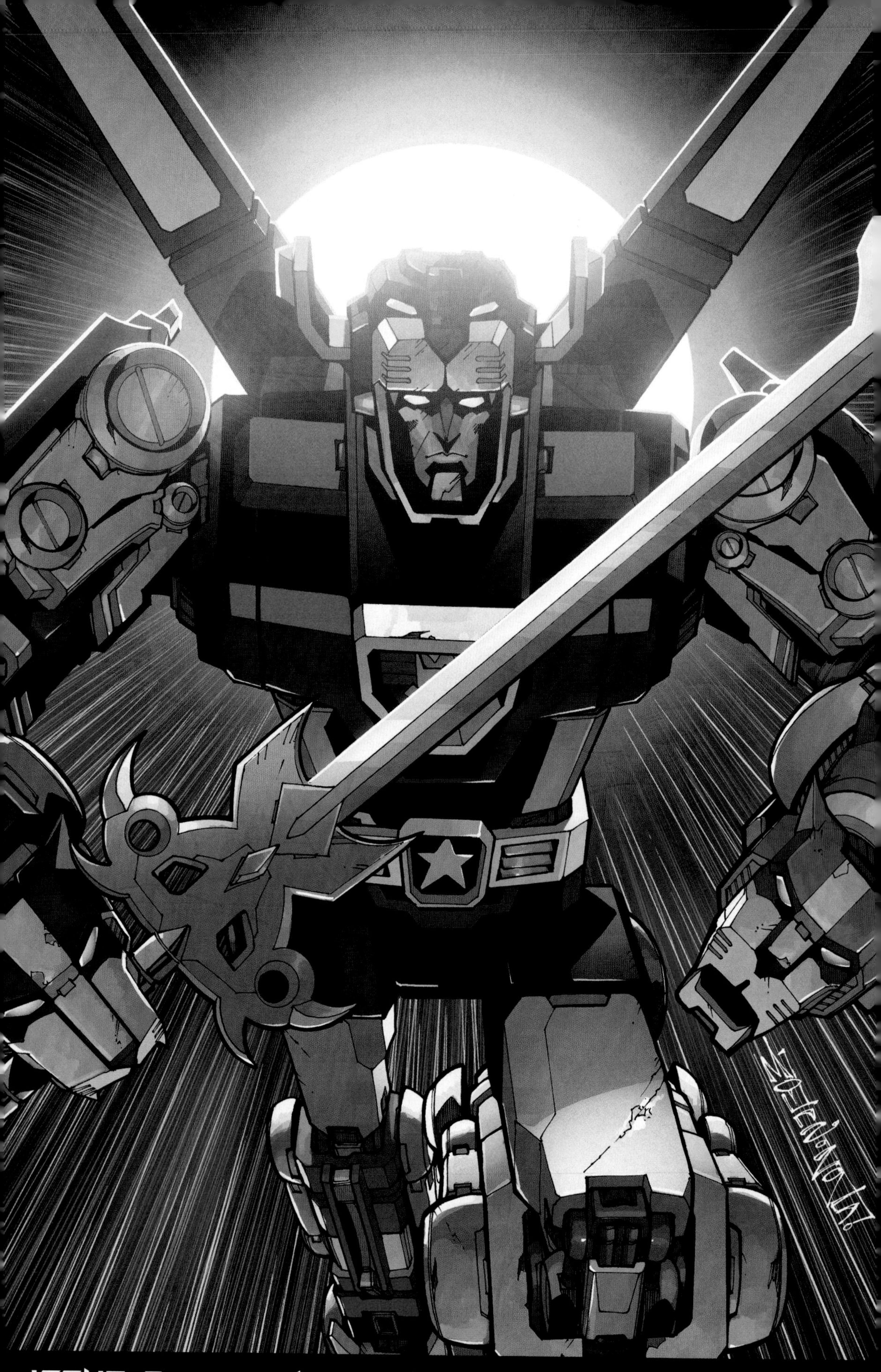

ISSUE 6 Cover by ALEX MILNE Colors by JOSH PEREZ

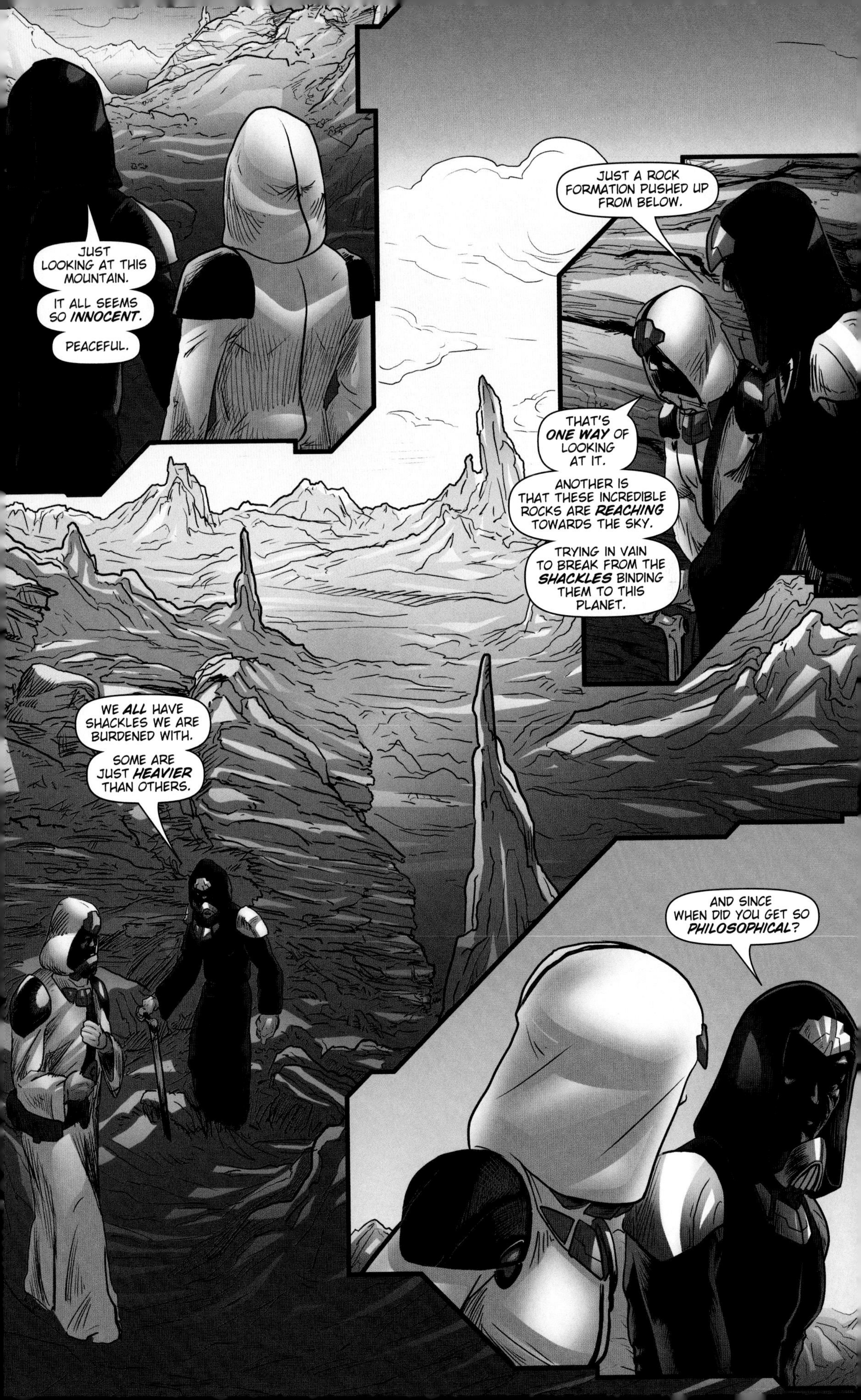
JUST LOOKING AT THIS MOUNTAIN.
IT ALL SEEMS SO *INNOCENT*.
PEACEFUL.
JUST A ROCK FORMATION PUSHED UP FROM BELOW.
THAT'S *ONE WAY* OF LOOKING AT IT.
ANOTHER IS THAT THESE INCREDIBLE ROCKS ARE *REACHING* TOWARDS THE SKY.
TRYING IN VAIN TO BREAK FROM THE *SHACKLES* BINDING THEM TO THIS PLANET.
WE *ALL* HAVE SHACKLES WE ARE BURDENED WITH.
SOME ARE JUST *HEAVIER* THAN OTHERS.
AND SINCE WHEN DID YOU GET SO *PHILOSOPHICAL*?

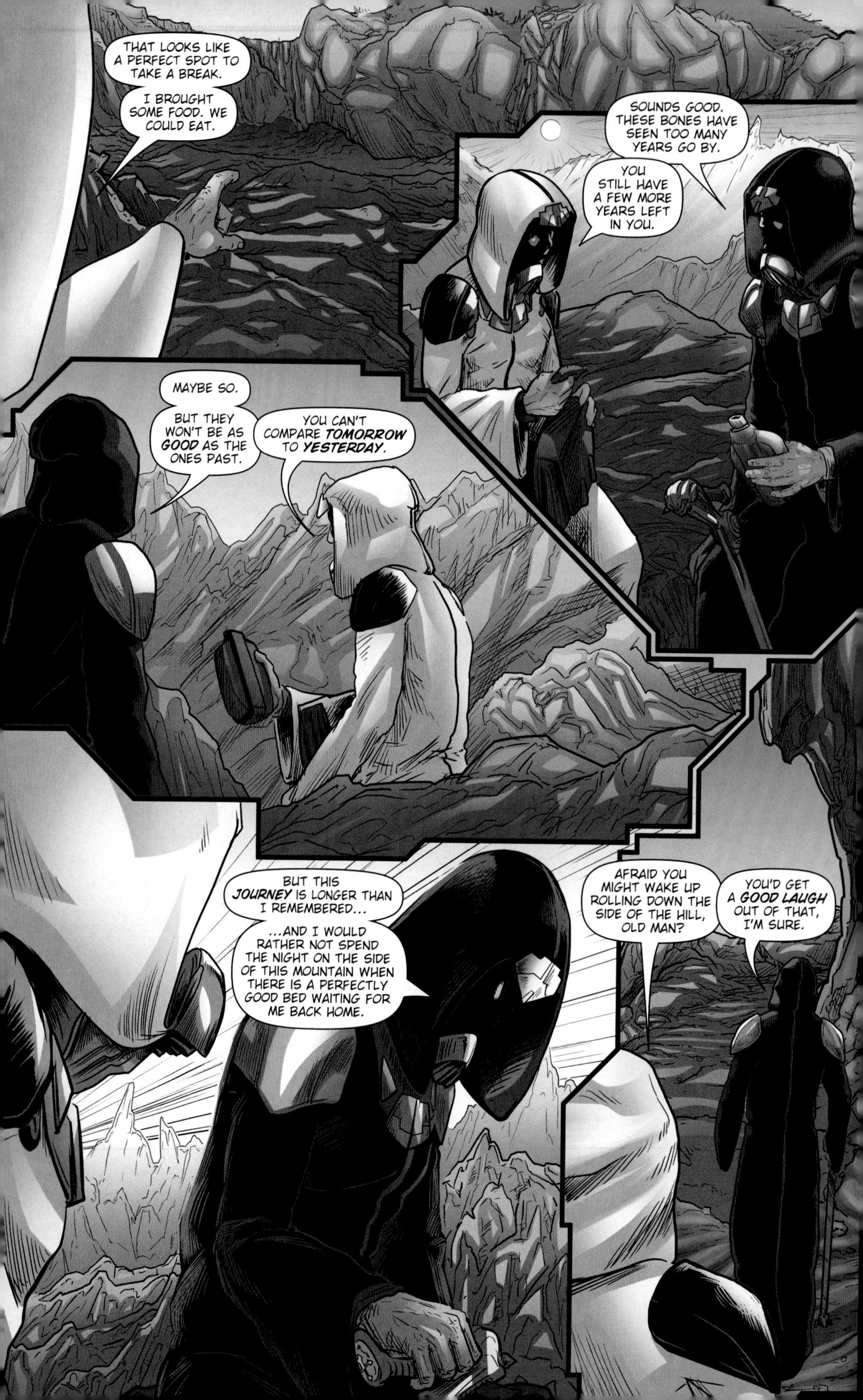
THAT LOOKS LIKE A PERFECT SPOT TO TAKE A BREAK.
I BROUGHT SOME FOOD. WE COULD EAT.
SOUNDS GOOD. THESE BONES HAVE SEEN TOO MANY YEARS GO BY.
YOU STILL HAVE A FEW MORE YEARS LEFT IN YOU.
MAYBE SO.
BUT THEY WON'T BE AS GOOD AS THE ONES PAST.
YOU CAN'T COMPARE TOMORROW TO YESTERDAY.
BUT THIS JOURNEY IS LONGER THAN I REMEMBERED...
...AND I WOULD RATHER NOT SPEND THE NIGHT ON THE SIDE OF THIS MOUNTAIN WHEN THERE IS A PERFECTLY GOOD BED WAITING FOR ME BACK HOME.
AFRAID YOU MIGHT WAKE UP ROLLING DOWN THE SIDE OF THE HILL, OLD MAN?
YOU'D GET A GOOD LAUGH OUT OF THAT, I'M SURE.

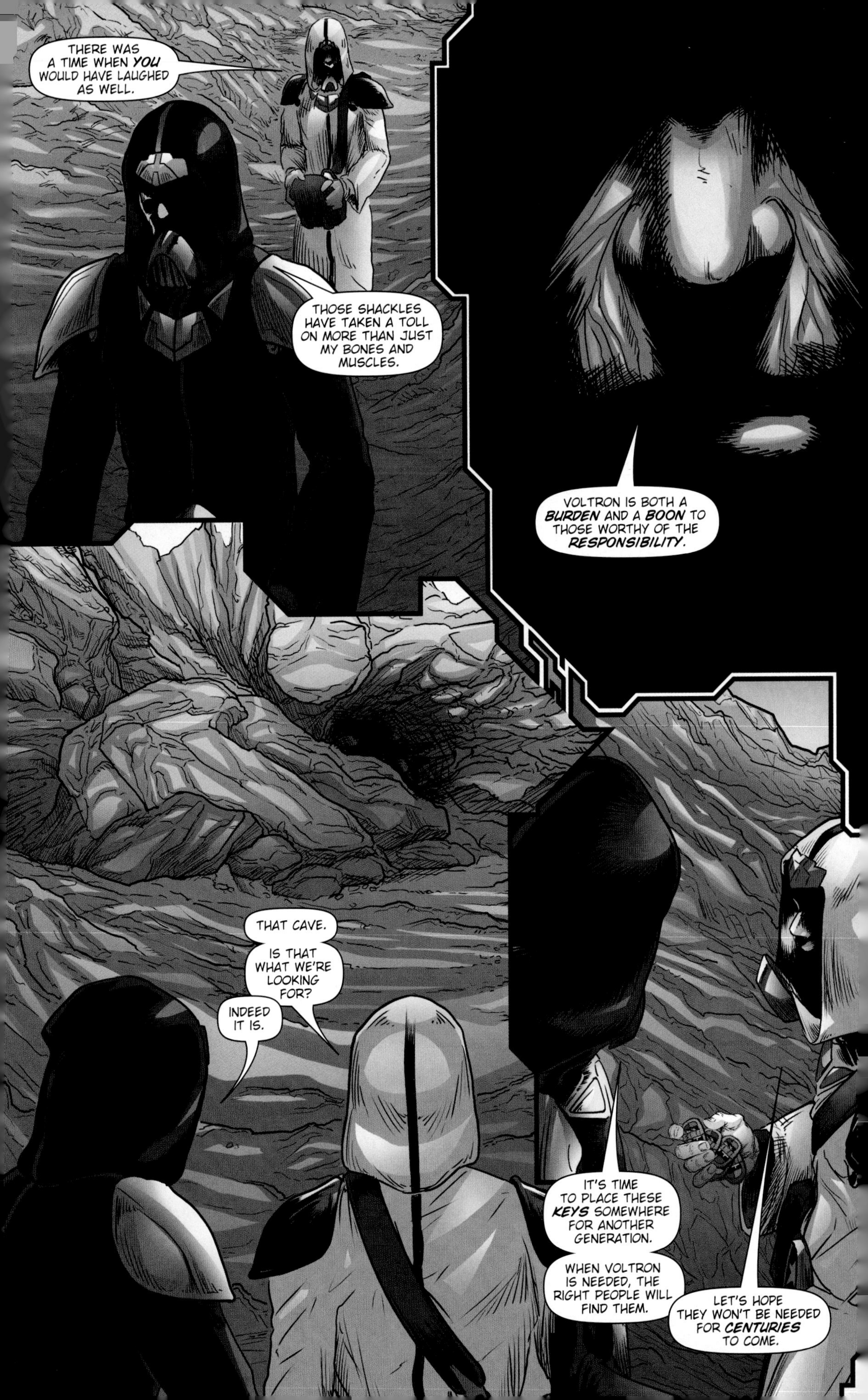
THERE WAS A TIME WHEN YOU WOULD HAVE LAUGHED AS WELL.
THOSE SHACKLES HAVE TAKEN A TOLL ON MORE THAN JUST MY BONES AND MUSCLES.
VOLTRON IS BOTH A BURDEN AND A BOON TO THOSE WORTHY OF THE RESPONSIBILITY.
THAT CAVE.
IS THAT WHAT WE'RE LOOKING FOR?
INDEED IT IS.
IT'S TIME TO PLACE THESE KEYS SOMEWHERE FOR ANOTHER GENERATION.
WHEN VOLTRON IS NEEDED, THE RIGHT PEOPLE WILL FIND THEM.
LET'S HOPE THEY WON'T BE NEEDED FOR CENTURIES TO COME.

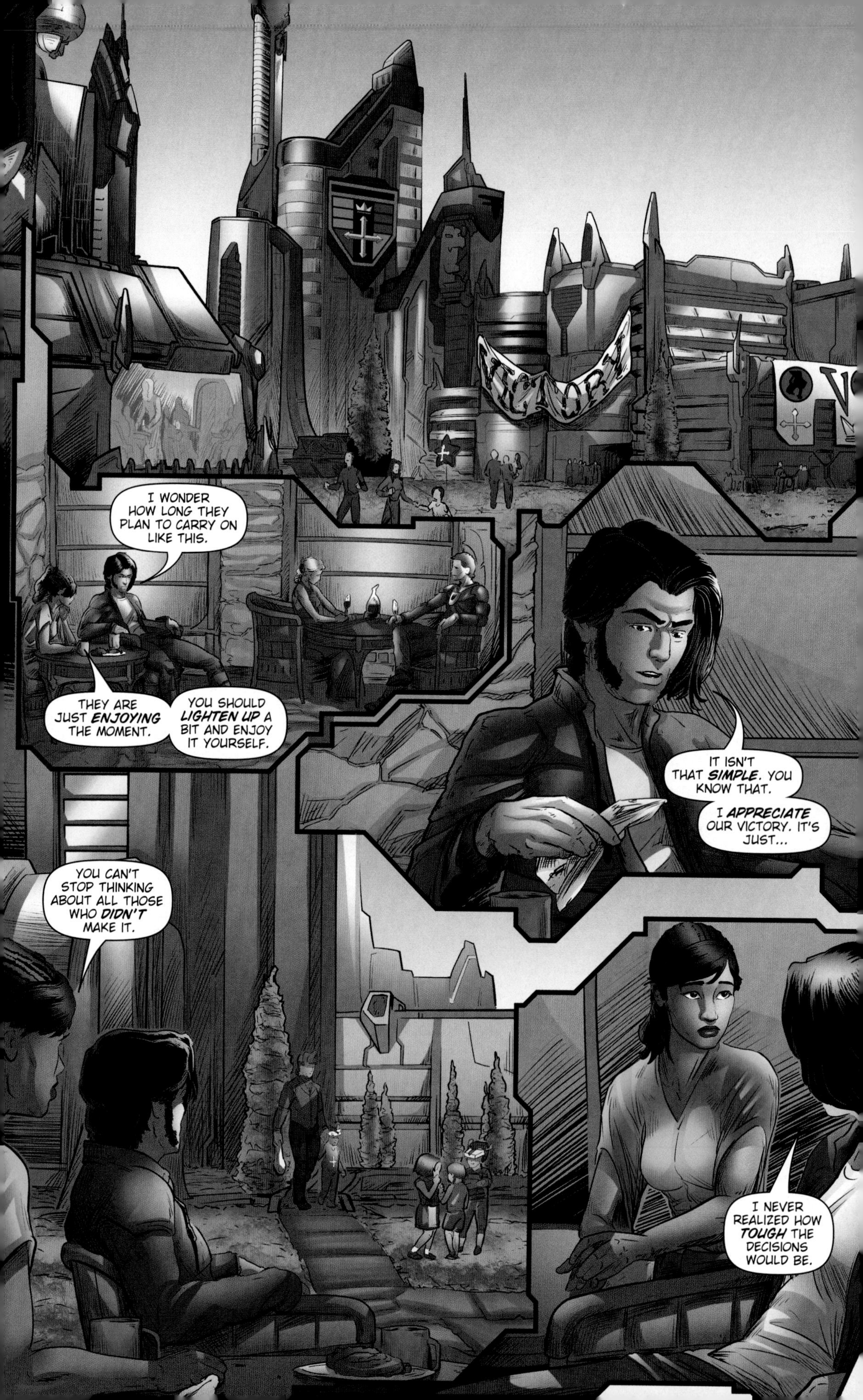
VICTORY
I WONDER HOW LONG THEY PLAN TO CARRY ON LIKE THIS.
THEY ARE JUST ENJOYING THE MOMENT.
YOU SHOULD LIGHTEN UP A BIT AND ENJOY IT YOURSELF.
IT ISN'T THAT SIMPLE. YOU KNOW THAT.
I APPRECIATE OUR VICTORY. IT'S JUST...
YOU CAN'T STOP THINKING ABOUT ALL THOSE WHO DIDN'T MAKE IT.
I NEVER REALIZED HOW TOUGH THE DECISIONS WOULD BE.

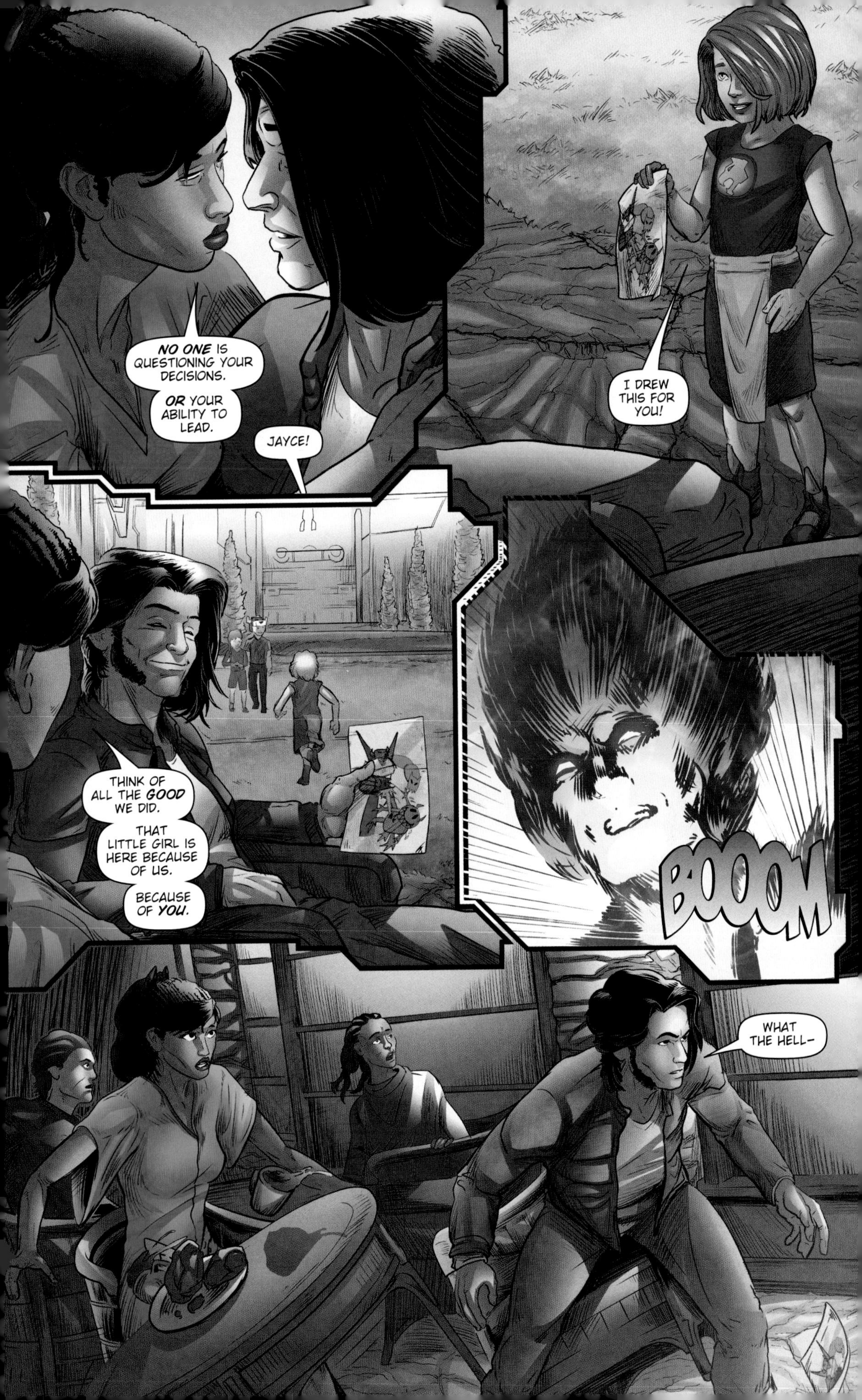
NO ONE IS QUESTIONING YOUR DECISIONS.
OR YOUR ABILITY TO LEAD.
JAYCE!
I DREW THIS FOR YOU!
THINK OF ALL THE GOOD WE DID.
THAT LITTLE GIRL IS HERE BECAUSE OF US.
BECAUSE OF YOU.
BOOOM
WHAT THE HELL-

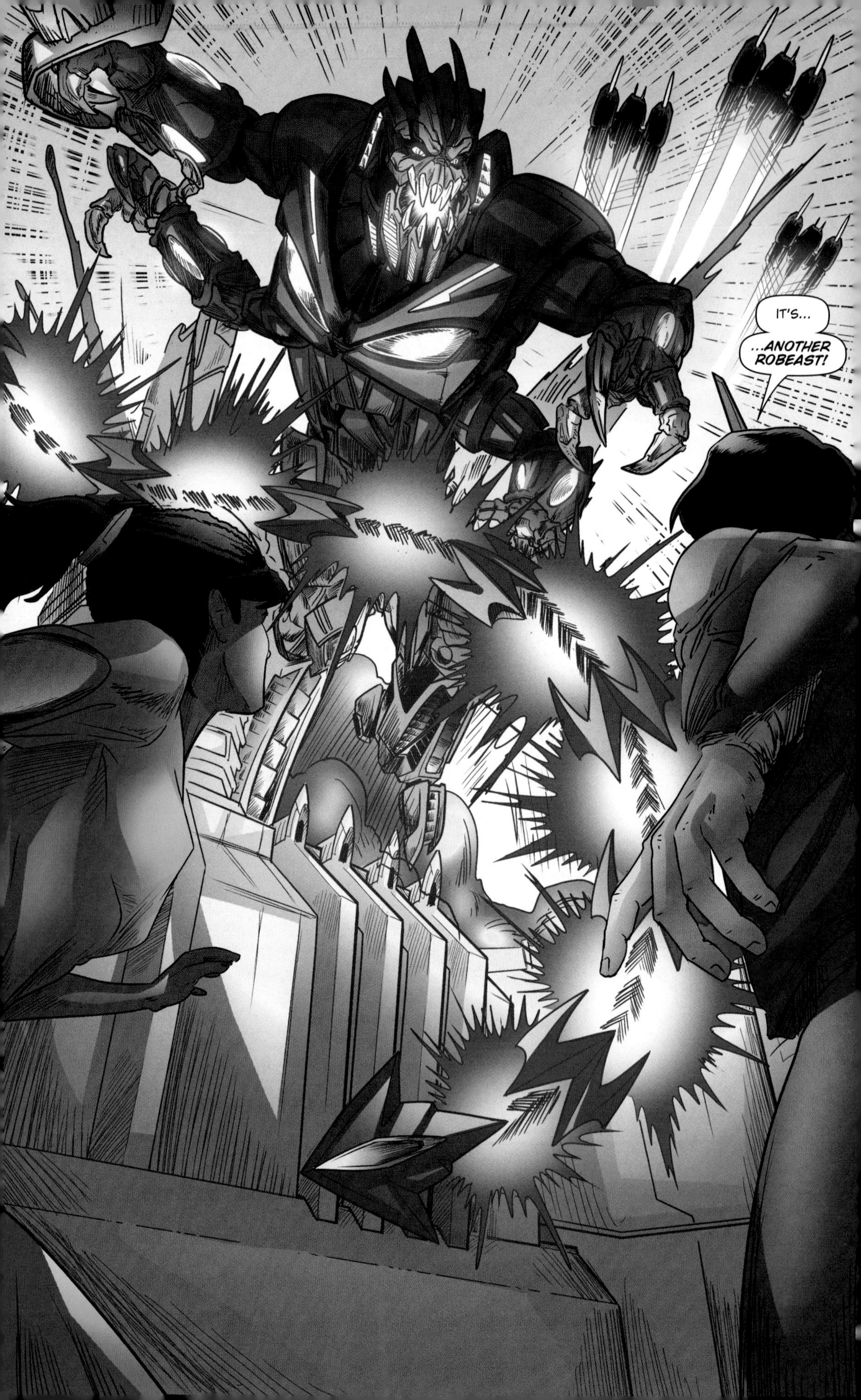
IT'S...
...ANOTHER ROBEAST!

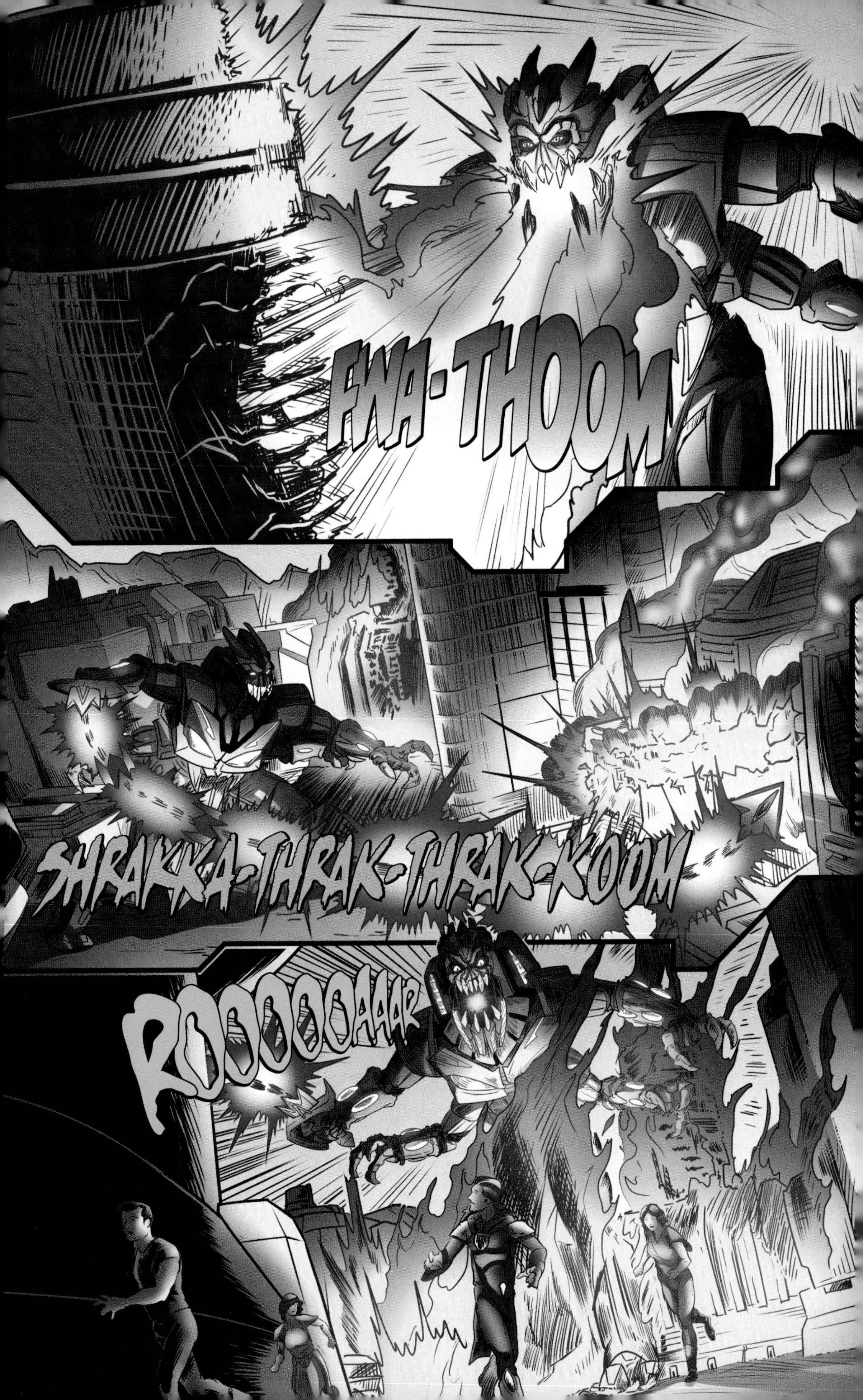
FWA-THOOM
SHRAKKA-THRAK-THRAK-KOOM
ROOOOOAAAR

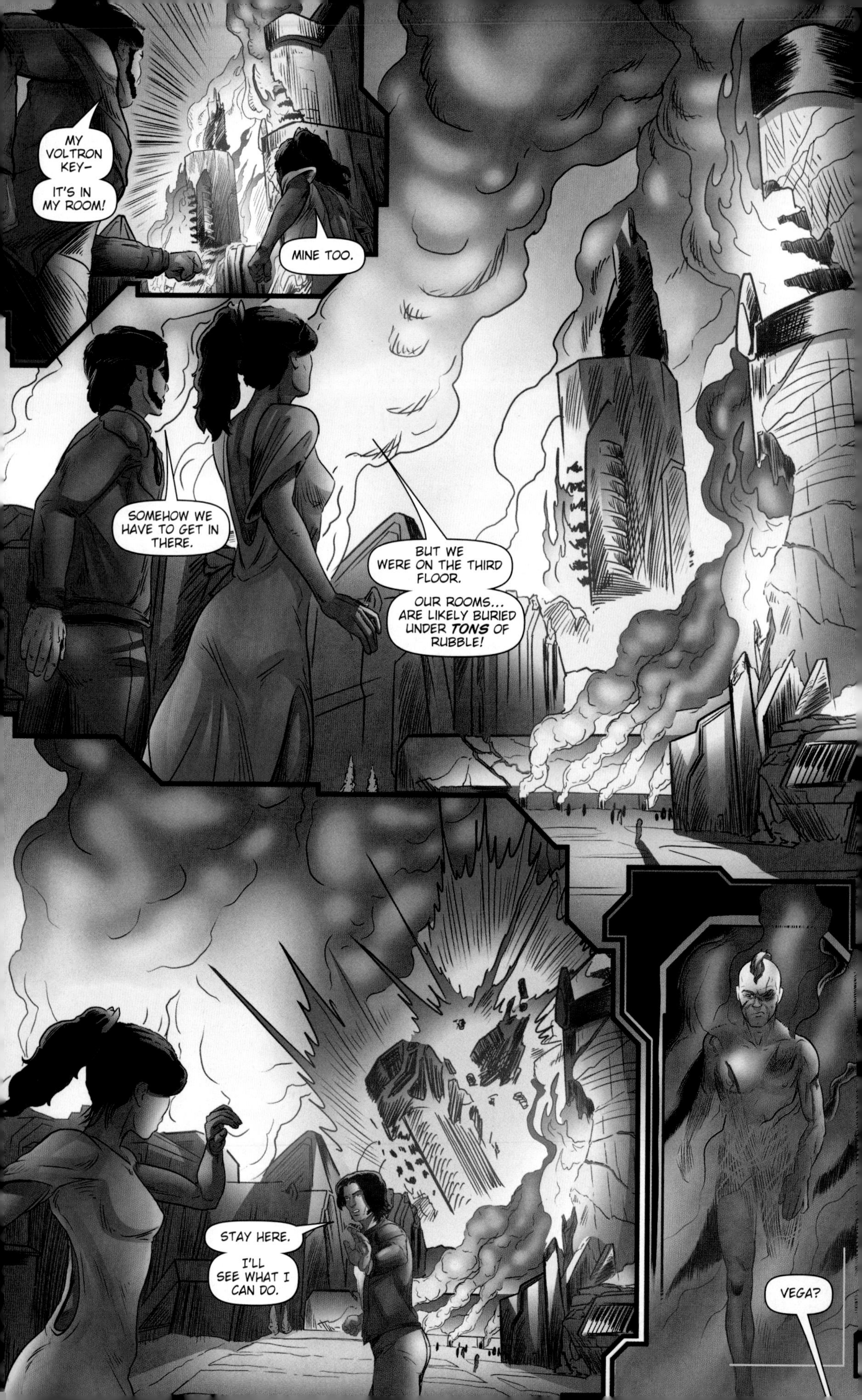
MY VOLTRON KEY-
IT'S IN MY ROOM!
MINE TOO.
SOMEHOW WE HAVE TO GET IN THERE.
BUT WE WERE ON THE THIRD FLOOR.
OUR ROOMS... ARE LIKELY BURIED UNDER TONS OF RUBBLE!
STAY HERE.
I'LL SEE WHAT I CAN DO.
VEGA?

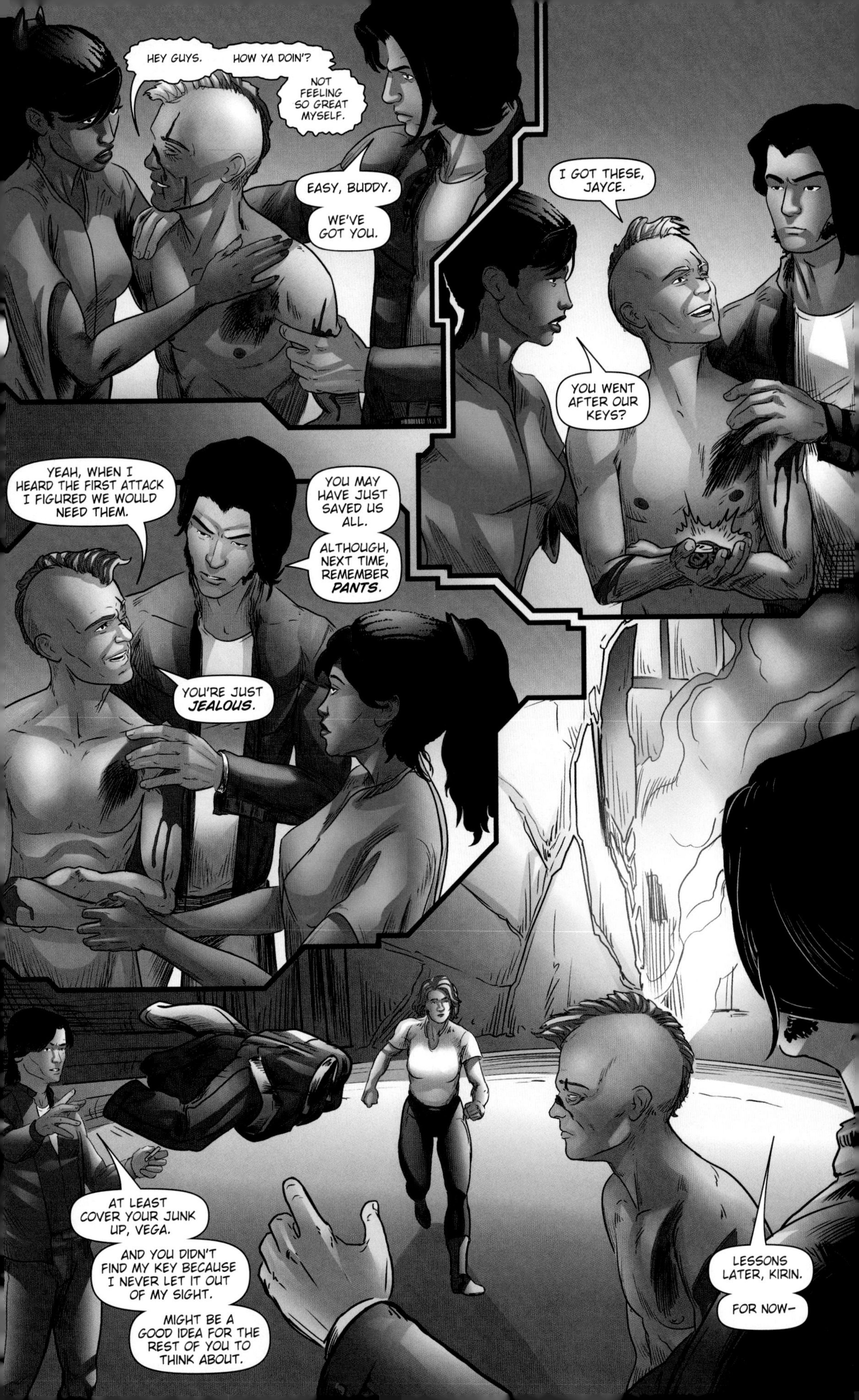

HEY GUYS. HOW YA DOIN'?
NOT FEELING SO GREAT MYSELF.
EASY, BUDDY.
WE'VE GOT YOU.
I GOT THESE, JAYCE.
YOU WENT AFTER OUR KEYS?
YEAH, WHEN I HEARD THE FIRST ATTACK I FIGURED WE WOULD NEED THEM.
YOU MAY HAVE JUST SAVED US ALL.
ALTHOUGH, NEXT TIME, REMEMBER PANTS.
YOU'RE JUST JEALOUS.
AT LEAST COVER YOUR JUNK UP, VEGA.
AND YOU DIDN'T FIND MY KEY BECAUSE I NEVER LET IT OUT OF MY SIGHT.
MIGHT BE A GOOD IDEA FOR THE REST OF YOU TO THINK ABOUT.
LESSONS LATER, KIRIN.
FOR NOW–

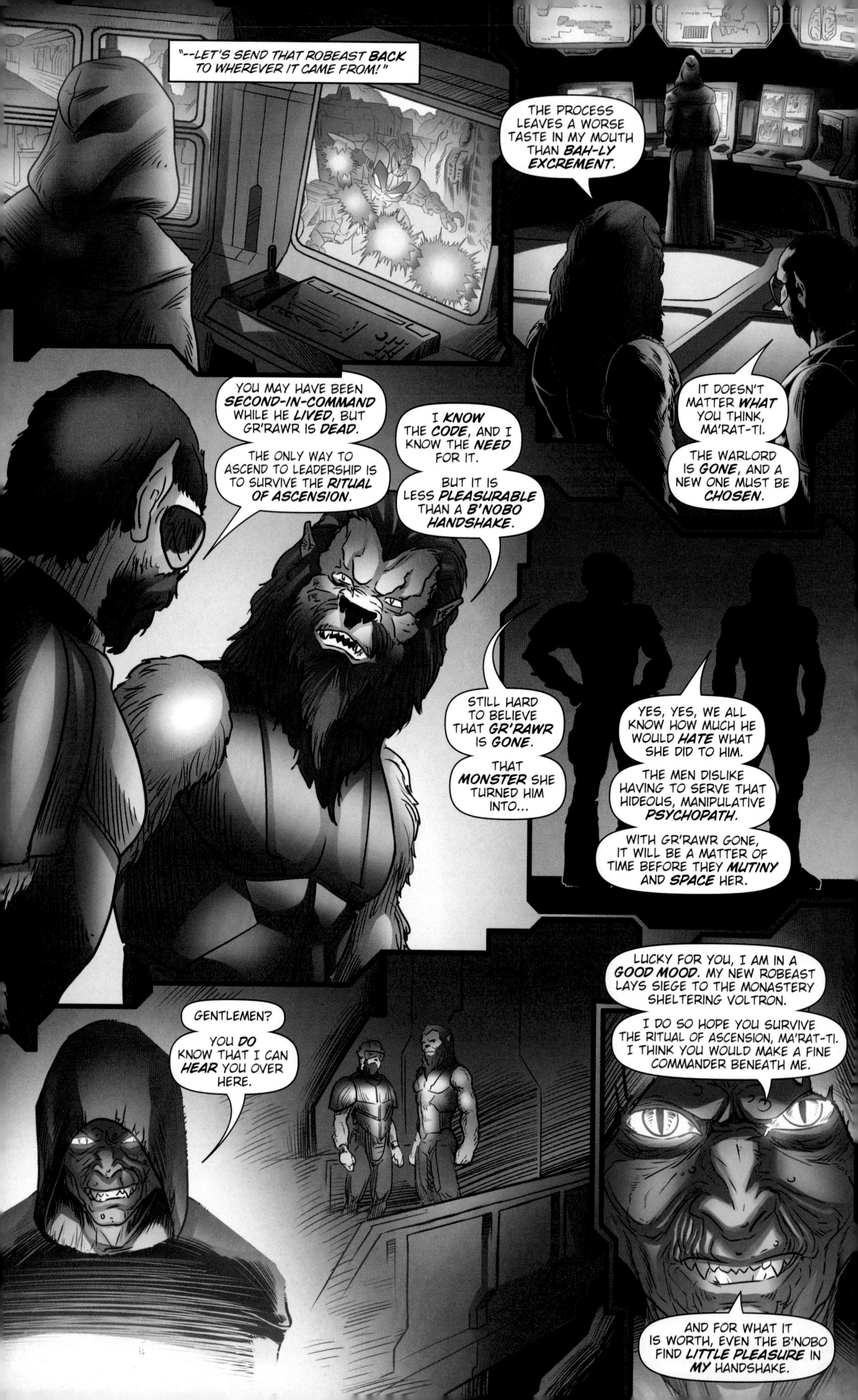
"--LET'S SEND THAT ROBEAST BACK TO WHEREVER IT CAME FROM!"
THE PROCESS LEAVES A WORSE TASTE IN MY MOUTH THAN BAH-LY EXCREMENT.
IT DOESN'T MATTER WHAT YOU THINK, MA'RAT-TI.
THE WARLORD IS GONE, AND A NEW ONE MUST BE CHOSEN.
YOU MAY HAVE BEEN SECOND-IN-COMMAND WHILE HE LIVED, BUT GR'RAWR IS DEAD.
THE ONLY WAY TO ASCEND TO LEADERSHIP IS TO SURVIVE THE RITUAL OF ASCENSION.
I KNOW THE CODE, AND I KNOW THE NEED FOR IT.
BUT IT IS LESS PLEASURABLE THAN A B'NOBO HANDSHAKE.
STILL HARD TO BELIEVE THAT GR'RAWR IS GONE.
THAT MONSTER SHE TURNED HIM INTO...
YES, YES, WE ALL KNOW HOW MUCH HE WOULD HATE WHAT SHE DID TO HIM.
THE MEN DISLIKE HAVING TO SERVE THAT HIDEOUS, MANIPULATIVE PSYCHOPATH.
WITH GR'RAWR GONE, IT WILL BE A MATTER OF TIME BEFORE THEY MUTINY AND SPACE HER.
GENTLEMEN?
YOU DO KNOW THAT I CAN HEAR YOU OVER HERE.
LUCKY FOR YOU, I AM IN A GOOD MOOD. MY NEW ROBEAST LAYS SIEGE TO THE MONASTERY SHELTERING VOLTRON.
I DO SO HOPE YOU SURVIVE THE RITUAL OF ASCENSION, MA'RAT-TI. I THINK YOU WOULD MAKE A FINE COMMANDER BENEATH ME.
AND FOR WHAT IT IS WORTH, EVEN THE B'NOBO FIND LITTLE PLEASURE IN MY HANDSHAKE.

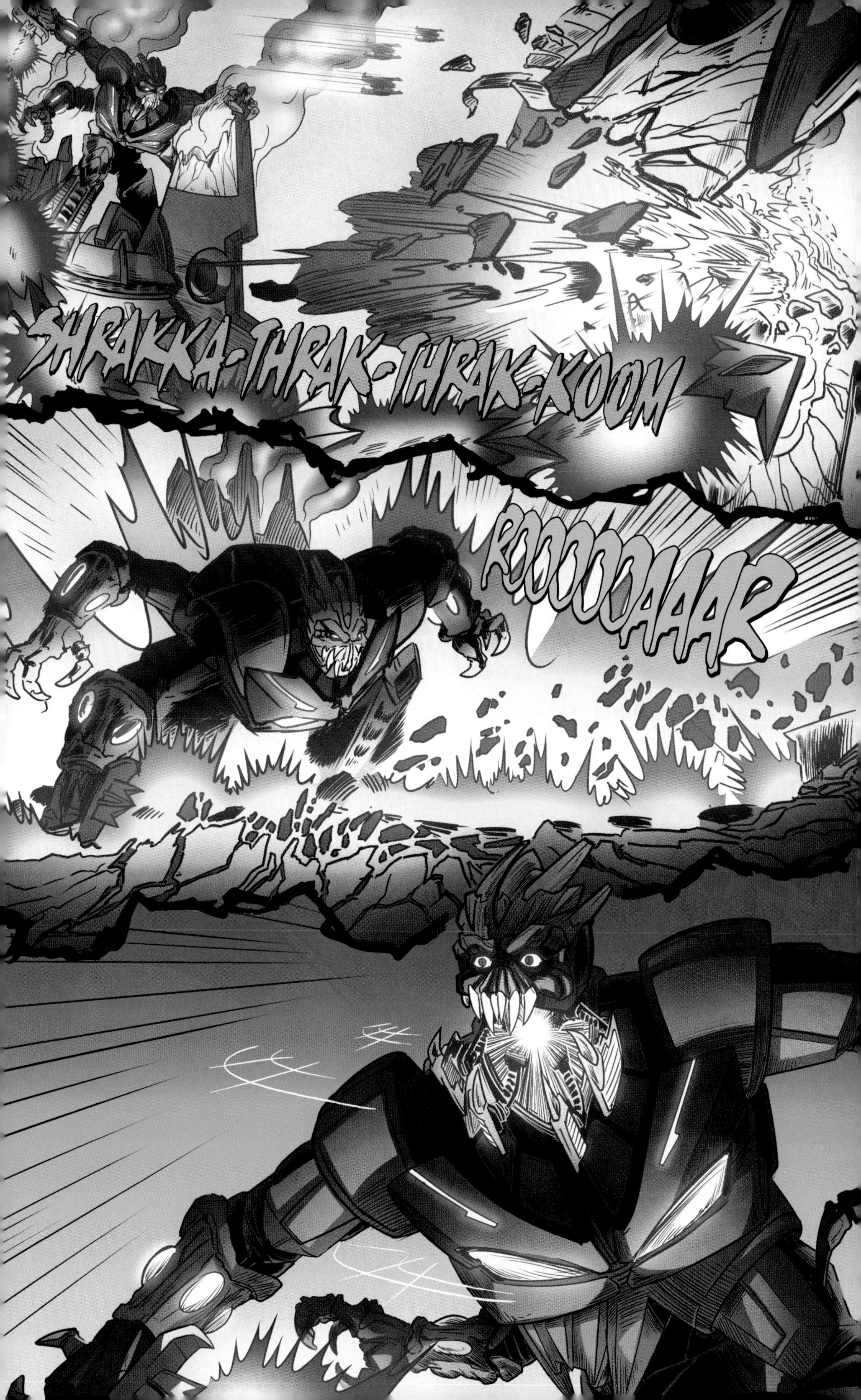
SHRAKKA-THRAK-THRAK-KOOM
ROOOOOAAAR

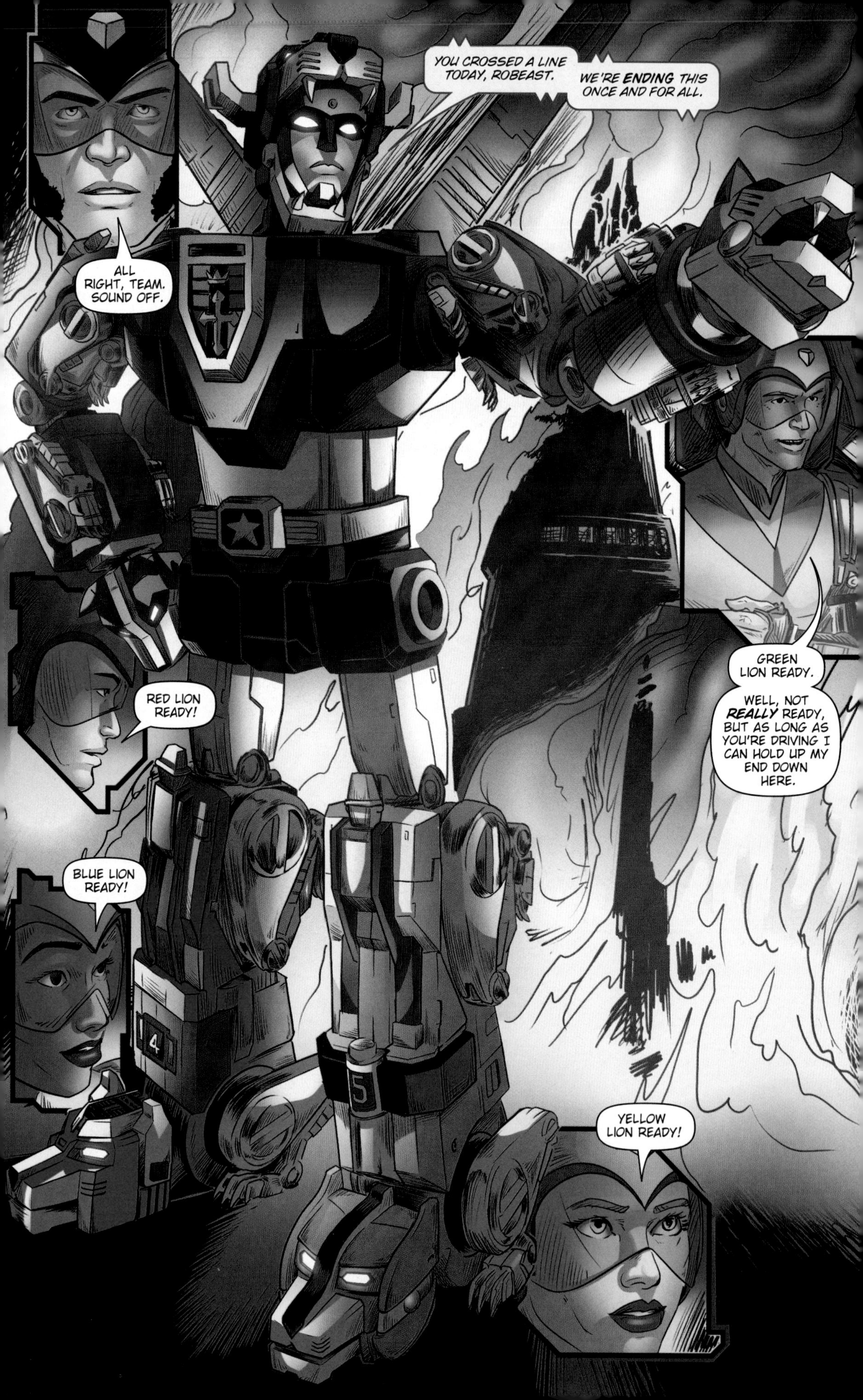
YOU CROSSED A LINE TODAY, ROBEAST.
WE'RE ENDING THIS ONCE AND FOR ALL.
ALL RIGHT, TEAM. SOUND OFF.
GREEN LION READY.
WELL, NOT REALLY READY, BUT AS LONG AS YOU'RE DRIVING I CAN HOLD UP MY END DOWN HERE.
RED LION READY!
BLUE LION READY!
YELLOW LION READY!

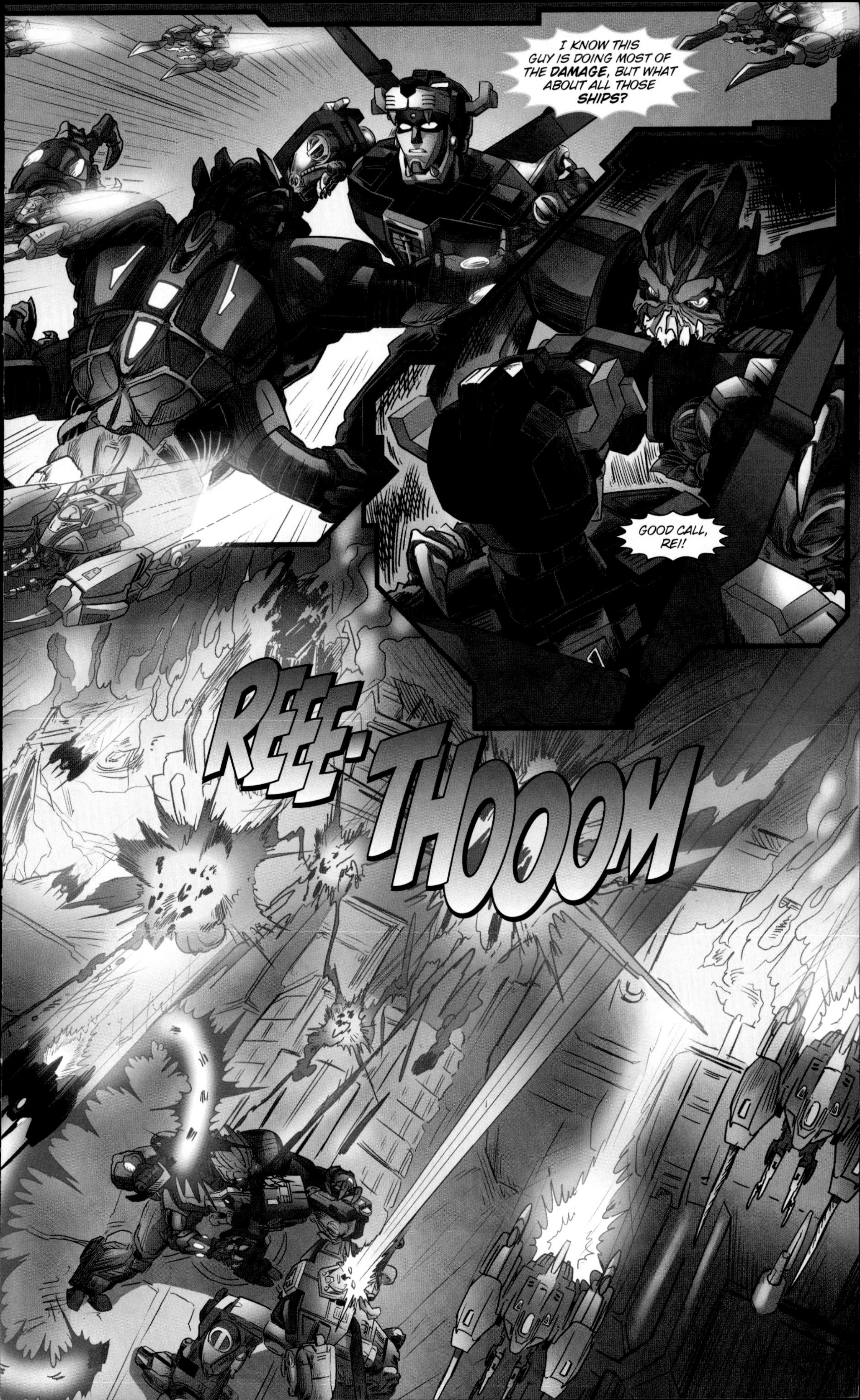
I KNOW THIS GUY IS DOING MOST OF THE DAMAGE, BUT WHAT ABOUT ALL THOSE SHIPS?
GOOD CALL, REI!
REEE-THOOOM

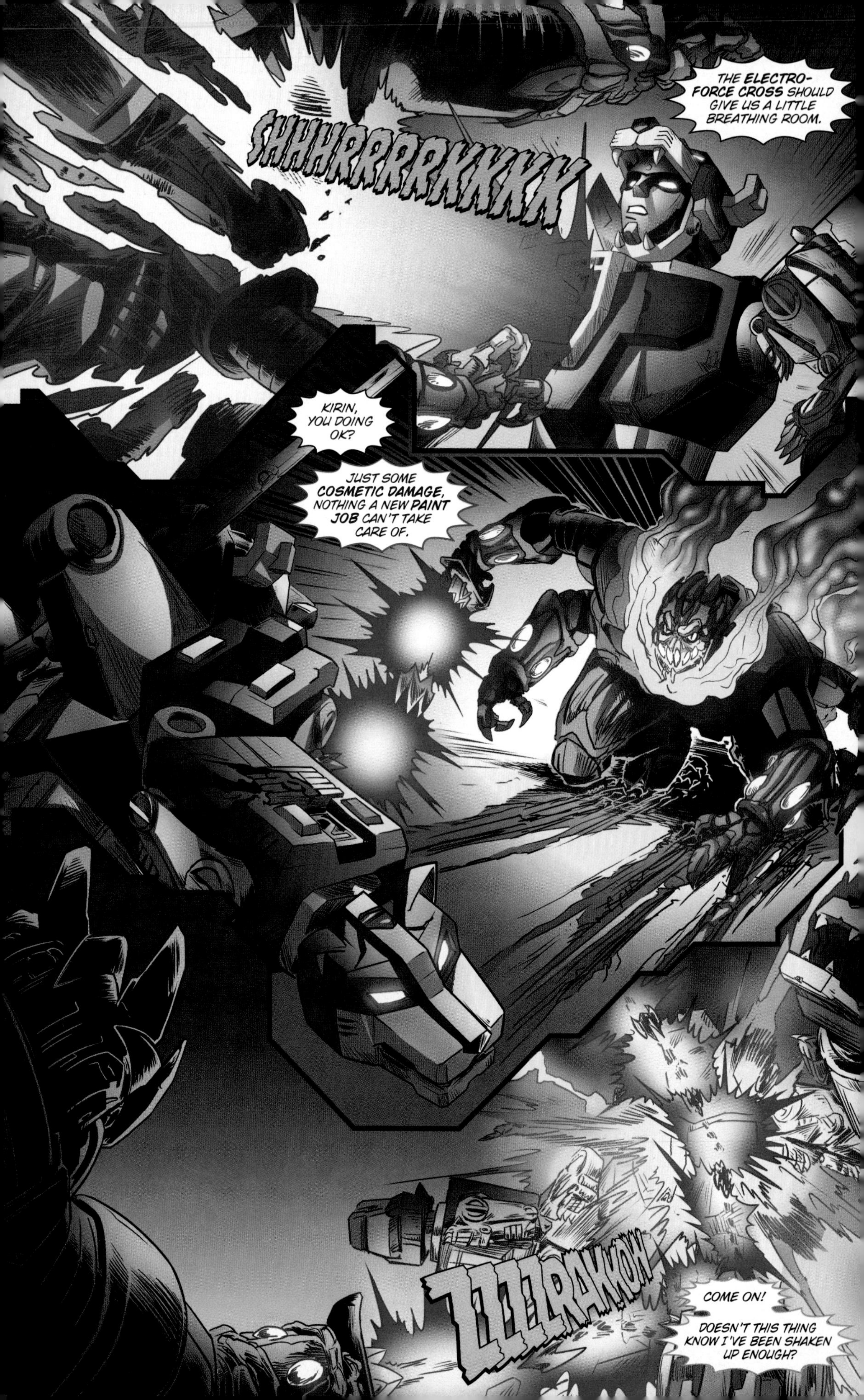
SHHHRRRRKKKKK
THE ELECTRO-FORCE CROSS SHOULD GIVE US A LITTLE BREATHING ROOM.
KIRIN, YOU DOING OK?
JUST SOME COSMETIC DAMAGE, NOTHING A NEW PAINT JOB CAN'T TAKE CARE OF.
ZZZZRAKKOW
COME ON!
DOESN'T THIS THING KNOW I'VE BEEN SHAKEN UP ENOUGH?

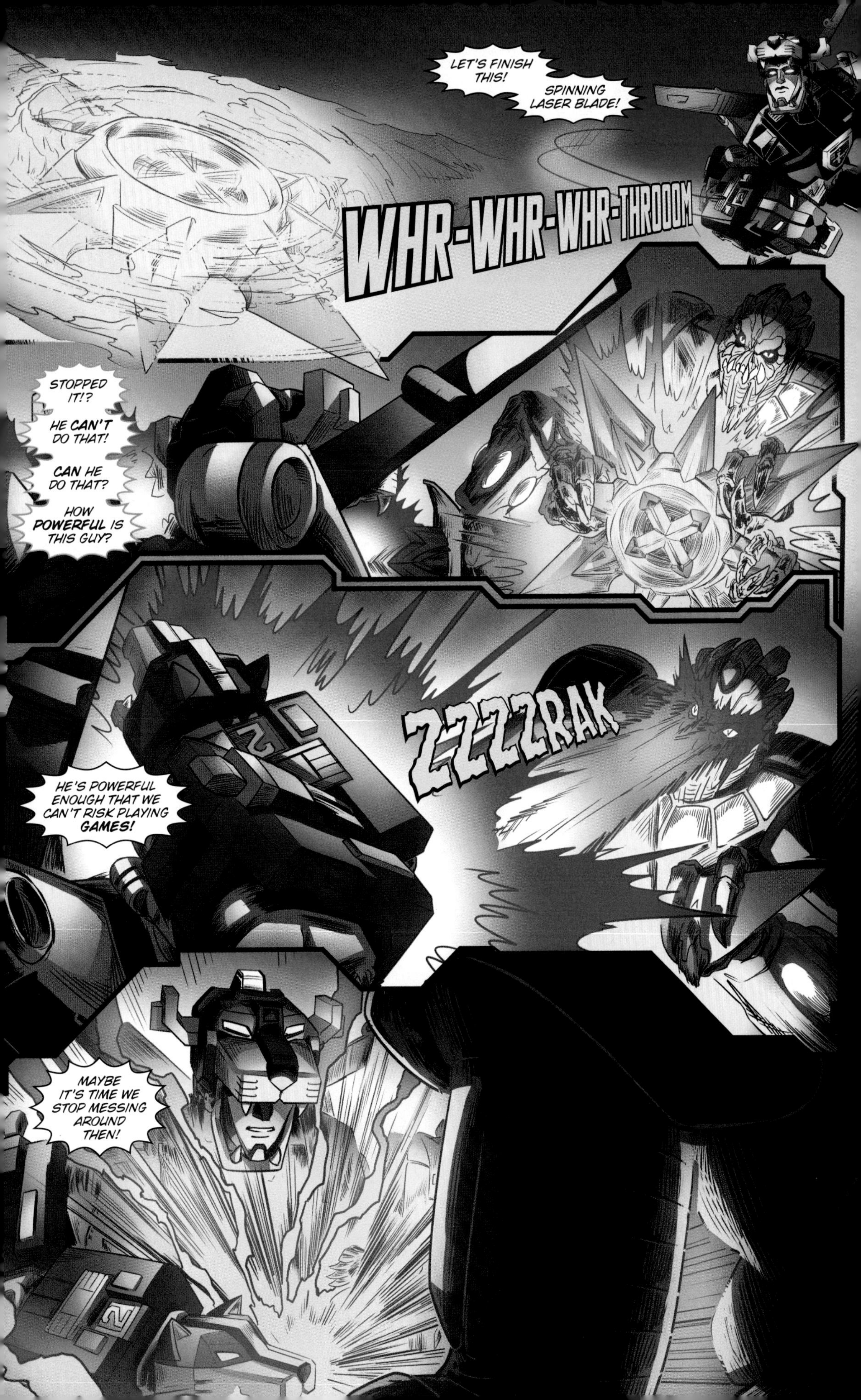
LET'S FINISH THIS!
SPINNING LASER BLADE!
WHR-WHR-WHR-THROOOM
STOPPED IT!?
HE CAN'T DO THAT!
CAN HE DO THAT?
HOW POWERFUL IS THIS GUY?
ZZZZZRAK
HE'S POWERFUL ENOUGH THAT WE CAN'T RISK PLAYING GAMES!
MAYBE IT'S TIME WE STOP MESSING AROUND THEN!

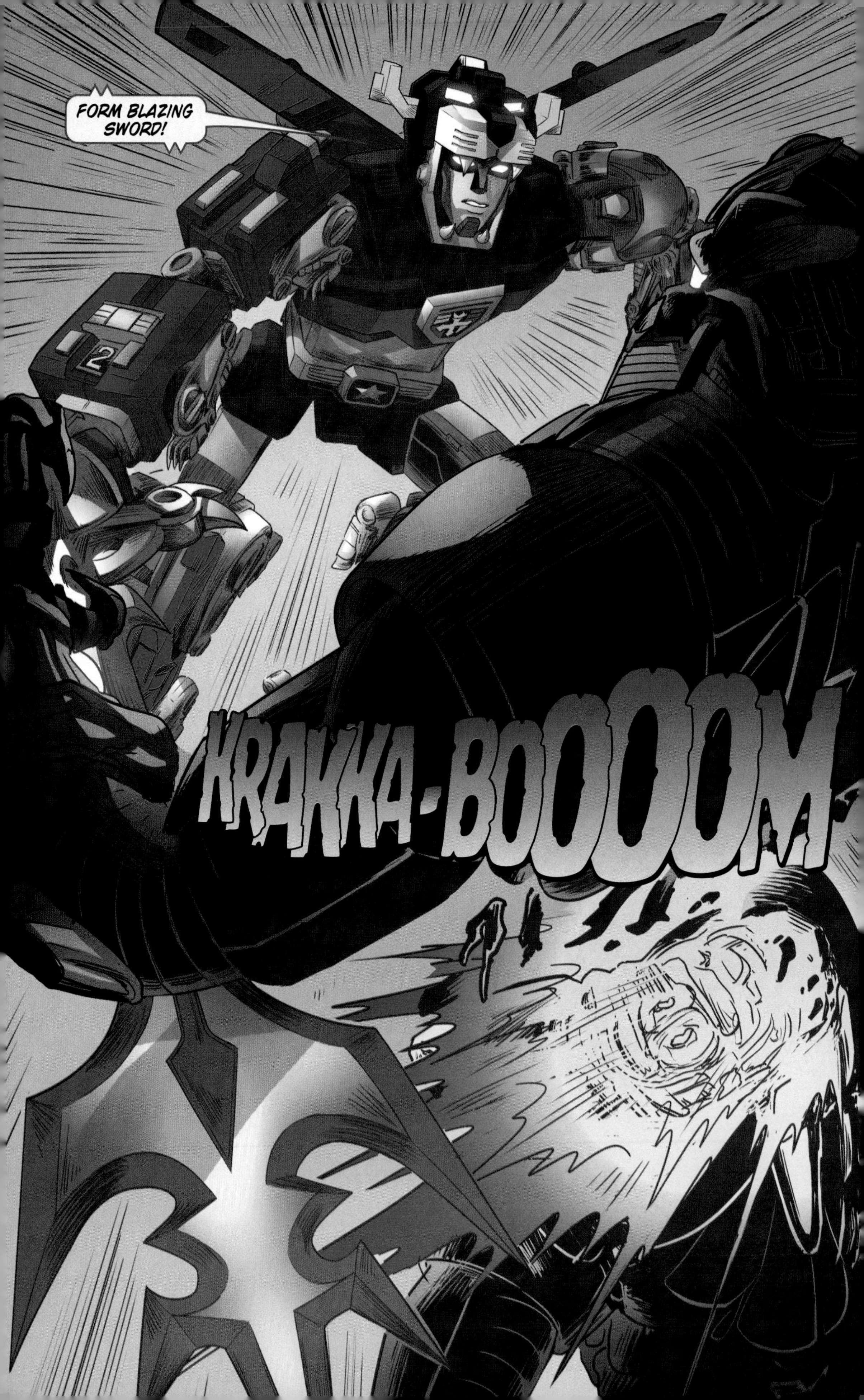
FORM BLAZING SWORD!
KRAKKA-BOOOOOM

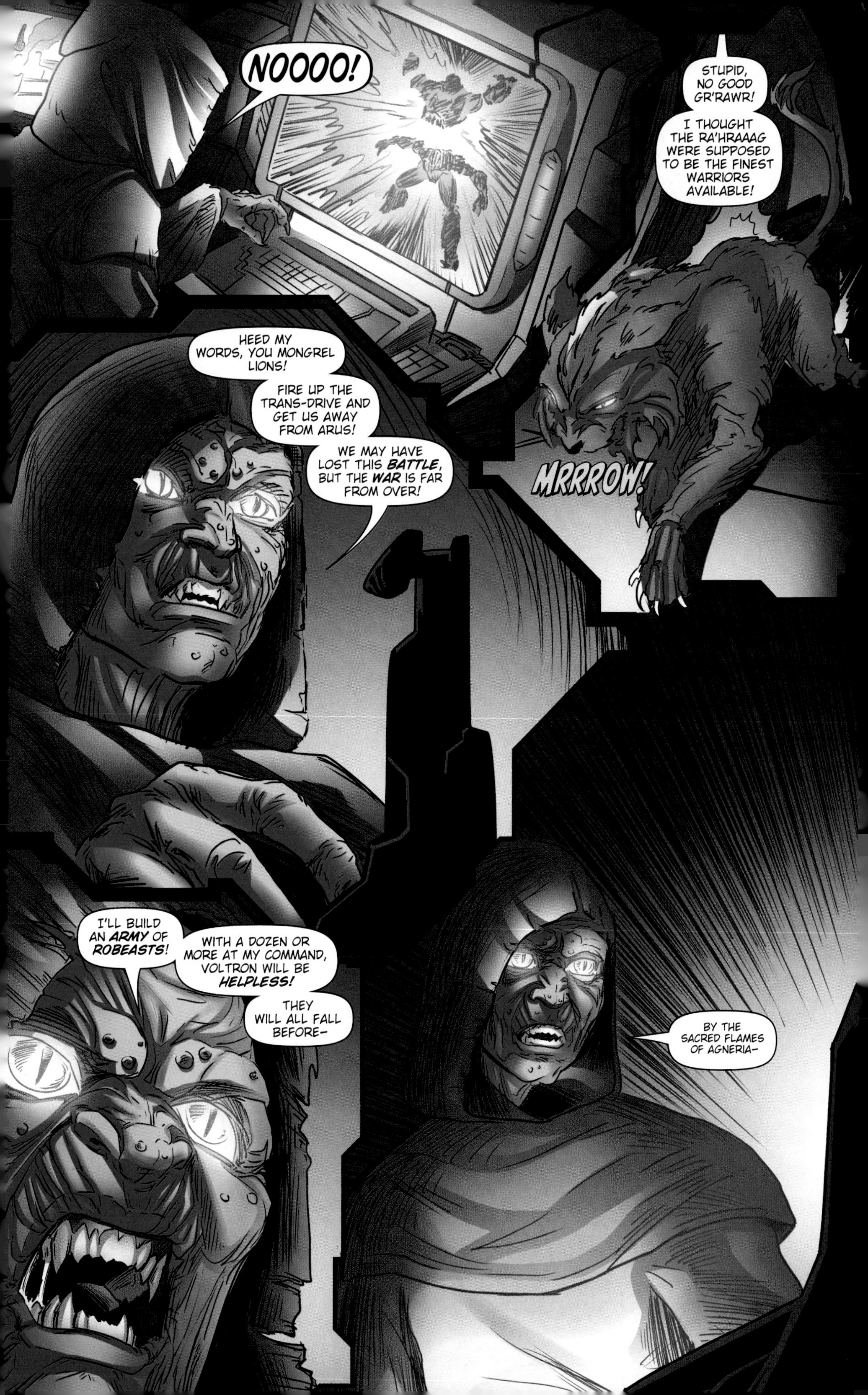
NOOOO!
STUPID, NO GOOD GR'RAWR!
I THOUGHT THE RA'HRAAAG WERE SUPPOSED TO BE THE FINEST WARRIORS AVAILABLE!
HEED MY WORDS, YOU MONGREL LIONS!
FIRE UP THE TRANS-DRIVE AND GET US AWAY FROM ARUS!
WE MAY HAVE LOST THIS BATTLE, BUT THE WAR IS FAR FROM OVER!
MRRROW!
I'LL BUILD AN ARMY OF ROBEASTS!
WITH A DOZEN OR MORE AT MY COMMAND, VOLTRON WILL BE HELPLESS!
THEY WILL ALL FALL BEFORE-
BY THE SACRED FLAMES OF AGNERIA-

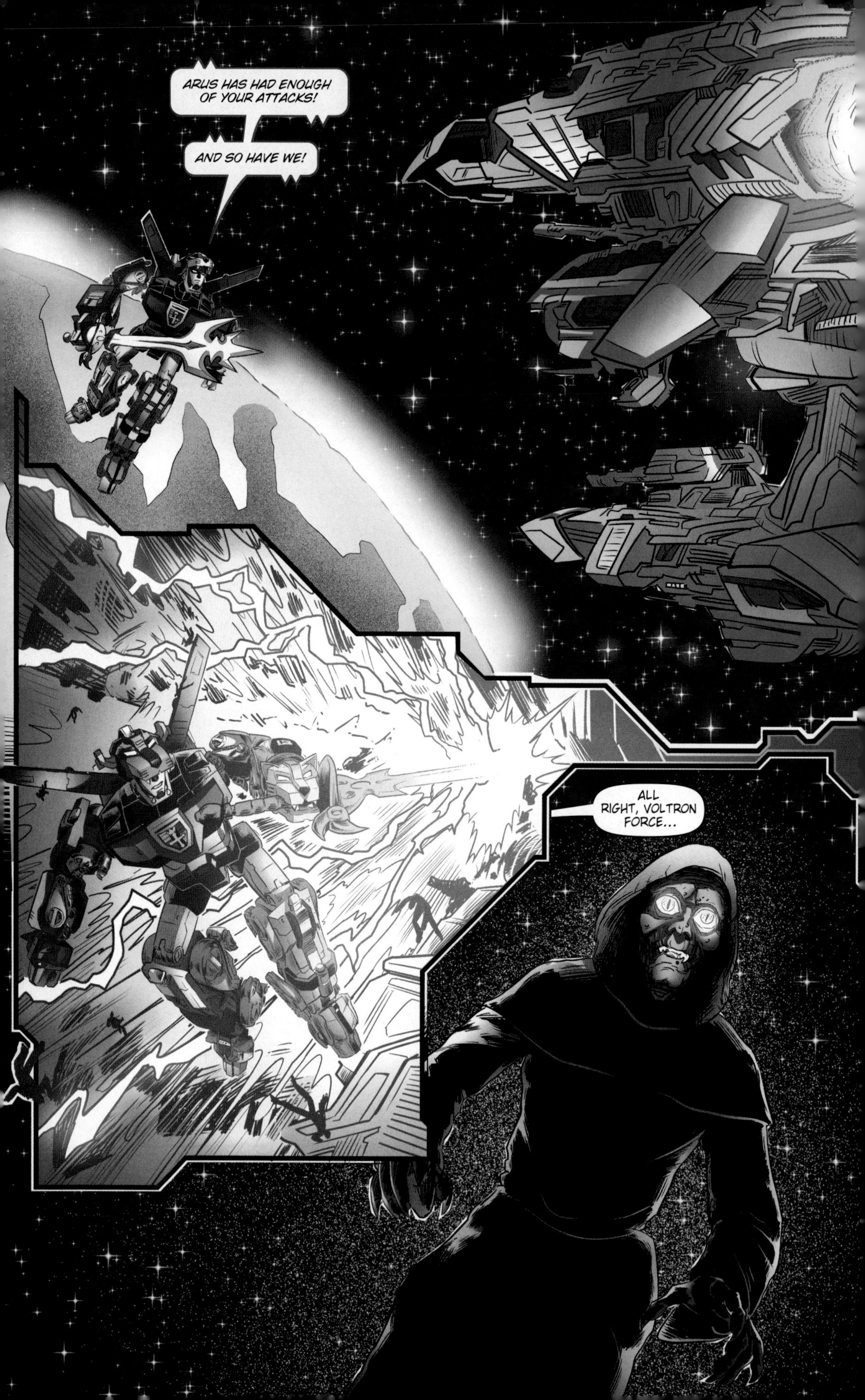
ARUS HAS HAD ENOUGH OF YOUR ATTACKS!
AND SO HAVE WE!
ALL RIGHT, VOLTRON FORCE...

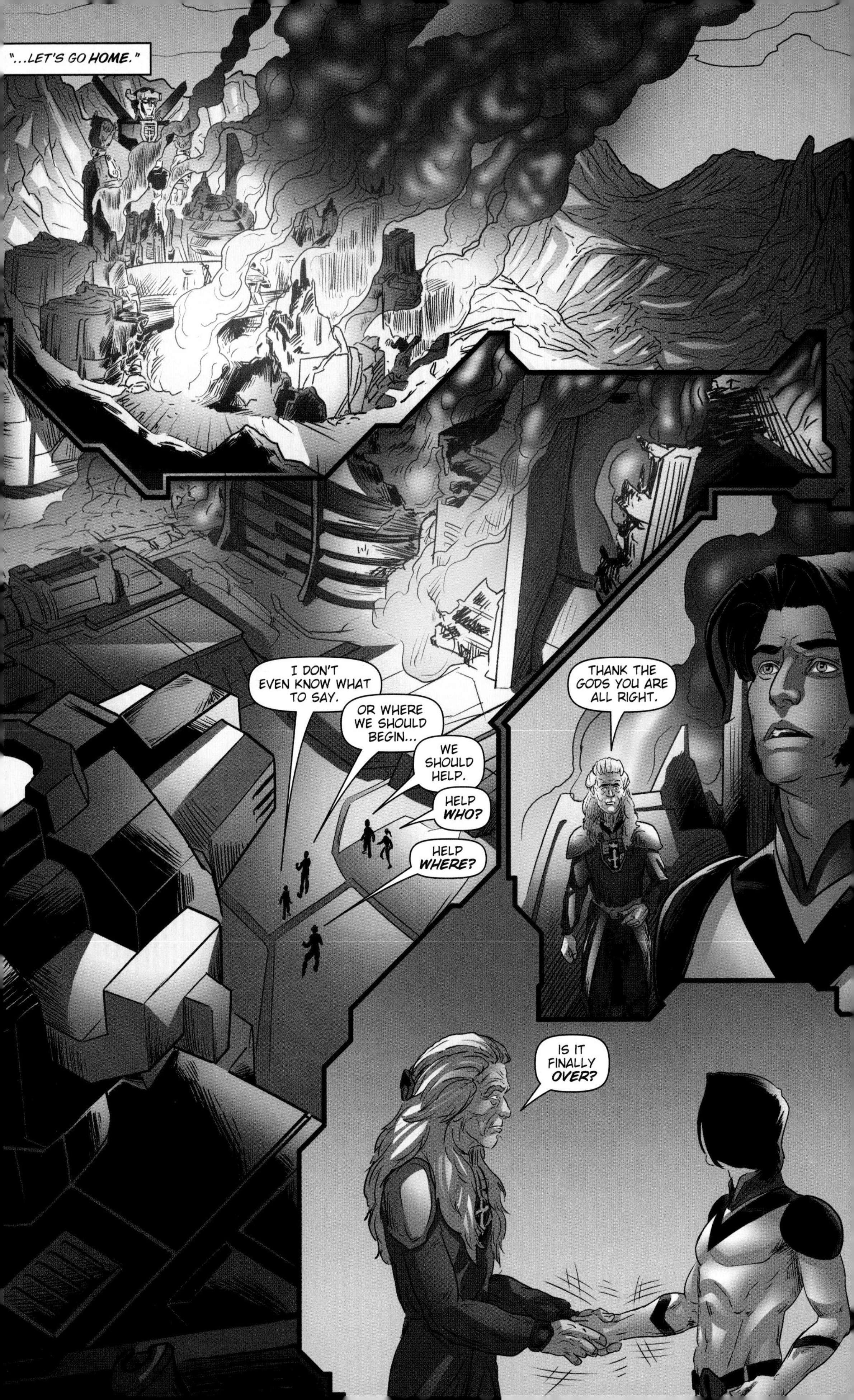
"...LET'S GO HOME."
I DON'T EVEN KNOW WHAT TO SAY.
OR WHERE WE SHOULD BEGIN...
WE SHOULD HELP.
HELP WHO?
HELP WHERE?
THANK THE GODS YOU ARE ALL RIGHT.
IS IT FINALLY OVER?

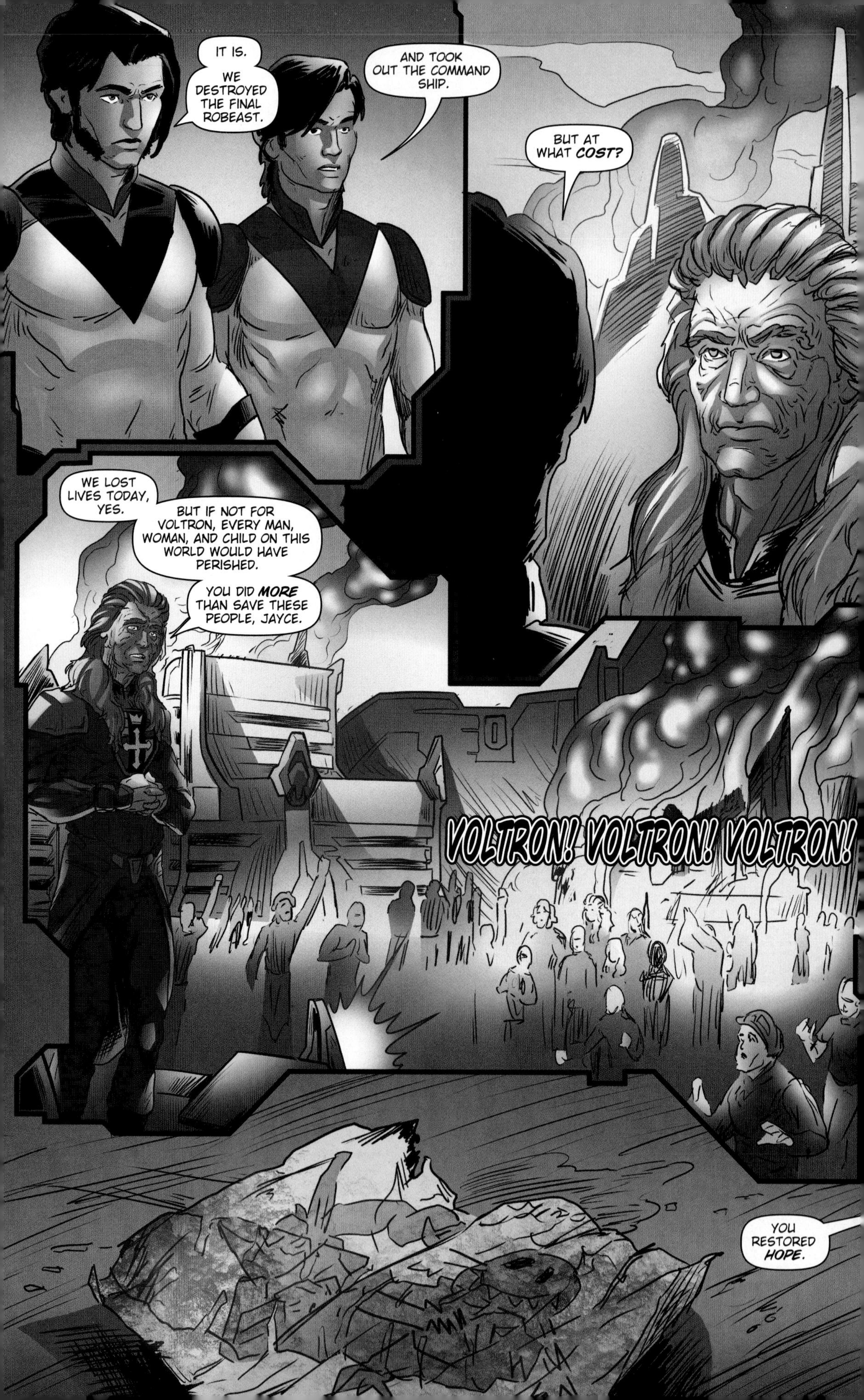
IT IS.
WE DESTROYED THE FINAL ROBEAST.
AND TOOK OUT THE COMMAND SHIP.
BUT AT WHAT **COST?**
WE LOST LIVES TODAY, YES.
BUT IF NOT FOR VOLTRON, EVERY MAN, WOMAN, AND CHILD ON THIS WORLD WOULD HAVE PERISHED.
YOU DID **MORE** THAN SAVE THESE PEOPLE, JAYCE.
VOLTRON! VOLTRON! VOLTRON!
YOU RESTORED **HOPE.**